**W9-CTW-122**

# DATE DUE

| | | | |
|---|---|---|---|
| | | | |
| | | | |
| | | | |
| | | | |
| | | | |
| | | | |
| | | | |
| | | | |
| | | | |
| | | | |
| | | | |
| | | | |
| | | | |
| | | | |
| | | | |
| | | | |
| | | | |
| | | | |
| | | | |

DEMCO 38-296

# Easterns, Westerns,
# and Private Eyes

# Easterns, Westerns, and Private Eyes

## American Matters, 1870–1900

Marcus Klein

THE UNIVERSITY OF WISCONSIN PRESS

Riverside Community College
Library
MAY    '96    4800 Magnolia Avenue
Riverside, California 92506

PS 374 .P63 K58 1994

Klein, Marcus.

Easterns, westerns, and
  private eyes

The University of Wisconsin Press
114 North Murray Street
Madison, Wisconsin   53715

3 Henrietta Street
London WC2E 8LU, England

Copyright © 1994
The Board of Regents of the University of Wisconsin System
All rights reserved

1      2      3      4      5

Printed in the United States of America

Library of Congress Cataloging-in-Publication Data
Klein, Marcus.
Easterns, westerns, and private eyes: American matters, 1870–1900 /
Marcus Klein.
228 p.        cm.
Includes bibliographical references and index.
ISBN 0-299-14300-7 (cl)      ISBN 0-299-14304-X (pb)
1. American fiction—19th century—History and criticism.
2. Popular literature—United States—History and criticism.
3. Dectective and mystery stories, American—History and criticism.
4. Literature and history—United States—History—19th century.
5. Alger, Horatio, 1832–1899—Criticism and interpretation.
6. National characteristics, American, in literature.
7. Western stories—History and criticism.
8. New York (N.Y.)—In literature.
I. Title.
PS374.P63K58        1994
813'.409—dc20        94-5675

*For Marian, Jenny, and Eric*

# Contents

# Illustrations

# Acknowledgments

Colleagues near and far have provided me with: texts, discoveries, instigations, insights, prose, and, best of all, their interest both in my subject and what I was trying to do with it. Vic Doyno especially brought materials to my attention and clarifications to my thinking. For their various gifts I wish also to thank Anne Coon, Leslie Fiedler, Keiichi Harada, Jay Martin, Scott Michaelsen, Robert Pack, Robert Rebein (late of Dodge City), Fred See and Myles Slatin.

Portions of this book have previously been published elsewhere. The author particularly wishes to thank the editors of *Chiba Review* and the University of Toronto Press for permission to reprint. Additional material is reprinted from *The Bread Loaf Anthology of Contemporary American Essays*, edited by Robert Pack and Jay Parini, copyright © 1989 by Bread Loaf Writer's Conference/Middlebury, by permission of the University Press of New England.

# Easterns, Westerns,
# and Private Eyes

# Introduction

THESE tales and figures define themselves in the following ways: they are distinctly American both in origin and usual association; they go back far enough that they can be said to be embedded in a history but are at the same time indisputably contemporary (by the measure, aside from everything else, that they are likely to occur on television every night); and they inform fictions high and low, and, as well, the writing of American history. In short, they prove to be both so broadly and so durably popular that it must be the case that their meanings are basic, which would be to say that they have American uses which are fundamental and continuous. By the same measure, moreover, these, if any, are the tales that bind; whatever the uses, the facts both of the acknowledged identity of the tales and the continuing history of their repetitions go in the first place to say that there is such a thing as a society which is American.

No doubt that they solicit study.

Sheer presence has a meaning, and the three categories of tale which here follow obviously do have it.

The story Rags-to-Riches, in part I, while it is no longer likely to be invested in children as it was in the original Horatio Alger version, in contemporary uses is not otherwise greatly different. But as a tale of abrupt success, specifically and bluntly in terms of money and prestige come to by pluck and luck, with accent on the latter, the story is perhaps so often before us, in forms ranging from the soaps to quiz shows, to tales of corporate climbing, in the news and on the screen, to the telling of political biography—the tale with its underlying thematics is so much a commonplace as perhaps after all to require some special effort to see it. And if the story as now it is told is most often accompanied by

3

a nice tang of cynicism, this enrichment first of all does not diminish the amount of the presence of the tale, while, as will be demonstrated, the spice of disbelief is also precisely the secret of the original. The Horatio Alger story is continuously relevant, continuously active, exactly by the implication of its implausibility. In the original as well, it undermined itself.

As for the sheerness of the presence of Westerns and Private Eyes, evidence surely is immediately redundant. Serious or comic, gravely or lightsomely, portentously or amusingly, these abound, and not only that, but they are seminal. It is with these that movies and television begin. In the case of these two, moreover, the transition from an actuality to mass audience is smooth and direct. Buffalo Bill once was real enough, and then he went into show business, and near the end, in the words of a historian of these matters, Loren D. Estleman, "the hand that shook those of Custer and Sitting Bull would work the crank of a Pathé camera." The real "cowboy detective" Charlie Siringo, who for months on the trail had tracked Butch Cassidy and the Wild Bunch, retired to Hollywood, where he wrote stories, acted in some movies, and published cowboy ballads thus providing material for the singing cowboy who shortly would succeed him. The ex-Pinkerton Operative Dashiell Hammett wrote for both the pulps and for Hollywood.

If only by the fact of their presence, it must be the case that these stories and figures indicate a consensus precisely as to what demands repeating, and it follows that the fact of persistence in the telling, in itself, has its own implication, namely that these figures and stories remain open-ended and suggestive and problematic. They are unique by the amount of their presence, and are related to each other by the same. They are enormously present and have been so for a century and more.

The obvious question, then, is, why? Why do they go on and on? Whatever else, it must be the case that they contain a history which still is unresolved, else they would not persist, and it follows from that, that some illumination should be had by discovery of these figures and tales in the context of their origins, which are not distant—and that discovery is what is attempted by this book. Distinctions between "high" and "low" literature have less meaning than ever, in this effort, and in fact disappear. From the nearly forgotten hacks of the fiction factories (nearly forgotten but not quite anonymous), to the writer who became president of the United States, the persons who made the tales and the figures in effect cooperated in creating this material that has lasted so terrifically. I have wanted to try to discover them in their common history and thus something of the content of their collective response to it, allowing of course for varieties within the response in common.

These tales and figures do not constitute "myth," given that that term usually means belief-beyond-question, validity prior to event. As will be seen, these tales are adamantly secular—despite not infrequent attempts to read universals into them having to do with death and human greed, and so forth. They arrive equipped with the reality which supplies them with their details, and even as they take on their rituals and their stereotypes of action and character, they do so by way of deep skepticism and repeated questioning of event. Altogether, indeed, they are characterized by their disbelief. They integrate and in the same motion interrogate. If anything, they confront whatever there might be of national pieties and are sarcastic and sinister.

The tales abide, but forward from a certain time. They take their distinguishing details (costumes, characterizations, landscapes) in texts which are quite available for study, which fact goes to indicate that they do not constitute "legend," either, given that "legend" suggests a matter of origins going back to dim prehistory. Granted the shapes by which we do recognize them, both the texts and the contexts of the origins of these stories are readily available. The tale Rags-to-Riches in its radical origins has to do, first, with persons who are in rags, and, second, who are introduced to an established business economy. They form an urban social class, located most probably in New York. The Western as we do actually recognize it has cowboys (but not many Indians), and the badmen and the schoolmarms, and the hats and the horses and the Colt 45s, and so does not begin with Hawkeye and Fenimore Cooper, nor even more remotely and vaguely in a dim European mythology of the lure of the West. And likewise the story of the Private Eye, who is not Poe's dandified, rather insouciant C. Auguste Dupin, nor Dupin's own predecessor, the Parisian Eugene François Vidocq, nor is the superior, rather indifferent Sherlock Holmes, nor the "cony-catcher" before him, nor is in any way heroic, but is at home among the metropolitan crooks and pols and especially knows the relationship between the two. He lives in the big city in America, where the little crimes have become dogmatic. His authority is that, as the law has come to be in its local and immediate application, he knows that there is no difference between law and lawlessness.

All of these tales in fact proceed from one certain originating moment, namely the one during which the United States entered into its modern time: the Gilded Age, and the time of the rapid urbanization of America, which is the time of the ghettoization of urban America, and is as well the time of the tremendous growth of the corporations, and the time which includes the first decades of the so-called New or Second Immigration, when the old urban centers were flooded with

Hungarians and Poles and Slavs and Sicilians and Russian Jews, and is the time of the great and bloody conflicts between Labor and Capital (the great railroad strike of the summer of 1877, the Burlington strike of 1888, the Homestead strike of 1892, to name a few saliences), and is also the time of the great acceleration of the growth of finance capitalism, along with much else. After Andrew Johnson, the presidents of the United States were: Grant, Hayes, Garfield, Arthur, then Cleveland, who sent the federal troops to Chicago at the time of the Pullman strike. These were the business presidents, in all candor. And this is the time when "anarchy" is ominous, both as an organized political force and generally, both in upper and in lower case.

Nor then is it surprising that these tales with their late–twentieth-century pertinences should have had the beginnings of their durability in this time, the years approximately 1870 to the turn of the century. They begin in the years of the modern and discover the modern, and they do so with frequently remarkable detail of reference to event and condition of the moment, as the following pages will show. If they continue to have bearing, that is to say, their relevance is finally not surprising because from their beginnings they have addressed a society we know.

When in 1866 the writer and ex-Unitarian minister Horatio Alger, Jr., set down the words to *Ragged Dick, or Street Life in New York,* that first of the juvenile fictions by which he would be defined, it was exactly "street life in New York" that had at once startled him and, perhaps perversely, inspired him. He had arrived in New York from a small town in Massachusetts. He had arrived at America's primary city and found himself confronted by a population of homeless boys and girls who lived on the streets and who survived by begging or theft, or by the practice of occupations not much removed from begging and theft, or who did not survive. When then he wrote his tales tracing the vector Rags-to-Riches, the theme was loaded with the particularities and the ironies of his immediate discovery. "Rags-to-Riches" might be Cinderella, or Benjamin Franklin, but the important part of Alger's telling was this consequence of life now in the American city.

And the same, again, with Westerns and the story of the Private Eye.

The Western obviously is not a Shepherd's Tale. First of all it does bear its weight of reference to the actual event of the settling of the American West in a period of about three decades at the end of the nineteenth century (with repeated appeal to what is just a handful of iconic figures based somewhat on their actual namesakes: Billy the Kid, Jesse James, Wild Bill Hickok, Bat Masterson, Butch Cassidy, and only a few others). To that degree the appeal of the Western has to do with bringing a recent past to present contemplation, but more to the point, the literary discovery of the West was conducted largely by easterners whose investment, high and low, was in the East. When Edward L. Wheeler of Philadelphia, author of the dime-novel stories of Deadwood Dick, had a grizzled old miner up in the hills, one Josiah Hogg, reflecting on Boss Tweed and Mayor A. Oakey Hall, both of New York, clearly it was not a western ore that Wheeler was mining. When at a more elevated but quite parallel level, the West was discovered by the trio of Theodore Roosevelt, Frederic Remington, and Owen Wister, the entire impetus for the construction of the fiction of the West had to do with the recovery of, as it were, a lost civilization, namely that of New York, Newport, Philadelphia, Charleston, and perhaps a few other places, as will be shown in the following pages.

Likewise, again, the story of the Private Eye: it secures its modern form and protagonist when the idea of what was crime came to the point of its modern ambiguity. When in 1873 Allan Pinkerton, founder and head of the Pinkerton National Detective Agency, having been hired by the Philadelphia and Reading Railroad, sent a spy, one James McParlan, into the Pennsylvania anthracite country to inform upon, subsequently to cause to be hanged, some supposed radical labor agitators recently emigrated from Ireland, then it might be said that the Private Eye story as we know it has its beginning. As will be seen in the following pages, McParlan lived in the intimate community of those Irish miners for some two and a half years, well beyond the time when mere ingratiation might possibly have served. Without ideology, he was on the side of the laboring man. He was one of them and was in truth an exploited young Irishman like the others. On the other hand, and fluently, he was on the side of his employers, to a degree of loyalty seeming to be neither more nor less than his loyalty to the Irish miners, at least until the denouement of the episode of the Mollie Maguires. (And the same ambiguous loyalty characterized events a few years later when the Pinkerton detective Charlie Siringo spent a year among the miners of the Coeur D'Alene in Idaho. He too served his employer with fine fidelity and managed at the same time to be a good companion to those he lived among and spied upon.) Real outrages of violence did occur in the Pennsylvania fields, and it is not the case that all of the activities of the miners might have been considered to be exculpable, but the point for character is that the detective was one who invested into his own activities no moral considerations at all, but, rather, did a job. And as with McParlan among the Irish miners, so with the detectives, public and private, who served in the cities and sometimes wrote books. They confirmed the character. As, again, with Dashiell Hammett's Continental Op to come and then as with the line of descent following upon that character, these forbears too made the very idea of crime, here and now, to be dubious. Therein was their authority and the glamour of the persona. Their social intimates were the "bank sneaks" and forgers and swindlers and burglars—who, in the repeated phrase of Thomas Byrnes, late Chief of Detectives in New York City, in his great book *Professional Criminals of America*, were persons "well worth knowing." Nor did Byrnes mean that they were well worth knowing only in the sense that one had to watch out for them. "Each thing's a thief. . . . All that you meet are thieves," so Detective Phil Farley was content to repeat, at once speaking the basic conviction of the Private Eye and putting the proper poetry to it: converting cynicism to a kind of whimsy.

These three categories of tales do occasionally intersect, in their nineteenth-century versions. Or they fold one into the other. In the dime-novel juveniles of the type of the Horatio Alger stories, the street boys will turn detective. (*Vide*: J. C. Cowdrick's *Broadway Billy, the Bootblack Bravo; or, Brought to Bay by a Bold Boy*, of 1886; *Bob o' the Bowery; or, The Prince of Mulberry Street*, by "Captain" Jo Pierce "of the New York Detective Force," of 1885.) And the figures of the Western, the same, as will be seen.

That these categories of tales are thus related is of course not surprising either, just because the three do occur at the same time and do respond to and address the same distinct history. From a distance, moreover, and regarding the three together, it might even be seen that they also have a serial nature and comprise a nice allegory for our times. Properly read, the tale Rags-to-Riches, in the Horatio Alger version, is assault from below and is not a celebration but an exposé of the pretensions of the systems of wealth now in America. It celebrates the anarchic energies pitted against the systems of Business. The Western in its turn is also an effort to cancel the modern moment, by law and arms. It would reimpose social hierarchies, at the beginning directly and not infrequently on the part of authors who consider that they are the dispossessed. And the tale of the Private Eye might then be seen to record the failure all around, of both the street boys of Lower Manhattan and the cowboys of Medicine Bow. Sly subversion doesn't work, nor does armed suppression, and what is left for election is a disengagement, which in its turn is so absolute as to constitute a style. (The first sentence of this book ends with the word "fancy," and the last with the word "style." "Fancy" fails, it being the "aggregative and associative power," in the classic formulation, and yields to "style," which is just theatrics and a joke, and has no power at all.)

These tales do not compose either "myth" or "legend," nor would "folklore" be the right word. "Folklore" intimates a peasantry, whatever else is meant by the word. The tales with which I am here concerned are neither anonymous nor are a stuff of traditional belief nor do they arrive via oral transmission, nor certainly are they fabrications of the unlearned. Horatio Alger, Jr., went to Harvard, graduating eighth in a class of eighty-eight, and liked the poetry of Alexander Pope. Nor are any of the writers of these tales to be accounted children of the Folk.

These tales on the other hand are so much attached to the singular and distinct social history of their origin, that they resonate it, much as once did the tales of King Arthur echo and elaborate a so-called "Matter of Britain," or as did tales of Charlemagne derive from and affect a so-called "Matter of France." So one might propose modern and American "Matters," granted that, by definition, they are neither antique nor finished. As in those other Matters, here too the tales and the history intertwine to compose a single narrative. Hence the *American Matters* of my title—although I also intend the pun, as to say that here are some things which matter.

# PART I

## Rags to Riches; or Horatio Alger, Jr., and the Dangerous Classes of New York

"That boy is an impostor."
—Horatio Alger, Jr., *Adrift in New York*

# Introduction

NO other American writer, nor any other American, has ever come more completely to represent any more distinctly or durably so American a fancy. It is the name of Horatio Alger that distinguishes the imagination of preposterous fame and fortune. Horatio Alger is not "Franklinesque," but certainly Benjamin Franklin is a Horatio Alger kind of a hero. Andrew Carnegie, Thomas Edison, Henry Ford, and others of the type likewise are confirmations of the bootblack Ragged Dick, Mark the Match Boy, Paul the Peddler, and Silas Snobden's Office Boy, while Horatio Alger is the poet. The name is a primary datum. And if just now, as indeed for approximately a century past and extending back into Alger's own time, that American idea of success which once was a plausibility is more often than not taken to be a fraud, or a locale for a familiar disillusion, or is a resource for wry comedy, the fact goes all the more to prove the persistence both of it and of Horatio Alger. He abides, the name becoming no less famous because it might stand for a fundamental disbelief.[1]

He is fixed, for one thing, by the history of his terrific popularity as measured in terms simply of the numbers, so far as they are to be had. Possibly no novelist anywhere has ever been more widely read. Near the end of his life, in 1899, Alger himself estimated that he had sold approximately 800,000 books, merely, but had no way of knowing for certain, and in any event the greater extravagance was to come later, after 1910 and in the 1920s. Alger, says his biographer Frank Gruber, "was the greatest selling author of his time, of all time" (27), and it is the evidence of his text that Gruber was not one to be carried away. Reasoned estimates of the sales by the several of Alger's biographers range from a stunning 16 million to a stupefying 400 million, but reason is the harder to come by because it is not known either how many juvenile novels Alger actually did write. For his boys' books he used at least four names in addition to his own. Under his own name he wrote at least 103 novels (although not more than 117). The numbers of the novels and the sales, moreover, and whatever their extravagance, testify still the less because these were juvenile fictions which were likely to be read repeatedly and likely to be passed from hand to hand. The number of the sales therefore is reasonably to be multiplied an indefinite several times, while the question whether there were 117 Alger novels, or 109, as is sometimes also said, or 103, hardly matters in this astronomy except for consideration of the fact that while the novels are not identical they are anyway very similar to each other, and therefore it follows that all of that infinity of readers read essentially the same story again and again.

The numbers mean still the less, moreover, because Alger was one of those marvelous and select writers whose chance it was to compose a tale of such grace that very soon, transcending its text, it would have an independent fate and would not have to be read at all. Among American writers Horatio Alger did that more certainly than for instance, Washington Irving, who drifted into quaintness, or even Mark Twain with his whitewashed fence or with even the journey down the river, or Harriet Beecher Stowe, who pertained mostly, if mightily, to her moment. Alger was a genius for whom the question of talent is irrelevant. If scarcely anyone anymore does actually read a novel by Horatio Alger, no one does not know what is meant by the Horatio Alger story. Daniel Boone and Paul Bunyan and Mike Fink, and other such heroes of the few accredited American folktales, as compared with Alger, are mementoes at best, to be salvaged by deliberate acts of research if salvaged at all any longer in order that they might be characters in a perpetuated drama of the American frontier, whereas Alger is the name of an unassisted archetype.

Horatio Alger is uniquely the measure of American imagination because no other American writer has been so surely, centrally, and continuously present in it.

# 1 Alger

THERE is comedy here which attaches to both the man and the myth, the two being related. To contemplate Horatio Alger is to consider national gospel, both of which might be seen to be alive with their ironies. Both contain their encoded dangers and realizations, without which they would both be dead. Lacking the ironies, the American dream of success would be only an antique piety without shrewdness and disillusion, while Horatio Alger would be just another of the many grubs of the later-nineteenth-century kiddie market, just another little sodomizing defrocked ex-minister.

The ironies are everywhere, not least in the successive exposés of the man.

The first biography of Alger, by Herbert R. Mayes, was published in 1928. In his book which he called *A Biography Without a Hero*, Mayes explained a great deal by retrieving an Alger who was a case study in repressions mostly sexual and sometimes literary. Mayes's Alger was the son of an iron-handed Unitarian minister, of Chelsea, Massachusetts, "a blue law by himself, diagnosing as sinful every human activity conducive to enjoyment" (14), who demanded that the boy prepare himself for the same, and of a Mrs. Alger who was warm but timid and who embraced the boy secretly when her husband was away.

> "Now you may sit on my lap," she said. He would climb up and nestle his head on her shoulder, putting his skinny arms around her, holding tight; and sometimes, out of a mutual mingling of joy and misery, their tears would drop together on her black, woolen dress. Those occasions, however, were not frequent; chiefly she was compelled to fondle him at a distance. (19)

Alger was a lonely boy, not unsurprisingly. The other fellows teased him and called him "Holy Horatio." But when at age sixteen he went to

Harvard, as Mayes discovered, Alger rebelled against the authority of the father, although not with entire success. Alger's favorite subject was un-Unitarian French, for he knew what people said about the French. Also, there was a girl in Cambridge, and her name was Patience Stires, but Alger, Sr., secretly interfered with that romance in order to preserve the boy for the ministerial calling, although in fact Horatio already really wanted to be a writer.

Then Horatio Alger went to Paris where, on a visit to the Morgue, he met Elise Monselet, a chanteuse in a sleazy cabaret, and on the night of a February 4th he lost his virtue. ("I was a fool to have waited so long," he wrote in his diary, as discovered by Mayes. "It is not vile as I thought. Without question I will be better off physically" [Mayes 76].) Then there was an English girl, Charlotte, and still later, after he had entered and left the ministry and had established himself as a writer, there was a lengthy relationship with a Mrs. Una Garth, whose husband fulminated and who herself was at once compassionate and condescending, both, with regard especially to Alger's continued ambition to be a serious writer. Alger when he traveled carried a bust of Shakespeare in his baggage.

All of this along with much else—Alger's diminutive stature (5′2″) and his sickliness, and a strange episode of amnesia in Manhattan, and visits to iniquitous caves in lurid Chinatown, and his adopting of a Chinese orphan, Wang, who unhappily not long thereafter "had his bowels kicked out when he fell under the hoofs of a runaway horse" (111), and episodes in which Alger prowled the city at night in disguise— all of this presented such a Horatio Alger that, in Mayes's words, "the Freudians, it may be supposed, would have had with him a glorious adventure" (107).

In fact there was a nicely intended, and peculiarly appropriate, gamesomeness in all of this. Some of the things that Mayes wrote were in fact true, if only by accident, and were verifiable, but for by far the greater part the biography was a sprightly fraud. It was "a deliberate, complete fabrication, with virtually no scintilla of basis in fact," said Mayes himself, fifty years afterwards. "Any word of truth in it got in unwittingly. I made it up out of nothing. Most of the few facts I uncovered were intentionally distorted." To a biographer, Edwin P. Hoyt, he would write, "Not merely was my Alger biography partly fictional, it was practically *all* fictional. . . . The project was undertaken with malice aforethought."[1] For a period of a generation and still lingeringly thereafter, however, Mayes was the accepted and authoritative source for information about Horatio Alger, alike for popular magazine pieces with such titles as "Horatio Alger Was No Hero," "Alger: No Alger Hero,"

"The Unholy Horatio Alger," for the entry in the *Dictionary of American Biography*, and for serious and keen Freudian interpretation, as in an essay by Norman N. Holland, "Hobbling with Horatio, or the Uses of Literature," in 1959.

Mayes's own chief source had been Alger's black, clothbound secret diary, which nobody else had ever seen because Mayes had invented it, too, but nobody else would seem ever to have looked for it, either, no doubt because it answered so generously to what was wanted in a true account of the real Horatio Alger. Only the critic Malcolm Cowley had raised a question about the diary, in 1945, in a brief review of some Alger reprints, to ask whether Mayes had copied it correctly, or whether the diary had ever existed, but he questioned only passingly and without apparent consequence. The Mayes book, *A Biography Without a Hero*, after all had created a hero of a kind that was especially wanted *circa* 1928 and lingeringly for a generation thereafter, in a time when debunking of eminent piety and prudery was itself a species of hagiography, as in instances ranging from Lytton Strachey's Florence Nightingale and Queen Victoria, to Gamaliel Bradford's Mary Todd Lincoln, to the Elmer Gantry of Sinclair Lewis. Mayes's Alger was a more pathetic if less tragic version of the Mark Twain of Van Wyck Brooks's provocatively entitled biography of 1920, *The Ordeal of Mark Twain*. As had been the case with Brooks's Twain, Alger's life as it was now to be truly known would reveal the morbidity of the rule in America of the twin spirits of Capitalism and Calvinism. Mayes's Alger was a pathetically comic hero. This Alger had tried repeatedly, if vainly and not quite consciously, but viscerally, as it were, to give the lie to that tremendous number of moral tracts which somehow he had written and which had come to identify him. Mayes's Alger was a representative man by virtue of his hypocrisy, however modest or frustrated that was.

Corrective to the fraud of the debunking arrived in 1961. The writer Frank Gruber collected Alger books. He published a bibliography prefaced by a short biography. The Mayes book, said Gruber, was "studded with such a vast number of factual errors and flights of the imagination that I am compelled to discard virtually everything in the book with one single exception, the date of his birth. Even the date of his death is wrong" (13). (But a subsequent biographer was to discover that Mayes had been wrong about Alger's birth date as well.) The truth about Alger, said Gruber, was that he was a singularly uninteresting figure except for the fact that he wrote an enormous number of books for boys which were successful beyond belief. Alger "did not drink, smoke or gamble. He remained a bachelor all his life. He led a quiet life, a lonely life" (11).

The few facts of relevance or of any interest whatsoever were these:

Alger had been born in 1832, in Revere, Massachusetts, the son of a Unitarian minister and the eldest of five children. The family had moved to Marlborough, Massachusetts, when Alger was thirteen. In 1848 Alger went to Harvard. In 1853 he entered Cambridge Divinity School, graduating in 1860 having taken time off from his studies for periods of teaching and writing and some work as an editor. Alger did at this point spend several months traveling in Europe, but never was there any Elise or Charlotte, and in 1861 he entered the ministry. In April of that year he was preaching in Dover, Massachusetts. Three years later he moved into another ministry, in Brewster, Massachusetts. Meanwhile, he had in fact had serious literary ambitions, dating from the time of his undergraduate years, and since his late teens he had been publishing poetry regularly, including a book-length volume of his work and a lengthy verse satire, and also adult fiction. In 1864 he published his first juvenile novel, *Frank's Campaign; or What Boys Can Do on the Farm for the Camp*, designed to aid the war effort. In 1866 he resigned from the ministry in Brewster, removed to New York City, and except for occasional travels lived there for the rest of his life.

He was not a recluse, Mayes to the contrary. He enjoyed the society of his fellow writers. The success of *Ragged Dick*, in 1867, made Alger welcome at the social institution known as The Newsboys' Lodging House, which became his second home. "He ate most of his meals there, sometimes slept in the dormitories with the boys," said Gruber, for "throughout his life, Alger was genuinely fond of children" (23).

And he died at the home of his sister Olive Augusta Cheney, also a writer of children's stories, in South Natick, Massachusetts.

Gruber claimed for Alger no exorbitance other than that he happened to have been "the greatest selling author of his time, of all time." Gruber's Alger, by way of relief from gaudy revelation, was temperate, sane, and honorable, and, if neither greatly inspired nor gifted, had been terrifically hardworking in pursuit of his craft. But all of that was after all worth remarking, for Gruber's demonstration of such modesty, and such plausibility, was delicious in its own way. Both the Horatio Alger story and the story of Horatio Alger were already absolutely in place when Gruber came to assess the man, and Gruber with his plain fact brought to the two fictions a new and a wholesome presumability which was more than demystification. He created a Horatio Alger who was rather like Alger's own typically humble heroes, except indeed that this Alger seemed to be real and rather like someone whom one might know.

But then Mayes, with all of his factual errors and flights of fancy and his candid lying, turned out actually to have had very nice instincts. Other biographies followed upon Gruber's brief account. One, by Ralph D. Gardner in 1964, elaborated upon Gruber at length. Another, a year earlier, by John Tebbel, oddly was derived entirely from Mayes and took no account of the debunking of the debunker. But in the 1970s new materials were uncovered which oddly confirmed the general sense of Mayes's book, to the effect that shocking things had indeed been hidden away. Particularly, some of Mayes's nastier and more fetching insinuations were confirmed.

In his romance for Freudians Mayes had provided Alger with: a distant father, a fondling mother, a series of sexual frustrations and frenzies, and a Chinese foundling boy. Now in biographics first by Edwin P. Hoyt and then Gary Scharnhorst, it was revealed that in 1866 Alger had left his ministry at Brewster and had gone to New York because an investigating committee of the Unitarian Society of Brewster had requested his dismissal, having charged him, in the words of the report, "with gross immorality and a most heinous crime, a crime of no less magnitude than the abominable and revolting crime of unnatural familiarity with *boys*, which is too revolting to think of in the most brutal of our race." Probably there had been earlier homosexual episodes. After the discovery of the pederasty Alger had written a seemingly confessional poem, beginning: "Friar Anselmo (God's grace may he win!)/Committed one sad day a deadly sin." Four years later he was still reeling with guilt, or perhaps was indulging his reeling. He had sought professional counseling, from William James. Henry James, Sr., in a letter to Henry, Jr., reported that "Alger talks freely about his own late insanity which he in fact appears to enjoy as a subject of conversation and in which I believe he has somewhat interested William."

And this was to put a different light on Alger's fondness for children, particularly wayward boys, and occasionally girls, both in life and in letters. As is often said of Horatio Alger, he was still the preacher when he wrote his juvenile fictions, only having transferred the venue of his ministry.

In later biography, by Scharnhorst, and by Scharnhorst and Jack Bales, Alger was a mostly lonely custodian of his guilty secret, although not a recluse. He did not sleep with the boys at The Newsboys' Lodging House, although he was probably sometimes a visitor and for certain was one of the institution's donors. He did not share the society of fellow writers, although once in 1853 Ralph Waldo Emerson had spent a night at his parents' house. Through family connections he also knew Henry James, Jr., but James shunned him. He was a member of the Harvard Club, for which he wrote occasional odes, and he was a man who possessed a considerable store of genteel learning. He had a special clientele among wealthy uptown German and Sephardic Jews in New York, whose place in American culture was perhaps in its other way as ambiguous as Alger's own. He was tutor to the sons of Joseph Seligman, later to Benjamin Cardozo and to the future The Honorable Lewis Einstein, a diplomat, and maybe to the future Governor Herbert Lehman—that last is disputed. Another of the ironies attaching to Alger is that such novels as *Herbert Carter's Legacy* and *Paddle Your Own Canoe; or the Fortunes of Walter Conrad* appeared first as serials in the magazine *Young Israel,* which Joseph Seligman had founded and which for many years was Alger's primary magazine publisher.

His relationship to American "society" was in fact nothing if not ambiguous. Alger was a man who had considerable learning and patrician credentials. He had Mayflower and Pilgrim ancestors. If Alger's father had been strict with his son, and also had not had much money, still the father had been a man of some secure consequence in towns in the neighborhood of Boston, and it is to be presumed that Alger himself had had at least some knowledge of the reputed "old clerical self-respect which," in the words of Alger's near-contemporary Henry Adams, "gave the Unitarian clergy unusual social charm." But Alger's tastes at least sometimes, apparently, ran to snobbish disdain, in a way befitting in a young man who had had an excellent education at Harvard, graduating eighth in a class of eighty-eight. He had at least a taste, or at least a momentary ambition, for lightsome social satire, if no talent for it at all, as he demonstrated in a four-hundred-line poem, dated 1857, entitled "Nothing to Do: A Tilt at our Best Society," about a languidly wealthy young man whose father had been a pawnbroker:

> Augustus Fitz-Herbert, as all are aware,
> Having crossed the Atlantic, and got a moustache on,
>     Likewise being son of a known millionaire,
>         Stands of course on the very top round of the fashion.
>     Being taught to consider himself, from his birth,
>     As one of the privileged ones of the earth
>     . . . . . . . . . . . . . . . . . . . . . . . . . . . . . . . .
>     In this model republic, this land of the free—
>     So our orators call it, and why should not we?—
>     'Tis refreshing to know that without pedigree
>     A man may still climb to the top of the tree;
>     That questions of family, rank, and high birth,
>     All bow to the query, How much is he worth?

And this was satire composed by the one American writer who beyond all others was to be celebrated for his celebration of the promise of lowly origins.

Again, if Alger did not carry a bust of Shakespeare wherever he went, the ironies were not fewer, for in his correspondence he did frequently cite Alexander Pope, and was a fond reader of the living poets including his former teacher Henry Wadsworth Longfellow and other such Brahmins as James Russell Lowell and William Cullen Bryant and Oliver Wendell Holmes, and was an avid reader of William Dean Howells. He was well-travelled. He was an accomplished classicist.

There was fine irony in the fact that this man of quite elegant tastes, or education at least, was to be known forever first of all as a writer of books for boys, and second as a writer of peculiarly crude and sensational boys' books which for decades were the object of the wrath, beyond contempt, of militant librarians. Libraries banned the books, on the ground that they were crude and sensational—beginning in 1879 with the Fletcher Free Library of Burlington, Vermont, and thereafter throughout the rest of the country through the 1920s. Especially after the turn of the century, those millions of middle-class boys who read the Horatio Alger story, read it behind the barn or behind the garage, for the great ideologue of Respectability was not considered to be respectable.

Moreover, for all of his literary education, Alger was not even a crafty writer. It is not to be supposed that he dashed off his tales in order simply to keep the pot boiling while all the while he was living a truer life elsewhere, at some higher level. The sheer amount of the labor required for the writing down of all of those words would deny that possibility. Presumably, he wrote as best he could, and then, obviously, that best proved to be both tremendously and persistently fetching for his juvenile readers—and it becomes a nice problem to know what after all it was that fetched them.

It was not sensationalism nor moral crudeness of any obvious kind. Alger brought to the novels a sensibility which would seem almost perversely to have denied any of the low qualities which might have served for the entertainment of children, and brought to the tales on the other hand a sense for fiction, or lack of sense, which made the novels to be almost unexceptionably bland, unadventurous, unoriginal in either plot or sentiment, but to be, rather, repetitive and simple-minded, while being nonetheless pedantic, and intolerably so, as one would suppose.

The very titles of the novels with their characterizing rhythmic alliterations—*Strive and Succeed, Do and Dare, Fame and Fortune, Try and*

*Trust,* and on and on—should have indicated that these were clichés more than they were stories.

Once again, the novels were not only didactic but were at once ruthlessly and irrelevantly informative, often with footnotes. When Ragged Dick wandered past the old Mercantile Library in New York City, in the novel of 1867 which bears his name and which remained one of Alger's most popular novels, an asterisk directed the reader to the bottom of the page where he learned that the library had a collection of one hundred thousand books. In a moment of what might have been climactic action in *Mark the Match Boy,* in 1869, the reader learned at the bottom of a page that banks in New York City were paying 10 percent on savings accounts—a noteworthy fact for someone, but not for the presumed juvenile reader of this novel, who just previously, in the novel *Rough and Ready, or Life Among the New York Newsboys,* had been instructed in the meaning of the Wall Street terms "bulls" and "bears", and the same previously to that, in *Ragged Dick.* ("The bulls is what tries to make the stock go up," says Dick, in dialect, "and the bears is what try to growl 'em down.") He or she also learned some principles of post–Civil war currency exchange: "I must here remind my New England reader, who is accustomed to consider a shilling about seventeen cents," said Alger midway in what was already a narrative digression, "that in New York eight shillings are reckoned to the dollar, and a shilling, therefore, only represents twelve and a half cents."

Digression, on the other hand, might have been the pleasant rule of these novels except that they were endlessly episodic, while in narrative line they were so arbitrary as to disallow suspense. Nor was there much violence to be found in the novels, such as boys, especially, of all ages, are presumed to love. The favored felony in them is abduction, wherein the boy heroes, and sometimes girls, are victims and are rendered passive—but even so, and allowing whatever suggestiveness there was in that, the suggestion was not usually confirmed by any physical cruelties. Alger's most serious juvenile fiction, as a matter of his intention, was *Phil the Fiddler,* in 1872. In it Alger set out to expose the so-called "padrones," alleged slave masters who bought Italian boys abroad and brought them to New York to be street musicians. It was said that the padrones beat the boys regularly. These children, said Alger, were "the 'White Slaves' of New York," and here Alger did put physical cruelty on the page, but even here and with serious justification, only briefly, while by its virtual uniqueness the instance suggests that his imagination found no excitement in this sort of thing, nor any comfort.

Nor even if one accepts the unlikely possibility that once, perhaps a century ago, American boys had a taste for capitalist homiletics, is the allure of the novels to be thus explained. Alger moralized about the virtues of savings accounts, and about honest dealing, indefatigably, and about readiness to serve one's employer, but for his boy heroes when they rose, although indeed they practiced those virtues, the practice of the virtues was never the proximate cause of the rising. In Alger's arithmetic of luck and pluck, the former always greatly outweighed the latter. Alger indeed was obsessive about luck. As John G. Cawelti has observed, "The chapter which contains the crucial turning point of the book is invariably entitled _____'s Luck" (115). Our hero comes to the right place at the right time to catch a thief, or to aid in an accident, or to help a stranger who has a reward to offer, or, more typically, to discover that he is the lost or the true heir. Sometimes he is lucky enough to be victimized in the right place at the right time. In 1888, in *The Errand Boy; or, How Phil Brent Won Success*, Phil Brent receives immediate promise of success because on the train to New York, from Planktown, he was cheated out of five dollars and was arrested for possession of stolen property but was saved by the old gentleman who was sitting behind him, who is the president of the railroad and who asks him to call at his offices. Typically, were our hero not so plucky as he is, he would not be able to capitalize on the luck, but the luck always comes first, as in fact Alger now and then candidly admitted. Thus of Frank Courtney in *The World Before Him*, of 1880: "[Frank] felt that it was largely owing to a lucky chance that he had been the means of capturing the bond robber. However, it is to precisely such lucky chances that men are often indebted for the advancement of their fortunes." And thus with minor qualification at the end of *Struggling Upward; or, Luke Larkin's Luck*, of 1890: "So closes an eventful passage in the life of Luke Larkin. He has struggled upward from a boyhood of privation and self-denial into a youth and manhood of prosperity and honor. There has been some luck about it, I admit. . . " The boys did strive and they did succeed, but they did not succeed only nor even primarily because they strove.

Nor did Alger provide his boys with much "character" at all, in the sense that, in fiction, motives to virtue, or to vice, are attached to a process of characterization. Complexity would not have been wanted, but Alger's heroes were not only incredible in their virtues, as were his villains in villainy, but were also monotonous. His plucky lads were nothing if not eager to enumerate their own virtues, while his villains were obsessed by wrong-mindedness:

"I don't smoke," answered Ben, hardly able to repress a look of disgust.

"So you're a good boy, eh? One of the Sunday-school kids that want to be an angel, hey? Pah!" and the tramp exhibited the disgust which the idea gave him.

"Yes, I go to Sunday school," said Ben coldly, feeling more and more repelled by his companion.

"I never went to Sunday school," said his companion. "And I wouldn't. It's only good for milksops and hypocrites." (*The Store Boy; or, The Fortunes of Ben Barclay*)

"You must be considerate of his feelings, Joshua. Remember that he has just lost his father."

"Suppose he has, there's no need of looking glum about it." (*Strong and Steady, or Paddle Your Own Canoe*)

"You may be a wealthy man!" said his mother impressively. "Cousin Hamilton is not so healthy as she looks. I have a suspicion that her heart is affected. She might die suddenly."

"Do you really think so?" said Conrad eagerly. (*The Store Boy*)

"It would not look well for you to go to the theatre just at the present," [Mrs. Preston] said.

"Why not?"

"So soon after your father's death."

Godfrey said nothing, but looked discontented. It was early to think of amusement while his father lay yet unburied in the next room. He left the room, whistling. He could not gainsay his mother's objection, but he thought it hard luck. (*Only an Irish Boy: or, Andy Burke's Fortunes*)

"Your poor mother is dead, Mark."

"Well, there was no need to wake me for that," said the boy, irritably. "I can't help it, can I?" (*The World Before Him*)

The stories existed in a dimension beyond clarity, where blatancy was of such degree that for all but the most naive of juvenile readers it might well have been understood to mock the clichés and formulas which it exploited:

He was a tall, dark-complexioned man, of perhaps thirty-five, with shifty black eyes and thin lips, shaded by a dark moustache. It was not a face to trust. (*Adrift in New York; or, Tom and Florence Braving the World*)

At this moment a poor woman, in a faded calico dress, with a thin shawl over her shoulders, descended the steps that led into the saloon, and walked up to the bar.

"Has my husband been here to-night?" she asked.

Tim Bolton frowned.

"Who's your husband?" he asked roughly.

"Wilson."

"No, Bill Wilson hasn't been here to-night. Even if he had you have no business to come after him. I don't want any sniveling women here."

"I couldn't help it, Mr. Bolton," said the woman, putting her apron to her eyes. "If Bill comes in, won't you tell him to come home? The baby's dead, and we haven't a cent in the house!"

Even Tim was moved by this.

"I'll tell him," he said. "Take a drink yourself; you don't look strong. It shan't cost you a cent."

"No," said the woman, "not a drop! It has ruined my happiness, and broken up our home! Not a drop!" (*Adrift in New York*)

The author of the words was a fond reader of the verses of Alexander Pope, and must have had some knowledge, even if suppressed, of the ways in which conceits will turn upon themselves and become satire, and in any event nothing is explained, certainly not the popularity of the novels, by saying that Alger's young readers would not have appreciated subtlety. Neither, it is to be supposed, would they have loved Temperance, and certainly they would not have loved having still more of the Temperance tractarianism which was inescapably everywhere else during the late nineteenth and early twentieth centuries. But present in such an instance as this of Tim Bolton, with its not unsubtle sequence of discordances—the information about the death of the baby followed by Tim's lyric of generosity, etc.—was perhaps an intimation concerning the nature of piety itself, whether or not Alger's readers would fully have understood.

Alger composed not only in clichés, as after all would have been right for his enterprise, but in clichés so flat and so thoroughly realized that they must at some level have implied their malign opposites, even in instances in which it is to be presumed that the issues were dear to Alger. No doubt that during the war years he was sincerely opposed to slavery and was concerned to rouse pity for its victims. His first juvenile novel, *Frank's Campaign*, in 1864, was a political statement in which in one important motif Alger upbraided northerners who were not better than southerners in their treatment of blacks. Frank intervenes when the bully is about to whip a little black lad: "You are not in Richmond, John Haynes," he says, "and you'll get into trouble if you undertake to act as if you were." On the other hand, our hero's and Alger's own affection for the same lad amounted to minstrelsy laid flat upon the page. Frank tries to teach the boy, Pomp, to read. Pomp tells Frank a fib about a lost book. And the novel says:

> "Doesn't your mother tell you not to lie?"
>
> "Lor', Mass' Frank, she's poor ignorant nigger. She don't know noffin'. . . ."
>
> "If you behave properly she won't whip you. You'll grow up a 'poor ignorant nigger' yourself if you don't study."
>
> "Shall I get white, Mass' Frank, if I study?" asked Pomp, showing a double row of white teeth.

Nor could this have been simple advice to his young readers that they had better study and not tell lies, because Pomp was not one of those readers and Pomp was considerably different. He was "a bright little fellow, as black as the ace of spades, and possessing to the full the mercurial temperament of the Southern negro. Full of fun and drollery, he attracted plenty of attention when he came into the village, and earned many a penny from the boys by his plantation songs and dances."

Nor could all of those readers have been charmed by the prose, for in fact the prose, far from being pleasantly simple or even lucid, was obstinately repetitious and expository and stilted, collapsing at every other moment into anesthetizing universals: "The little [Italian] fiddler, who had never before been invited into an elegant house, looked with admiration at the handsome furniture, and especially at the pictures upon the wall, for, like most of his nation, he had a love of whatever was beautiful, whether in nature or art." "The picnic came off on Saturday afternoon. The weather, which often throws a wet blanket upon the festivities of such occasions, was highly propitious, and several hundred persons, young and middle-aged, turned out *en masse.*"

Nor, finally, did Alger, for all that he was entranced by his alliterations, ever write a story called "Rags to Riches," nor would he have because, as all his readers have known, the repeatedly stated goal never was Riches but, rather, was Respectability. His heroes' monetary reward typically was modest, and even when not, always was arbitrary. The time and place offered egregious actual models. Alger might have described the budding of Rockefellers, Philip Armours, Jay Goulds, Andrew Carnegies. But he didn't. Alger's boy readers would not have found fulfillment for their own presumed greedy fantasies in these novels.

Alger's hero receives a new suit and/or a pocket watch, or an indoors job in a store or a "counting house," or an opportunity for a cautious investment, or a new name signifying either new or reclaimed family, in a modest republican version of Freud's family romance. In the first of the Ragged Dick series, Dick is happy as he contemplates taking the cut in his earnings which will be the result of his transferring to a counting room from the bootblacking business. He is happy with the new lesser enterprise because status is more than money for him. He says: "I want to grow up 'spectable." Tom Dodger, in *Adrift in New York*, prays for all of the boys when he begs a wealthy young lady, "You think I could be good if I tried hard, and grow up respectable?" Julius, in *The Street Boy Out West*, represents all of the boys in his having "a vague idea of what is meant by respectability," which idea beckons him forward. Julius acquires a guardian, a last name, and a reward consisting of a cash grant of 250 dollars which, upon the advice of his guardian whose daughter he has just rescued from a kidnapper, he invests in real estate. "I have endeavored," said Alger in his Preface to the novel, "while giving characteristic sketches of Julius and his companions, to show how, in his new surroundings, my young hero parts with the bad habits contracted in his vagabond life, and, inspired by a worthy ambition, labors to acquire a good education, and to qualify himself for a respectable position in society." And so did they all, except that many having come from good family from which they were only temporarily lost, were qualified already.

The money just in itself was the least of it, although these heroes were almost always very quick with figures. Julius will triple his net worth by the end of the novel in 1874, two years after his initial investment. We may know that this is no more than reasonable, however, because in 1878, in *Joe's Luck*, Alger would advise his juvenile readers that Joe, who had bought real estate in San Francisco in the 1850s and had made a killing, had been lucky, nothing more. "The day has passed," Alger warned, when "such rapid progress was possible. California is no longer a new country. . . . Success is always attainable by pluck and persistency, but the degree is dependent on circumstance." In *Adrift in New York* Tom Dodger gets a thousand dollars, prior to discovering that his name is really Harvey Linden, and Mark, of *Mark the Match Boy*, comes into an inheritance of exactly $2524, including interest, together with a lost grandfather. Nor could there have been allure in the money for itself even when the payoffs were greater because in all instances the rewards were essentially fortuitous.

And despite everything—the pedantic irrelevancies, the endless digressiveness, the clichés of situation and of piety and of characterization all inevitably brought to a flagrancy, the terrible discursiveness, the randomness of nearly all eventualities, and despite everything else— it remains the case that somehow, once, the story made by Horatio Alger was stunningly popular, that then it did come to be a locale for an abiding myth, and that the defrocked Unitarian minister, having got himself embedded in the imagination of children, came to be a national metaphor.

No doubt that there was a message here, and a provocation as well, and a system of innuendo, in some way known alike to young readers and their librarians.

# 2    Adrift in New York

ALGER distributed his heroes variously. The tales take place in villages in New England, in western mining towns, sometimes in Australia, where Alger had never been, and elsewhere, but the site for major exploitation was the City, and among cities chiefly New York City; in the typifying novels Alger's boys either are natives of Lower Manhattan, or if they have their homes in the village or the country, then from the country they go to New York to have their adventures. Or if they have happened to leave the streets of New York in order to find adventure in foreign parts, they take their New York habits and knowledge with them, because you can deport the boy from the City but you can't take the City out of the boy.

Alger was already an established moralizing hack writer of juvenile fictions when in 1866, after the Brewster affair, he himself removed to New York. In his new situation he looked for new materials, and evidence suggests that very soon he realized that in the streets of New York he had come upon something promising for both fiction and social concern. *Ragged Dick*, the first of the New York novels, would be serialized in the children's magazine *The Student and Schoolmate* beginning January, 1867. In December of 1866 Alger was writing to his sometimes sponsor William T. Adams ("Oliver Optic"), "Frankly, this tale of life in the streets almost writes itself, as there exists in New York today an unruly horde of boys in straits so desperate as to seem unbelievable," and, "There appears to be an endless supply of material here, for [in addition to bootblacks] there also are newsboys, luggage carriers and messengers who exist by wits and initiative in a dozen different ways." He had come upon such boys as these earlier, in 1863, on a brief visit to New York, but now with the end of the Civil War there were many more of them and their numbers were increasing daily. "Among the older boys," he observed to Adams, "are a number who ran away from farm homes to serve as drummers and foragers with the troops, and many of the children—there are girls among them—followed the armies, becoming mascots or begging or stealing to live. At any rate, they somehow made their way to the city, and now accept constant struggle as a part of their daily lives." Nor did Alger rush to sentimentalize them. Many, he said, continued to live by begging or by stealing, or by "imposing upon smaller boys of their class, and other despicable ways."[1]

Institutional philanthropies were already in place, notably the Newsboys' Lodging House, which had been established in 1854. The extent of Alger's association with it is disputed, but at the least he did contribute money and there can be no doubt of the decidedness of his association with the cause it represented. He wrote magazine articles about the Newsboys' Lodging House by way of raising interest and soliciting donations. In the Preface to the book edition of *Ragged Dick*, he announced that it was his intention to write a series of volumes "to illustrate the life and experiences of the friendless and vagrant children who are now numbered by thousands in New York and other cities," and then not only did he do that, but the matter became his essential subject.

Alger was sympathetic. He committed himself. More than that, manifestly he was enthusiastic. No doubt that he liked outlaw young boys. ("Nothing delighted him more than to get a lot of boys between the ages of 12 and 16 years in the room with him," so his sister Augusta would later write, "and while they were cutting up and playing about he would sit down and write letters or a paragraph of a story.")[2] But the special appetite aside, his address to the reader now changed by becoming excited and peremptory. In *Frank's Campaign*, in 1864, Alger had begun in long, leisurely, bucolic, not inelegant perspective, after an eighteenth-century manner, perhaps Goldsmith or William Cowper—

> The Town Hall in Rossville stands on a moderate elevation overlooking the principal street. It is generally open only when a meeting has been called by the Selectmen to transact town business, or occasionally in the evening when a lecture on Temperance or a political address is to be delivered. Rossville is not large enough to sustain a course of lyceum lectures, and the towns-people are obliged to depend for intellectual nutriment upon such chance occasions as these. The majority of the inhabitants being engaged in agricultural pursuits, the population is somewhat scattered, and the houses, with the exception of a few grouped around the stores, stand at respectable distances, each encamped on a farm of its own.

One Wednesday afternoon, towards the close of September, 1862, a group of men and boys might have been seen standing on the steps and in the entry of the Town House . . .

Now *Ragged Dick* was to begin: " 'Wake up there, youngster,' " spoken by a rough voice. Followed by:

Ragged Dick opened his eyes slowly, and stared stupidly in the face of the speaker, but did not offer to get up.
"Wake up, you young vagabond!" said the man.

And hereafter as a usual case the novels would begin imperatively in an immediacy of dialogue.

If Alger was sympathetic to the plight of these children, as no doubt he was, nevertheless there was an energy here which was not to be accounted for only in terms of a devotion to social service. There were other, if related, sources of excitement. The novels which were "to illustrate the life and experiences of the friendless and vagrant children," while in their way they did do that, more plainly were books about the City, especially the early "Ragged Dick" series, and they reported what were doubtless Alger's own eager discoveries of it. When Alger's young victim of a reader was advised that the old Mercantile Library had a collection of one hundred thousand books, or that savings banks in New York were paying 10 percent, with much else of the same, plainly the passages were in the books because Alger himself was fascinated.

No matter indeed the humiliation connected with Alger's having removed to New York, the novels spoke of an arrival. When he had been in New York the once before, in the autumn of 1863, his response in fiction had been that of a visiting rustic, easily overwhelmed. In *Paul Prescott's Charge*, of 1865, Alger's second juvenile novel, Paul would visit Broadway and feel the spell: "Paul at last sat down in a doorway, and watched with interest the hurrying crowds that passed before him."

Everybody seemed to be in a hurry, pressing forward as if life and death depended on his haste. There were lawyers with their sharp, keen glances; merchants with calculating faces; speculators pondering on the chances of a rise or fall in stocks; errand boys with bundles under their arms; business men hurrying to the slip to take the boat for Brooklyn or Jersey City—all seemed intent on business of some kind, even to the ragged newsboys who had just obtained their supply of evening papers, and were now crying them at the top of their voices.

But Paul's experience had been brief, and had been peculiarly literary in quality, as well, therefore second-hand. In Paul's cadences there had been much of Walt Whitman, for one evident thing.

Now Alger really was here and in residence, and was abrim with data. Dick has his first lucky chance when he is hired by a rich man to be a guide to the man's young swell of a nephew:

> "So you are a city boy, are you?"
> "Yes, sir," said Dick, "I've lived here ever since I was a baby."
> "And you know all about the public buildings, I suppose?"
> "Yes, sir."
> "And the Central Park?"
> "Yes, sir. I know my way all round."

And for a half of the novel Dick takes the nephew across and up and down Manhattan, from Chatham Street to Broadway, Broadway to Madison Square. The boys have exemplifying city encounters in which Dick demonstrates that he knows more than geography, but the sense of place just in itself, as it inheres in the street names, and in the details of transit, and in the public buildings, is constant and compelling, for Dick as for Alger:

> Chatham Street, where they wished to go, being on the East Side, the two boys crossed the Park. This is an enclosure of about ten acres, which years ago was covered with green sward, but is now a great thoroughfare for pedestrians and contains several important public buildings. Dick pointed out the City Hall, the Hall of Records, and the Rotunda. The former is a white building of large size, and surmounted by a cupola.

> The Third Avenue and Harlem line of horse-cars is better patronized than any other in New York, though not much can be said for the cars, which are usually dirty and overcrowded. Still, when it is considered that only seven cents are charged for the entire distance to Harlem, about seven miles from the City Hall, the fare can hardly be complained of. But of course most of the profit is made from the way-passengers who only ride a short distance.

In later novels of the City, this kind of touring would be less candid and relatively less extensive, but some such information was always likely to be in the books. Paul of *Paul the Peddler*, in 1871, lives in Pearl Street off Centre, having persuaded his mother to move from Harlem in order that he might find a way of doing business in Nassau Street. Young Frank Courtney, of *The World Before Him*, in 1880, seeking an apartment upon his arrival in New York, learns from a little "baggage smasher" that

Mott Street is not a good neighborhood, while the area of Bleeker and Clinton Place is better. Even away from New York, knowledge of New York was a boy's capital. When Julius emigrates west to rural Wisconsin, in 1874, he teases Abner, the hired man, and Mr. Slocum, the village schoolmaster, for their ignorance of New York. Mr. Slocum pretends to know Chatham Street, but it is proved that he does not. Abner in good faith accepts information that cows are pastured in Central Park and that there are bears in Wall Street.

Alger was fascinated, and so, evidently, were his young readers, but evidently his readers were not fascinated because they themselves were illiterate fourteen-year-old bootblacks who might identify with Ragged Dick nor because they planned to rent an apartment in Lower Manhattan. Nor is there any evidence, either, that just in this moment there was any large movement of persons from farm and town into New York such that it might be presumed that guide books offering merely practical information would have commanded a general interest. During the war years New York had lost population. An extraordinary number of young men from New York had been killed in the war—more than 53,000 of a total general population of under 800,000. After 1865 there had been a net increase in the population of Manhattan (to 940,000), but that was due entirely to foreign immigration, according to census studies, while the inflow of native Americans from the hinterlands was exceeded by an outflow.[3] And in any event it is not likely that anyone of any age ever, actually, in the years just after the Civil War or thereafter, took any practical information from Alger's guide books. The reasons for the allure had to have been other—in the exoticism of Alger's New York rather than its plausibility.

New York was in fact largely a foreign city. In 1870 already almost half the population was foreign-born, mostly Irish and German. Children who had two American-born parents constituted a mere 17 percent of the population.[4] This population, moreover, greatly concentrated as it was in Lower Manhattan, was dense and swarming, and therefore alive with both dangers and possibilities. (In 1870 in the area of the Lower East Side the population was already 450.2 to the city block, on its way to a density of 867.2 to the city block in 1910.)[5] New York was a place where one might lose one's way, perhaps deliciously. It provided geography for wickedness. It was "the modern Gomorrah," in the words of the prominent clergyman the Reverend T. DeWitt Talmage, of Brooklyn, uttered sometime in the mid-seventies.[6] The rush and the thronging and the clamor in the areas where the docks and the warehouses were, and in the hustled roadways of the Lower East Side, and in the commercial streets like Nassau and Wall and Canal, and in the labyrinths of alleyways in between, along with the inevitabilities of vice and violence, conditioned depravity perhaps, and mystery certainly.

Alger's novels were gazetteers to a New York which as a matter of substantial fact was enticing by reason of its terrific energy and its promises of iniquity.

On the other hand, the novels were of a piece with a larger industry devoted to mythologizing of the City. Alger's novels, quite with their presumptions of didactic intention and with their seeming piety, as well as in details of their adventures, directly echoed the extensive and lurid sub-literature made up of guides for unwary presumed rustics who were planning to visit New York, which flourished throughout the second half of the nineteenth century. Alger's novels directly echoed that other literature, and as well borrowed an extra measure of vitality from it. Thus it was that the pages of *Ragged Dick* intimated things other than what was said—darknesses and delightful revelations, which perhaps would be explicit, or perhaps not, in another book at another reach of vulgarity.

Alger's boys, or girls, adventured in a milieu which otherwise was established, for instance, by the anonymous author of *Snares of New York; or, Tricks and Traps of the Great Metropolis, Being a Complete, Vivid and Truthful Exposure of the Swindles, Humbugs and Pitfalls of the Great City,* in 1879, whose book was offered for fifty cents, who revealed interlinearly that he knew a great deal about proper strategies for faro, poker, and keno, and who, in accents very like those of Horatio Alger, offered service:

> Considering that the number of daily transient visitors to New York city in each twenty-four hours is almost as great as the total population of the whole State of Connecticut, and that there are classes of people in the city who rely upon the pillage of these strangers for their daily bread—to say nothing of diamond pins and other trifles regarded as equally essential as daily bread by this fraternity—it is evident that there are a great many persons who are—or ought to be—interested in knowing about the Snares of New York, and the Tricks and Traps of the Great Metropolis (13).

That writer was surpassed in moral urgency, in 1888, by the twin authors of *In Danger; or, Life in New York. A True History of a Great City's Wiles and Temptations,* which was a compilation of *True Facts and Disclosures by Howe and Hummel, The Celebrated Criminal Lawyers,* who were not sanguine and who sold their book by subscription:

> By hoisting the DANGER signal at the mast-head, as it were, we have attempted to warn young men and young women—the future fathers

and mothers of America—against the snares and pitfalls of the crime and the vice that await the unwary in New York. . . . With the desire that this book shall prove a useful warning and potent monitor to those for whose benefit and instructions it has been designed, and in the earnest hope that, by its influence, some few may be saved from prison, penitentiary, lunatic asylum, or suicides' purgatory, it is now submitted to the intelligent of America. (iv)

Howe and Hummel, meanwhile, had been preempted in piety by J. W. Buel, author of *Mysteries and Miseries of America's Great Cities*, in 1883. Buel, who had previously written *Border Outlaws, Heroes of the Plains*, and *Exile Life in Siberia*, among other handbooks, was unctuous, in a manner not unlike that of Horatio Alger on occasion. In his "Prologue," subtitled "Why the Veil Has Been Uplifted," Buel explained: "The following pages . . . have been prepared solely for purposes of enlightenment, which, it is my earnest hope, may be regarded in the light of wholesome revelation. While the descriptions are devoted to unmasking social evils, they are not prompted by pessimistical reflections, but rather to show the dark and ominous sides of national life, that the beauties of refinement and purity may appear nobler by comparison" (1).

J. W. Buel's reflections encompassed several cities, including Washington, San Francisco, Salt Lake City, and New Orleans, as well as New York, but the author agreed with general opinion in thinking that New York was primary. "First in the category of American cities," he said, "stands that [sic] of New York; first in size, first in wealth, and first in all the abominations which curse humanity" (25). "For several reasons," he said, "New York must have a larger percentage of licentious men and women than any other American city," and for a fact, he said, "There are more insane people in New York in proportion to the population than can be found in any other city of America" (62, 30).

For a certainty this New York was ill-governed. Said the (respected) journalist Junius Henri Browne, in 1869, in *The Great Metropolis: A Mirror of New York:*

> New York is growing more and more like Paris in respect to the police. . . . They have almost everything in their own hands, and are prone to make the law a terror to all but evil doers. That they have entirely too much power is beyond question; and that they abuse it is a matter of hourly observation. . . . The reputation of the tribe is bad; and men are rarely better than their reputation. They are compelled to associate with vulgarians and scoundrels of all grades; are exposed to every species of temptation; act unfavorably on each other, and have no restraining influences beyond their own intelligence, which is not very great, and their fear of exposure, which is not probable. (50)

And the reputation of the police was superseded by that of the volunteer fire departments, comprised notoriously of gangs of looters and probable arsonists.

New York was darkly, unnaturally foreign. The police themselves consisted of two classes, said Junius Henri Browne, the better of which was "American." "The worst class, which is two, perhaps three, to one of the other," he said, "are generally foreigners" who were "fond of arresting innocent ruralists, charging them with some heinous offence, and frightening them out of their wits and pocket books at the same time" (53). And Mrs. Helen Campbell, one of the authors of *Darkness and Daylight; or Lights and Shadows of New York Life*, in 1891, in a backward look, agreed: "The brutal American is of the rarest. It is because New York is less an American city than almost any other in the United States that the need for the 'Society for the Prevention of Cruelty to Children' was so sore. As the foreign element increased, and every form of ignorance with it, drunkenness as well as natural brutality worked together. Women no less than men were guilty of almost unspeakable crimes" (170). Howe and Hummel meanwhile, a few years earlier, having had better experience of unspeakable crimes, had noticed that in New York young girls were special prey. "Sometimes," they observed, "the ever-watchful and lynx-eyed Chinaman singles out some pretty little girl, on the pretense that he has some curious things to show her in his laundry," with the consequence that: "Many of these girls become closely identified with the lives of Chinamen, and it is astonishing how fond some of these girls become of their almond-eyed protectors" (17, 23).

According to their historian Richard Rovere, Howe and Hummel, who were "beyond dispute the greatest criminal lawyers of their day and quite possibly the greatest in American history," were nevertheless always on the lookout for clients, and with *In Danger* had written what was in fact an advertisement. They were engaged in enticing the larcenous, with descriptions, in their words, of the "elegant storehouses, crowded with the choicest and most costly goods, great banks whose vaults and safes contain more bullion than could be transported by the largest ships," and so forth, while explaining the methods of the most successful jewel thieves, the workings of a dozen skin games, and numbers of cunning devices for ease in shoplifting. The book, in Revere's words, was "in fact a kind of Real Estate Board brochure apprising out-of-town criminals of the superior facilities offered by New York and of the first-class legal protection available on Centre Street at 'what we may be pardoned for designating the best-known criminal law offices in America.' "

But if the celebrated lawyers were ultimately commercial in their intentions, that did not mean that they did not offer sweetness. Sin, so they promised, was everywhere in New York, not infrequently attached to addresses. Howe and Hummel warned the visitor of the pleasures of Harry Hill's Dance House, Billy McGlory's, and the French Madame's on Thirty-first Street (all of whom happened to be clients of Howe and Hummel). And in this the lawyers were merely following a convention of the literature. Said the composite author named "One Who Knows" in *The Spider and the Fly; or, Tricks, Traps, and Pitfalls of City Life*, in 1873:

> Startling as is the assertion, it is nevertheless true, that the traffic in female virtue is as much a regular business, systematically carried on for gain, in the city of New York, as is the trade in boots and shoes, dry goods and groceries. Within three miles of the City Hall are four hundred houses of ill fame, containing not less than four thousand abandoned females; and the police returns show that the whole number of professedly dissolute women in New York cannot be short of *twenty-five thousand.* (2:9)

Diligence had been rewarded in the case of the author of *Snares of New York*, for after much searching he had discovered the whereabouts of the Low Show called the "Lively Flea" featuring "POSES PLASTIQUE." It took place in a hall in back of a bar-room "perhaps twenty-five feet long, by fifteen feet wide, bare walls, and the floor carpeted with nothing but tobacco juice and cigar stubs." That this offering of nude tableaux vivants—including "Venus Rising from the Sea," "The Greek Slave," "Susannah in the Bath," and a "Grand Olympian Dance"—could "exist in our midst," he said, "is impossible to believe, and the sooner it is rooted out the better" (76ff). To just that end, meanwhile, J. W. Buel gave explicit directions. "Of the large number of concert saloons and *maisons de joie* which once lined Water street," he said, "only two remain as reminders of the past and its gross iniquities," one of which was located at Number 337 1/2 where were to be found "eight highly painted and seasoned girls, in a theatrical make-up of tights and tonsorial stockings." Another place was Number 96 James Street, where there was a concert hall with "more than a score of brightly dressed bawds, each giving a cunning display of bust and limbs while whirling through the room in lascivious suggestiveness." There one was forced to "minister to the remorseless cravings of the girls" by buying two dollars worth of stale beer, or ten wine glasses "full of that demoralizing liquid at the very reasonable rate of twenty cents each" (45–46).

The street names and numbers were important beyond the matter of advertising, exactly indeed as in the novels of Horatio Alger, and

An underground stale beer dive late at night in Mulberry Street bend. From Mrs. Helen Campbell, et al., *Darkness and Daylight: or Lights and Shadows of New York Life* (Hartford: A. D. Worthington, 1891), facing page 230.

it was the same small area of Lower Manhattan that was named. The names and the numbers made for a density of inference, wherefore in an essential way J. W. Buel and Horatio Alger were appropriating the same mysteries. Alger's boys did business near City Hall on Chatham Street (Park Row, after 1886), Nassau, Centre, Pearl, and Broadway, Bowery, and Forsyth north to Canal, and knew their way around Mott Street, where Ragged Dick although not Frank Courtney takes his first apartment, and Pell, Mulberry, Baxter, Hester, and Bayard. In the guide-book version of Little Old New York one read of "the many dives in the cellars of Chatham street, the houses of prostitution in Forsyth, Hester, Canal, Bayard and other streets"—as recorded by Howe and Hummcl (20). "The purchaser of clothing on Chatham street is pretty certain to be swindled" (474), said Mrs. Campbell—a notable fact because it was just there that in his first novel Ragged Dick had gone to shop, and had known better than to be swindled. By 1869 the notoriety of "The Five Points," at the intersection of Worth, Park, and Baxter streets, had become international, but, said Junius Henri Browne, "The moral suppuration extends far beyond the Points, into Mulberry and Mott, Elm and Centre, Pell and Dover, James and Roosevelt streets. Within half to three-quarters of a mile to the north and southeast of the Points, poverty and depravity, ignorance and all uncleanliness, walk hand in hand, with drunken gait and draggled skirts. Wherever one turns, his gaze is offended, his sensibility shocked, his pity and disgust excited at once" (273). Nassau Street was the very center of Alger's world, and Nassau Street, said Browne, was "crooked, contracted, unclean, with high houses and low houses, marble palaces and dingy frames," and was "New York in miniature" (381). "If you don't want your hat knocked off," he said, "or your boots trodden on, or your coat torn, or your nose thumped, or your eyes put out, don't go to Nassau street":

> I have seen sensitive and impetuous gentlemen who, in the Avenue, would have knocked the fellow down that looked displeasure, submit, without a murmur, to be hurled against a lamp-post until their spine cracked in Nassau street. I have noticed delicate dandies, with lavender kids, violets in button-hole, breathing dainty odors, upset by an ash-cart, and smile serenely in the gutter. I have known nervous capitalists to have their pockets picked, without ever turning to look at the rogue who robbed them. . . .Newsboys play hide-and-seek between your legs. . . .A malignant urchin in the form of a boot-black, puts a shine upon your white pantaloons as you are wedged into a corner, and coolly asks for fifteen cents for "doin' it extray, boss." (386)

"Nassau street," he added, pertinently, "has material enough for half a dozen volumes, if it were written up thoroughly" (388).

Most of all, this touring literature was a tour of swindles, tricks, traps, and humbugs, as was the case in the novels of Horatio Alger. What Ragged Dick knows primarily, beyond geography although intricate with the geography of New York, is the ways of the thieves and sharpers. Coming upon the first of the stores on Chatham Street, he advises Frank, who is young and full of wonder, "It's a swindlin' shop. I've been there." He knows the intentions of the man who has pretended to find a dropped pocketbook full of bills, and he can tease and then out-sharp the would-be sharper. He saves the money of a visiting rustic and can do that because he knows not only the confidence game, the work of a "check operator" in this instance, but the perpetrator of the confidence as well. "A feller has to look sharp in this city," Dick says, "or he'll lose his eye-teeth before he knows it." And those who come to the city for business, learn quickly. Paul the Peddler, new to peddling, loses a diamond ring, his mother's diamond ring, to a deceiver pretending to be a jeweler from Syracuse. ("Beware of any jewelers hailing from Syracuse," says the thief when he is caught.) That happens in 1871. In 1872, in *Phil the Fiddler*, Paul reappears briefly to deal with a pawnbroker in behalf of Phil, and successfully chaffers, reducing the price of a violin

from $5.00 to $2.25. Come to New York from Pentonville, Ben Barclay
the Store Boy is approached by a stranger who says, "Why, Gus Andre,
when did you come to town, and how did you leave all the folks in
Bridgeport?" Foolishly, Ben corrects the stranger, and a moment later
is approached by another who says to him, "Are you not Ben Barclay of
Pentonville?", but Ben has suddenly become sophisticated, and exposes
the bunkum.

Sharpers, so the guides said, were to be found at every street
corner. "The rural or provincial visitor who, with well-stored purse, goes
down to New York on business or pleasure, is very liable to become a
victim," said Buel (129). "Even before he reaches the city," advised
the author of *Snares*, "the advance guard of Swindledom will be ready
to meet him on car or steamboat" (13). Preparation included being
advised as to such formal eventualities as "pocket-book dropping," the
"patent safe," "thimble rigging," the "trick knife," "the euchre game,"
"the stone watch" (substituting a stone for a watch), "mock auctions,"
and learning to recognize such specialists as "the confidence roper,"
and "the check operator" who offered a bogus check as security for
the loan of a small amount of cash. It was best to be wary as well of
the beautiful damsel, a former schoolmistress of Jamestown, New York,
who traveled the New York Central inviting gentlemen to a friendly
game of draw poker: "as for learning the mysteries of draw-poker," said
the *Snares* author, "it was not supposed to be a possibility for woman.
In fact, few of the sterner sex, even with the assistance of Schenck's
manual, have mastered the game, although they have striven diligently
and paid heavy tuition bills" (25). And speaking of which, it was best
to be wary, too, of the "Store Girls" who served as bait for the dealers
in ready-made fabrics, for "Who has not noticed how the tall, slender-
framed girls, with their graceful movements and flexible spines, their
long, smooth throats and curved waists, are drafted off to stand as
veritable decoy-ducks? Who has not observed the grace and ease with
which they wear risky patterns and unusual *façons*, and so delude the
arrogant but ungraceful customer?"

A writer who had unusual authority in these matters and was less
winking was the great Inspector Thomas Byrnes, in 1891 Chief of the
New York Detectives, who wrote the third volume of *Darkness and Daylight: or Lights and Shadows of New York Life*. He had seen many cases
wherein "men of standing and respectability, including authors, politicians, divines, and even famous generals of America and Europe [had]
become easy prey for sharpers, and have been roundly fleeced by con-
fidence-men and buncosteerers." Of the latter he observed:

Having comfortably settled themselves in a suitable apartment, the rogues are ready for business. The hand-shaker then sallies forth, and at the first opportunity grasps a stranger by the hand and exclaims:

"Why, how do you do, Mr. Brown; how are all my friends in Greenville?"

The stranger, surprised at the warmth and unexpected friendliness of the reception, invariably responds,

"You've made a mistake, sir. My name is not Brown. I'm Mr. Jones, of Oshkosh, Wisconsin."

Then the rogue apologizes, hurries off, and reports to his confederate, the steerer, who hurriedly produces a book from his pocket, and hunts up Oshkosh, Wis. The book is a bank-note reporter, and gives a list of all the banks in the country, with a complete list of their officers. . . . Then he hastily follows Mr. Jones, accosts him in the street, shakes hands with him, calls him by name . . . (728ff.)

And so forth, a few years after Ben Barclay had had opportunity to confound exactly the same. (In 1873, similarly, a Chicago journalist, writing about "Western Confidence Men," in the volume of "One Who Knows," *The Spider and the Fly,* advised: "Whoever has read Hermann [sic] Melville's 'Confidence Man' will have formed a very clear and accurate idea of this species of the genus homo, as exhibited in many of his chameleon-like phases" [51].)

As a special case but insistently and remarkably, the guides for those who would go to New York warned against the myriad children who lived in the streets, and who were Horatio Alger's valorized boys. These children were both rude and very cunning, so it was regularly said. They were always to be pitied, and in certain ways and not infrequently were to be admired, but they were also threatening, if not actively then no less than implicitly. "The child of the slums frequently has beauty, but on all of them is the look of experience, of cunning, or a self-reliance born of constant knocking about," observed Mrs. Campbell, before embarking on a particular examination of newsboys and bootblacks. "The bootblack," she said, "has many idle hours, and, as surplus energy must be worked off, he gives them to tossing pennies, gambling in easy forms, cheating, and fighting. They are often practiced pickpockets, and in brushing a customer's coat will steal a handkerchief or other light article with the skill of their brethren in the same trade" (151). The "gamin," said Junius Henri Browne, was everywhere in Manhattan at every hour of the day or night. "Go where you will, you find him looking shrewdly from under his unkempt locks and fragmentary cap; standing in his great and broken boots, which he has either found in an ash-heap or purchased at a second-hand shop in the Bowery; proffering his services in some manner, if you indicate any need of them; or if you don't staring at you half-curiously, half-critically, and evidently seeing your every grotesque or peculiar point" (426). And Junius Henri Browne, too, remarked particularly on the ways of the bootblack and the newsboy, observing of the former: "He does not flatter you. He does not tell you your feet are small, or your boots neat. . . . On the contrary, he vows your boots are big and dirty; intimates that it must have been a long time since they were 'polished up,' and that you're not what you pretend to be, if you do not give him an extra five cents" (428).

More thoroughgoing, if not quite in the same sense a guide for the unwary, was the study called *Street Arabs and Gutter Snipes: The Pathetic and Humorous Side of Young Vagabond Life in the Great Cities, with Records of Work for Their Reclamation,* by George C. Needham, in 1887. Needham, previously the author of *The True Tabernacle,* here was writing another missionizing book, with distinct intimations of pederasty. "The 'Arab' hunter must be prepared for endless freaks and multiplied dodges, else he will find himself outwitted in the end," Needham said (50). Nor, after the tracking, was the capture of the Arab by any means an easy task. He recalled "spending a night on the streets with two friends, looking into nooks and corners, visiting low lodging-houses and thieves' dens in pursuit of this game." "We met with many homeless boys," he said, "wretched, shivering atoms of humanity, but could induce only five to accept our proposal of lodgings, food, clothing, and education *free*" (413). But nevertheless hunt the Arab he did, diligently and so well that he could invent a typology. "Waif" was the comprehensive term and referred to deserted children, merely. "Gutter Snipes," he said, were children who were weak mentally and physically. "Like snipes, they are creatures of suction." "Arabs," however, so-called originally by the late Lord Shaftesbury, were distinct for looking and acting like their oriental namesakes, and they put one to one's mettle. The name "Arab" might sound "rough, uncharitable, offensive, and degrading," said Needham, but truly the "street Arab" was "a very Bedouin in the midst of the thronging city multitude." Of them, he said, as of the Arabs of the desert it might be said:

> Ishmaelites by descent, they are Ishmaelites in disposition also; their hand against every man, they trust no man thoroughly, save their own brotherhood. Uncertain, vindictive, and selfish, they are the source of apprehension to every traveler. Living in clans or hordes, for self-protection, however, rather than for love's sake, their one pre-eminent object in life is subsistence—food, shelter, clothing.

And regarding the juvenile hordes in Manhattan, in particular, he added, "From childhood they *prey*; and by experience learn to overcome *might* by *cunning*" (21–23).

Bootblacks and newsboys were especially to be distrusted, but, as was pointed out in the 1879 *Snares of New York*, the "industrious class of little girls to be found peddling fruit, candies and peanuts" turned out often to include young prostitutes and blackmailers (62). And Howe and Hummel, on the basis of their convincing experience, concurred. For little girls the selling of newspapers was sometimes merely a pretext, affording opportunity for conversing with men until such time as they might engage regularly in a life of shame. Newsboys, it was said, were largely responsible for leading these girls into the paths of vice, while the littlest of the girls who were to be seen begging on the streets, of five and six years of age, in many cases had been "sent out as decoys by the larger ones to 'rope in' customers." The old-time procuresses themselves, often, formerly had been newsgirls.

Observations of this sort in this literature were no doubt appealing because prurient, and were not entirely appalling because they

Waifs and strays of a great city—a group of homeless New York newsboys. From left to right: Whitey, Dutchy, Yaller, Slobbery Jack, King of Bums, King of Crapshooters, Bumlets, Sheeny, The Snitcher, Snoddy, Kelly the Rake. From Mrs. Helen Campbell, et al., *Darkness and Daylight: or Lights and Shadows of New York Life* (Hartford: A. D. Worthington, 1891), facing page 124.

A group of bootblacks. From Mrs. Helen Campbell, et al., *Darkness and Daylight or Lights and Shadows of New York Life* (Hartford: A. D. Worthington, 1891), p. 152.

were largely drawn from convention. The City is where the sin always had been. On the other hand, what these guidebooks said was also considerably authorized by social fact, soberly observed, and especially with regard to the children. In 1890 in his epochal *How the Other Half Lives*, the reformer Jacob Riis, too, observed of "the street Arab" that "acknowledging no authority and owing no allegiance to anybody or anything, with his grimy fist raised against society whenever it tries to coerce him, he is as bright and sharp as the weasel, which, among all the predatory beasts, he most resembles" (67–68).

And just after the turn of the century serious socialist reformers such as Ernest Poole and John Spargo were testifying to much of the same. In a pamphlet prepared for the "Child Labor Committee" in 1903, *Child Labor—The Street*, Poole particularly regarded the cases of the

A gutter snipe. From George C.
Needham, *Street Arabs and
Gutter Snipes* (Boston: D. L.
Guernsey, 1887), p. 25.

newsboys and the bootblacks of New York. Newsboys in the thousands
worked the streets late into the night, so he reported, and, their shrewd
wisdom and amazing precocity being proverbial, imitated much of what
they saw. They were often intimates of prostitutes. In a sample of five
hundred newsboys, between 70 and 90 percent had contracted venereal
diseases by age fifteen. And even so, as between newsboys and bootblacks, as everyone testified, the former were much the higher in standing and promise. The bootblack, said Poole, was "the most ignorant of

all street workers," having relatively brighter prospects when dishonest. Hundreds of bootblacks, he said, "drift naturally into the humbler walks of crookdom, becoming petty thieves and pickpockets" (23–26).

And like Poole, Spargo, in 1906, in *The Bitter Cry of the Children*, approached the street children as a special case of child labor and discovered that among them, as opposed to children in factories, "the grosser forms of immorality" prevailed with special forcefulness. "The

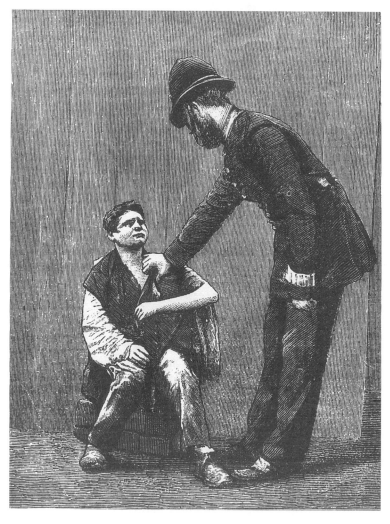

Catching an "Arab." From George C. Needham, *Street Arabs and Gutter Snipes* (Boston: D. L. Guernsey, 1887), p. 417.

proportion of newsboys who suffer from venereal diseases is alarmingly great," he reported, as had Poole. Glancing westward, in particular he called attention to the statement of the superintendent of the John Worthy School of Chicago, that: "One-third of all the newsboys who come to the John Worthy School have venereal disease, and that 10 percent of the remaining newsboys at present in the Bridewell are, according to the physicians' diagnosis, suffering from similar diseases" (184–85), and Spargo repeated statistics which he had found in Poole, to the effect that of 600 boys in detention in the New York Juvenile Asylum, 125 were newsboys, charged with crimes ranging from "ungovernableness" to grand larceny (187).

Throughout the second half of the nineteenth century the great authority on the problem of the street children was Charles Loring Brace. He had been principal founder of the Children's Aid Society of New York, in 1853, and was its secretary until his death in 1890. The Children's Aid Society in turn was the parent organization to the Newsboys' Lodging House, so that Brace was intimately involved in its founding as well, and thereafter with promotion, administration, and justification of the institution. He was cited by everyone, including George C. Needham, Mrs. Campbell, and Horatio Alger. His work was esteemed among the gentry, where the money was. He had received his first subscription from Mrs. William B. Astor. Horatio Alger may never in fact have had a meal at the Newsboys' Lodging House, but Teddy Roosevelt's father dined there every Thanksgiving and Christmas, as Roosevelt recalled in his *Autobiography*. Roosevelt remembered that his father had been "a staunch friend of Charles Loring Brace".

More persuasively and more officially than anyone else, it was Brace who characterized the children of the streets in New York, certainly in order to benefit them. His word was to be accepted. And it was a matter of a singular persuasiveness that his chief account of his work with homeless boys and girls, published originally in 1872 and cited by everyone, was called *The Dangerous Classes of New York*.

In that book he acknowledged and confirmed a general perception. When Mrs. William B. Astor had given him her fifty dollars, he knew that she had been responding to a social threat (88). Describing the need for the establishment of the Newsboys' Lodging House, Brace sounded not unlike the later George C. Needham with his Arabs, only with a twist of the metaphor:

> There seemed to be a very considerable class of lads in New York who bore to the busy, wealthy world about them something of the same relation which Indians bear to the civilized Western settlers. They had

no settled home, and lived on the outskirts of society, their hand against
every man's pocket, and every man looking on them as natural enemies;
their wits sharpened like those of a savage, and their principles often
no better. Christianity reared its temples over them, and Civilization was
carrying on its great work, while they—a happy race of little heathens
and barbarians—plundered, or frolicked, or led their roving life, far
beneath. (97)

Their potentiality for violence, he said, had been proved by their actions
in the New York Draft Riots in the summer of 1863. The danger of
these dangerous classes also was more than that of the same classes in
European cities: "The intensity of the American temperament is felt
in every fibre of these children of poverty and vice. Their crimes have
the unrestrained and sanguinary character of a race accustomed to
overcome all obstacles. They rifle a bank, where English thieves pick a
pocket" (26ff).

Brace did nonetheless like and recommend these youngsters beyond both pity and fear. Brace was himself a very Christian gentleman.
His later books included a theological tract, *Gesta Christa*, and a Christian meditation, *The Unknown God*. But apparently he was also aware
of an excitement in challenges to piety. He recalled that a precursor
of the Children's Aid Society, the so-called "Boy's Meeting," which
had consisted essentially of sermons addressed to assembled boys, had
foundered upon shoals of piety because "the street-boys," said Brace,
"as is well-known, are exceedingly sharp and keen, and . . . are soon
tired of long exhortations, and somewhat given to *chaff*." "The platform
of the Boy's Meeting seemed to become a kind of chemical test of
the gaseous element in the brethren's brains," he said. "One pungent
criticism we remember—on a pious and somewhat sentimental Sunday-
school brother, who, in one of our meetings, had been putting forth
vague and declamatory religious exhortation—in the words *'Gas! Gas!'*
whispered with infinite contempt from one hard-faced young disciple to
another" (79ff). Unrestrained or even sanguinary as these boys might
be, in some matters they were also discerning. " 'Life is a strife' " for such
children as these, Brace observed in his *Dangerous Classes*, "and money
its reward; and, as bankruptcy means to the street-boy a night on the
door-steps without supper, he is sharp and reckless." If ungovernable,
moreover, these boys were also ungoverned, wherefore when establishing the Newsboys' Lodging House, Brace had determined that first of
all it was necessary to "treat the lads as independent little dealers" (100).
They were to be given nothing without payment but were to be offered
more for their money than could be had elsewhere.

It was with some respect, again, that Brace said of the streetboy in his *Dangerous Classes* that "his views of life are mainly derived from the more mature opinions of 'flash-men,' engine-runners, cock-fighters, pugilists, and pickpockets, whom he occasionally is permitted to look upon with admiration at some select pot-house" (98). Brace's own repeating of not only the facts but the raffish terms for the facts implied no doubt an acknowledgement of a vital source of learning, one which obviously was unavailable to other boys, and which was available only vicariously to Charles Loring Brace himself. Among themselves the boys had a code of honor, it was said—they paid their debts, they did not poach on one another's newspaper beats—but to observe that fact was in a manner to say that they were a brotherhood, closed to outsiders, engaged presumably in the guarding of a secret truth. Visitors came to the Newsboys' Lodging House, and that it was some such perception as this that was encouraged is indicated by what Brace chose to quote from them in his book. He copied at length from the journal of an unnamed "visitor from the country":

> It requires a peculiar person to manage and talk to these boys. Bullet-headed, short-haired, bright-eyed, shirt-sleeved, go-ahead boys. Boys who sell papers, black boots, run on errands, hold horses, pitch pennies, sleep in barrels, and steal their bread. Boys who know at the age of twelve more than the children of ordinary men would have learned at twenty; boys who can cheat you out of your eye-teeth, and are as smart as a steel-trap. They will stand no fooling; they are accustomed to gammon, they live by it. No audience that ever we saw could compare in attitudinizing with this. Heads generally up; eyes full on the speaker; mouths, almost without an exception, closed tightly; hands in pockets; legs stretched out; no sleepers, all wide-awake, keenly alive for a pun, a point, or a slangism. (110)

Like everyone else, Brace made much of the fact that these boys liked to waste their money on the theater, when they were not gambling. That was an accepted wisdom although uttered always in wonder. Many years earlier, in the 1854 novel *The Newsboy* by Mrs. Seba Smith, the first of the fictions of the newsboy and taken sometimes to be an inspiration for Horatio Alger, it had been reported of the newsboy that "a fondness for dramatic display is the one passion with him. He will endure any amount of privation that he may indulge this passion" (25). That that was a low passion was not to be doubted. The gamins were to be found at the Old Bowery Theatre and at Tony Pastor's opera-house, where, as was reported by Junius Henri Browne, they indulged their excessive fondness for "sensational dramas founded upon robbery, seduction, elopement and desperate encounters; tragedies in which ranting, blue-fire, bloody villains and horrid murders form the chief features" (430). And of Ragged Dick himself it was said at the beginning: "However much he managed to earn during the day, all was generally spent before morning. He was fond of going to the Old Bowery Theatre, and to Tony Pastor's, and if he had any money left afterwards, he would invite some of his friends in somewhere to have an oyster stew." Col. Thomas Knox, a journalist, in a section of Mrs. Campbell's *Darkness and Daylight,* recalled the 1860s at the Old Bowery Theatre, remembering that the pit, at a price per admission of twelve and a half cents, "was generally filled with newsboys, bootblacks, and other youngsters" who ate peanuts and participated noisily.

> When a favorite actor entered he was greeted with three cheers, given in a somewhat disorderly fashion. Woe to the unfortunate actor who became unpopular with the "boys." He was received with cat-calls, hisses, and other demonstrations of dissatisfaction, and they were so loud and prolonged that it was impossible for him to proceed with his part. Occasionally he was the recipient of solid remonstrances in addition to vocal ones; they took the shape of eggs or vegetables that had passed their period of usefulness. . . . All the actors at this theatre fully understood the situation; in the language of the time they "played to the pit." (462)

What the boys liked particularly, said Colonel Knox, was broadsword duels and blood-curdling melodrama. The association of theater with juvenile delinquency was reflected in New York's "Theatre License Law" of 1872, which required theatrical managers to pay five hundred dollars a year license fee for the sole use of the Juvenile Delinquent Society.

But then that was not to say that the low amusement was not instructive. For one thing, the melodramas which the boys saw quite likely included mid-nineteenth century plays with such titles as *New York as It Is, The Poor of New York* (in later version *The Streets of New York*), *A Glance at New York, Out of the Streets,* and *New York Burglars; or Wedded by Moonlight,* which exploited crime and low life in the streets of New York, for these plays were numerous and popular, and that would have meant that for their entertainment these boys saw and greatly approved crude fictions about themselves and about the lives they very well knew, certainly with consequences for their ironical sense of things. For another thing, as Charles Loring Brace observed in his *Dangerous Classes,* "being accustomed to theatrical performances," the street boys had a nice ability for discriminating between oratory and "gas" (80). For Brace nothing indeed would seem so well to have distinguished these boys as a rhetoric which, like that of the theater, was parodically florid, and which was subversive of propriety just by the fact that it alluded to the theater and therefore to low associations, and which was continuously impertinent in its assertion of a street vocabulary which in its turn implied a life unknown to propriety.

In the language they spoke these boys of the dangerous classes were cheeky or sarcastic or assaultive, and Brace quoted them at length, with apparent relish in their speechifying at meetings of the Lodging House. As:

> Bummers, snoozers, and citizens, I've come down here among ye to talk to yer a little! Me and my friend Brace have come to see how ye'r gittin' along, and to advise yer. You fellers what stands at the shops with yer noses over the railin', smellin' ov the roast beef and the hash— you fellers who's got no home—think of it how we are to encourage ye. [Derisive laughter, "Ha-ha's," and various ironical kinds of applause.] I say, bummers—for you're *all* bummers (in a tone of kind patronage)— *I was a bummer once* [great laughter]—I hate to see you spendin' your money on penny ice-creams and bad cigars. (110)

And:

> Boys, gintlemen, chummies: Praps you'd like to hear summit about the West, the great West, you know, where so many of our old friends are settled down and growin' up to be great men, maybe the greatest men in the great Republic. . . . If you want to be snoozers, and rummeys, and policy-players, and Peter Funks men, why you'll hang up your caps and stay round the groceries and jine fire-engine and target companies, and go firin' at haystacks for bad quarters; but if ye want to be the man who will make his mark in the country, ye will get up steam. . . (111–112)

The old Boy's Meeting had failed upon the turns of language, implying fundamental differences of knowledge and putting naive idealism to the test of rich experience:

> "In this parable, my dar boys, of the Pharisee and the publican, what is meant by the 'publican'?"
> "Alderman, sir, wot keeps a pot-house!" "Dimocrat, sir!"
> "Black Republican, sir!" (80)

And it was these boys who were Horatio Alger's prime materials for a fiction, with all of their complexity at once of challenge, threat, and appeal.

They were really there. They were already notorious. When Alger's boys were in touch with the streets, as typically they were, they confirmed a life which was well known as both fact and fancy.

Alger's novels, with all of their thinnesses and schematics of characterization and their arbitrarinesses of plot, did after all, that is to say, have their substantial subject matter. Horatio Alger wrote juvenile stories about an urban juvenile underworld. His boys, and sometimes girls, for all that they lacked absolutely in any personal psychological depth, and for all that their discrete adventures in a fiction would likely finally have no moral significance whatsoever, did know a certain ominous geography, and although they were honorable in themselves, they were sophisticated in ways of conniving and thievery and lived lives independent not only of parents but of law generally, and knew the appropriate language and were ready to offer instruction, and they therefore continuously insinuated a known and celebrated and alluring danger.

# 3   The Impostors

THE stated goal, repeatedly, was not Riches but Respectability. Ragged Dick says: "I want to grow up 'spectable." Tom Dodger yearns: "You think I could be good if I tried hard, and grow up respectable?" But there was a moment, in 1869, when the newsboy Rufus, in *Rough and Ready, or Life Among the New York Newsboys*, twitted an old lady from Danbury. She had been searching the newspaper for a marriage announcement. She says that she has forgotten her specs, and Rufus, offering service, plays a trick on her. He pretends to read: " 'In Danbury, Miss Roxanna Jane Pinkham to Pompey Smith, a very respectable colored man from New York,' " whereat the old lady, presumably sharing the benign racism of her author, splutters: "Massey sakes! Has Roxanna married a nigger?" We are told that upon her return to Danbury she spread the slander everywhere—and this might have raised several questions, having to do first perhaps with the author's ideas about race, then having to do with the author's ideas about newsboys, then more pertinently with his ideas about nice old ladies (this old lady is also a dissembler, it happens, for she does not know how to read), but then more pertinently still, the passage might have raised doubts about the author's real attitude toward "respectability," no matter the explicitness or quantity of his statements elsewhere. Obviously Alger knew that in this instance he was writing an easy joke, for in the eyes of nice old ladies from Danbury, and not only they, the idea of a respectable black man was absurd and quite likely frightening as well. For such as they, "respectability," whatever it was supposed to look like, would after all not be available to everyone. As with gentility, breeding was required, probably in a biological sense.

In this same novel Rufus in fact demonstrates remarkable aptitude for recognizing and playing upon ideas of propriety. He is a virtuoso of prejudices. He is a chameleon of ideology, and that is why he is good at being a newsboy. "He could tell by a man's looks whether he wanted a paper," it is said, "and oftentimes a shrewd observation enabled him to judge which of the great morning dailies would be likely to suit the taste of the individual he addressed." Thus:

> "Here's the 'Tribune,' sir," he said to a tall, thin man, with a carpet-bag and spectacles, who had the appearance of a country clergyman. "Here's the 'Trib-une,'—best paper in the city."
>
> "I'm glad you think so, my lad. You may give me one. It's a good sign when a young lad like you shows that he has already formed sound political opinions."

But the next customer is "a sallow-complexioned man, with a flashing black eye, and an immense flapping wide-awake hat," to whom Rufus offers the "World." "What's that,—the Tribune?" he asks. "None of your Black Republican papers for me. Greeley's got nigger on the brain. Do you sell many 'Tribunes'?" And Rufus answers, "Only a few, sir. The 'World's' the paper! I only carry the 'Tribune' to accommodate a few customers." After that he offers the "Herald"—the "smartest paper in the city!"—then the "Times" which is the "best paper in the city" for its being sound and dignified.

Thereby it is demonstrated that Rufus is an attractively saucy urchin, but at the same time, insinuatively but no less certainly, what is indicated is the bluster and the essential whimsicality and finally the stupid arbitrariness of the ideas of the buyers of the newspapers, and of those of the great editors as well. Horace Greeley is a "brick," so Rufus says, but so also are James Gordon Bennett, of the Herald, and Henry J. Raymond of the *Times*, all of them alike and alike dismissable. What was being offered was not only the sauciness and spunk of the character but a serious impertinence. These—writers and readers alike—were after all the people who ran things, and demanded respect, and had it, except among street boys who had their own privileged perspective.

Alger's youngsters typically had very good knowledge of the ways of respectability, much like such of their contemporaries as Tom Sawyer and Huckleberry Finn, and like them had a deftness in their confrontations with it. But Alger's boys also knew the street and its mysteries. Alger sometimes inveighed against the influence of that so-called dime fiction which boys seemed unhappily to love, but the proper literary brethren of his own boys were in fact the heroes of novels of the type of *Broadway Billy, the Bootblack Bravo, or Brought to Bay by a Bold Boy*, by J. C. Cowdrick, and *Bob o' the Bowery, or The Prince of Mulberry Street*, by Jo Pierce ("Of the New York Detective Force"), or *Fergus Fearnaught; the New York Boy,*

*A Story of the Byways and Thoroughfares by Daylight and Gaslight,* by George
L. Aiken, which is to say that Alger's boys were generically disreputable,
that their literary as well as their social milieu was one which had no
respectability to begin with, and that therefore in the ambitions of these
boys there was an inherent irony.

The important difference between Alger's and the usual run of
Street Arab dime fiction was in fact Alger's boldness, indeed the flip-
pancy of his assent to confrontation as the condition of the relationship
between his boys and the decent folk.

Among Alger's peers only an occasional genius like Edward L.
Wheeler, author of *Fritz, the Bound-Boy Detective; or, Dot Leetle Game mit
Rebecca* and much else in a short life, managed anything like the same
quantity of affront, and then in quite a different voice. Wheeler played
lightly upon high literary tropes, elaborating them only just beyond the
point of parody, thereby to sass the gentry which loved them. Prior to
the return of Fritz to the streets of the city, one read:

> "Fritz!"
>
> No answer to the call, which was shrill and authoritative; and a
> frown of displeasure mantled the brow of Mrs. Jerusha Shrimp, as she
> stood in the vine-wreathed gothic arbor of her pretty farm-house, and
> gazed searchingly through a well-kept fruit orchard, now just in full
> bloom, which surrounded the house. . . . The Shrimp family parlor was
> no elegant affair, but was rather cozily furnished; boasted of some nice
> pictures, a piano, and last but not least, three human ornaments in the
> persons of the three Misses Shrimp; the elder Shrimp of the masculine
> gender had long since passed away, peace be to his ashes.

While other writers of the dime juveniles seldom sentimentalized
the children, they also did not call romantic sentiment itself into question. Broadway Billy and Bob o' the Bowery, and the others, are sturdy
lads who do good deeds, mostly by finding the true heir. They are good
detectives, and are so because at once they belong to a netherworld
and individually are nearly invisible, but what might have been an ominous implication (that that other world did exist, that the multitudes
of anonymous baggage smashers and bootblacks and newsboys were
terrifically competent) was conventionally resolved in exigencies of plot,
although sometimes in a slangy sweetness of dialogue:

> "W'ot d'ye take me fer? Do I look like a box o' blackin'? Not any,
> fer Joseph. I ain't that kind o' a ham sandwich. I'm a merchant in good
> standin', I be; b'long ter the Board o' Trade an' ther Royal Silk-an'-Satin
> Highfalutin' Club. Do these hyar hands look ez ef they ever flourished

the bristles 'round tanned cowhide? Not any, fer Joseph!" (Pierce, *Bob o' the Bowery*)

"See here, ma'am. I mean no offense, fer I'm very thankful fer all ye've done fer me; but if you think 'a counter-jumpin' dude is more of a gentleman than a bootblack, ye miss yer fire. That is, pervidin' the aforesaid bootblack is honest and true-blue, like yours truly. No sir-*ee*! I don't take no back seat fer any of 'em." (Cowdrick, *Broadway Billy*)

Alger's boys, with all of their plausibilities of honest ambition, were never so ingratiating, and therefore were truer to the possibilities of their origins in both social and literary fact. In Alger's novels the whole of the plotting, everywhere, finally was a measuring of the low against their supposed betters, and the implicit result of that measuring was everywhere as much a pulling down as a struggling upward—was in fact much more a pulling down and a humbling of vanity. The obvious and typical villains in Alger's fictions were finally only two in number, the stepparent, usually a stepfather, and the young snob. What those two had in common was hypocrisy, which was to be exposed instantly and repeatedly. Moreover, while hypocrisy was not uninteresting in itself, and while its exposure by those canny street boys was satisfying, the adventuring did not end there. The boys struggled upward by imitating their putative betters, just as piety encouraged them to do, but in the nature of the genre and as a given of social fact, this imitation was always potentially a mockery, and not infrequently was so specifically.

It was not infrequently so even with respect to the money. The boys would choose Respectability rather than Riches, but that was not to say that there was no relationship between the two of those virtues, especially in the time and the place. The models of Respectability whom the boys encountered were as often as not great pretenders to fair reward, indeed to generosity, who in truth were experts in small change. After Julius, of *The Street Boy Out West*, has saved Mr. Taylor's daughter who had been kidnapped by an Indian, and has received his reward of $250, and has taken to heart Mr. Taylor's advice to invest the money in a $15,000 piece of property, he learns about interest. Mr. Taylor will hold the mortgage on the property, and will collect, for Mr. Taylor has recovered from being distraught: when at first his daughter had been abducted he had declared that rather than lose his darling he would give half his fortune. Again, Colonel Preston, of *Only an Irish Boy: or, Andy Burke's Fortune*, who makes a cool 12 percent on his investment in the local woolen mill, will give Andy $100 for having saved his life from the highwayman who was going to kill him.

(And Andy, understandably, is reluctant. He has had some previous experience with skinflints. To the local deacon he has had occasion to say, "I'm a poor boy, but I don't work an hour and a half for two cents," but here the deacon had the last word: "'That's a cur'us boy,' said the deacon, slowly sliding the pennies back into his pocket.") The good Silas Snobden, the commission merchant of *Silas Snobden's Office Boy*, declares his liberal intentions and at the same time takes out insurance: "I have made up my mind that it is better to pay a boy a living salary than have him help himself"—while Horatio Alger, with his ear educated by Alexander Pope, would have known and intended that in his very naming of "Silas Snobden," he was mocking small rectitude. Young Rufus the newsboy, known also as "Rough and Ready," at the end of the talc receives $200 and a job in a brokerage for having saved Mr. Turner's life, and is the recipient as well of a wonderfully self-complacent gesture of benevolence: "As to salary," says Mr. Turner, "I shall for the present give you the same as you have been earning by selling papers,—that is, eight dollars a week. It is nearly double what I have been accustomed to pay, but that is of no consequence."

Thus Rufus enters into business on Wall Street and reasonably asks with respect to himself, "Why should he not rise to a position of importance like the men whom he had heard of and seen, whose beginnings had been as humble as his own?"—a terminal question which the novel has already answered, for we know now the secret of both Mr. Turner's calculating success and Rufus's shrewdness. Rufus certainly can do as well as Mr. Turner. On the street he had been a master of petty hypocrisies. "As a rule," said Alger, speaking in this instance of peddlers like Paul the Peddler but also for many of his heroes, "they are sharp, and know how to turn a penny as well as their elders. Though the integrity of some is not above suspicion, I am afraid the same thing may be said of some older merchants, who do business on a considerably larger scale."

The place for the final salvation of New York's street children, so it was widely supposed, was the country. The Children's Aid Society of New York took as one of its main tasks the organizing of "Emigration," that is, the sending of boys and girls to farms, chiefly in the midwest. Charles Loring Brace was particularly proud of this effort, and was so in good part no doubt because the effort would have been particularly subsidized by what the historian R. Richard Wohl terms "The 'Country Boy' Myth" of the nineteenth century:

> The country boy was famous for being inured early to hard work (life on the farm was never easy); and for his singleminded devotion to making

a place (for which read, a farm) for himself in the world or so, at least, the existing literature of bucolic nostalgia claimed. He was described as abstemious (life in the country was simpler than in the city), steady and saving (cash was always scarce in the country), he mastered depression and defeat (living close to nature gave him spiritual and psychic resources unknown to the city boy). (105)

By means of "Emigration," city boys were to be made over into country boys. They were to become shepherds. The myth harkened to ancient pieties. The sanity, indeed the prophylaxis of "Emigration" was beyond question—despite the apparently open secret that in fact and practice the policy resulted frequently in a form of indenture, to which Mrs. Astor contributed heavily.

And Horatio Alger went along, intoning the goodness of removal to the country and occasionally attempting to secure fiction from emigration. But here too what Alger said effectively was denied as soon as it was said. Perhaps in the beginning Alger had made a genuine discovery beyond the capacity of institutional social service, when he learned that his street boys often ran away from the farms to which they had been sent. Johnny Nolan, a fourteen-year-old bootblack who figures by name in the first pages of *Ragged Dick* and in later fictions, was a real child on the New York streets and the first of the street boys whom Alger actually came to know, and Johnny Nolan in the moment of his first appearance in fiction is in flight. He is being pursued by a man in a brown coat who had secured the place far off in the country for him. "Didn't you like it?" asks Dick, and Johnny says, "No, I had to get up too early. It was on a farm, and I had to get up at five to take care of the cows. I like New York best." He had had plenty to eat, and a good bed, but had felt lonely. And Alger, being at this early time seemingly open-minded and anxious to learn, had opined: "Johnny could not exactly explain his feelings, but it is often the case that the young vagabond of the streets, though his food is uncertain, and his bed may be any old wagon or barrel that he is lucky enough to find unoccupied when night sets in . . . is accustomed to the noise and bustle and ever-varied life of the streets, and in the quiet scenes of the country misses the excitement in the midst of which he has always dwelt."

But if in 1867 Alger was somewhat surprised by Johnny Nolan's refusal, soon thereafter he seems to have been persuaded, at least at the level of the fiction itself, that Johnny had had other good reasons to flee, beyond missing the bustle of the streets. Alger intoned the pieties, but they were converted to irony because the tales went otherwise. "Though as a class our Western farmers are intelligent, they lack . . . refinement and cultivation" (*Julius*), so Alger would say by way of mild qualification of the accepted idea. There might have been an odd presumption here, that refinement and cultivation were in fact consequential for the tales of his street boys, but then the observation was not irrelevant because here was a matter which was almost always disregarded, in behalf of a supposed wholesomeness. Moreover, country folk who pretended refinement were fit objects for ridicule. So it was said in *Strive and Succeed* in 1872, concerning the country poetess Melinda Athanasia Jones, who has been rejected by *Atlantic* and *Harper's*: "'It is because I am a Western *Literati*,' she exclaimed to her brother with a lofty contempt for grammar. 'If I were a Boston or New York *literati*, they would be glad to get my productions.'" She has written the lines: "Breathes there a girl with soul so dead,/Who never to herself hath said,/Wisconsin is my native state?" And country folk who pretended to cosmopolitan knowledge were ripe targets for Alger's boys, as is the case with Julius's foolish country schoolmaster. The country is at best the place of country dullness. "In the country there aint no murders, nor burglaries, nor nothin'," says Patrick Riley in the book of *Julius*. Perhaps unlike Charles Loring Brace, who had spent his early years in Hartford, Alger would after all have had some actual knowledge of country life. Country and village were what he had left, albeit by urgent invitation. The farm was the breeding-place of farmers, who as likely as not were both dull and cunning. Thus in the adventure of Ben Barclay, *The Store Boy*, on his visit to Pennsylvania: "A little way from the house was a tall, gaunt man, engaged in mending a fence. He was dressed in a farmer's blue frock and overalls, and his gray, stubby beard seemed to be of a week's growth. There was a crafty, greedy look in his eyes, which overlooked a nose sharp and aquiline." Ben has been sent forth to outwit him because he has been robbing the wealthy New York widow who is Ben's patron. As between Fifth Avenue and the Farm, Fifth Avenue owns the virtue while the Farm is the locale of witless mean spirits.

As for the actual workings of Emigration, the good Republican Alger imagined something like a slave auction. Mr. Charles O'Connor, who in life was Superintendent of the Newsboys' Lodging House, would gather fifty children taken from the streets and put them on a train for Wisconsin. (O'Connor appeared frequently in Alger's pages. Alger apparently did know him. Presumably he would have agreed with Brace that O'Connor was a man unsurpassed in the skills of imposing order upon wild boys. "The Superintendent has had a very good preliminary experience for this work in the military service," said Brace, in *Dangerous Classes*, "having been in the British army in the Crimea?" [99ff].) Having arrived at the rural village, as was to be discovered in *Julius, or the Street Boy Out West,* the children were drawn up into a little company on the train platform where "many curious eyes were fixed upon them by those who had come to meet them, and some were already selecting those whom they desired to adopt."

> The next day was to witness the dispersion of the little company which had come out to try their fortunes in the great West. Notices had been circulated in the neighboring villages that a company of boys had arrived, and farmers and mechanics who needed a boy on the farm or in the shop came to Brookville; and at eleven in the forenoon the hall presented a busy and animated sight. While the new-comers scanned attentively the faces of the boys, or opened conversations with them, to guide them in the selections, the boys again were naturally anxious to obtain desirable guardians and homes.

Our hero here does obtain one of the good places but that, explicitly, is because he is lucky. No matter the expressed faith in Emigration and the solemn recapitulation of its benefits—"There are hundreds now living at the West," said Alger in his Preface to *Julius,* "respected and prosperous citizens" who owed to this admirable work all that they were—this story discovered something else, namely that Horace Greeley's advice as invoked upon the children, resulted in sending children to the block. And Julius, who in the previous volume, *Slow and Sure,* had been stepson to a burglar, would have been the proper lad to lead an author to that discovery.

Everywhere in Alger's fictions, finally, the country boy was exactly the boy the hero did not want to be. According to the basic plot everywhere, the country boy went to the city, or if he did go the other way, it was as a city boy that he went, whether naturalized or native-born, practiced in shams.

Those librarians who banned Alger's books ostensibly for their being crude and sensational, would after all have had better reason than that, inferable if not explicitly realized. The boys in the books were not what they should have been. They were not boys, for instance, like the little newsboys named "Nibsy" and "Skippy" in the juvenile fictions composed by Jacob Riis in accompaniment to his reforming, who tended to die pathetically. They were not occasions for facile pity. Nor were they lovable scamps.

In particular they were not the "bad boys" whose adventures were escapades, who provided delight in the extensive wholesome literature of childhood which flourished in Horatio Alger's years. Those years were the golden ones of children's literature. The time was that of

Louisa May Alcott (*Little Women* was published 1868–69, *Little Men* in 1871), of James Whitcomb Riley's barefoot boy with cheek o' tan (*The Old Swimmin' Hole* was published in 1883), thunderingly of Frances Hodgson Burnett, whose *Little Lord Fauntleroy* was published as a book in 1886, of Thomas Bailey Aldrich's *The Story of a Bad Boy*, published 1870, of George W. Peck, whose "Peck's Bad Boy" first appeared in book form in 1883, and of Mark Twain.

Thomas Bailey Aldrich's "bad boy," by way of particular illustration, had been the author himself, recalled in twinkling sedateness by a man who was not yet thirty-five years old, who set the tone for a genre:

> This is the story of a bad boy. Well, not such a very bad, but a pretty bad boy; and I ought to know, for I am, or rather I was, that boy myself.
>
> Lest the title should mislead the reader, I hasten to assure him here that I have no dark confessions to make. I call my story the story of a bad boy, partly to distinguish myself from those faultless young gentlemen who generally figure in narratives of this kind, and partly because I really was *not* a cherub. (7)

Growing up in Portsmouth, New Hampshire, this bad boy along with some companions had once fired off some old canons dating back to the War of 1812 and had alarmed the town. Another memorable moment was the time when, responding to a question about what the people of Boston did with the tea at the Boston Tea Party, a schoolmate had said they "chucked it"—"for which happy expression he was kept in at recess" (73).

Aldrich, whom Mark Twain thought to be the wittiest man in seven centuries, brought a glow to scampishness, and was rewarded with tremendous prestige and universal acceptance.

Not so, indeed, or not so in the same way, the midwestern journalist George W. Peck, whose "bad boy" was a deliberate and not infrequently macabre prankster, whose "Pa," the constant butt of his pranks, was a drunk and a womanizer, and whose language solicited violence: "O," he said, "it was the offulest smell I ever heard of, except the smell when they found a tramp who hung himself in the woods on the Whitefish Bay road, and had been dead three weeks" (*Peck's Bad Boy* 2:133); and "Some men can get full and not show it, but when Pa gets full, he gets so full his back teeth float, and the liquor crowds his eyes out, and his mouth gets loose and wiggles all over his face, and he laughs all the time, and the perspiration just oozes out of him" (*Peck's Bad Boy* 2:150). But Peck was otherwise a man of good will who winked at the patricidal ambitions of his "Hennery." "Of course all boys are not full of tricks," he would say, "but the best of them are. That is, those who are readiest to play innocent jokes, and who are continually looking for chances to make Rome howl, are the most apt to turn out to be first-class business men" *(Peck's Bad Boy* 1:28). And George W. Peck, author of *Mirth for the Million*, went on to become governor of the state of Wisconsin.

Horatio Alger's boys never were so crude as "Hennery," but were much more seriously subversive, and therefore were to be forbidden, as the "bad boys" were not. *The Adventures of Huckleberry Finn*, too, was banned, by the Library Committee of Concord, Massachusetts, for being rough, coarse, and inelegant, when it was no such thing but was duplicitous and disturbing. The custodians of the libraries evidently were not so trivial as to exclude crudeness merely.

But Huck Finn was also quickly redeemed for chuckling readers because despite all of the novel's challenge to right and duty, the amount of danger in his book, too, as in Thomas Bailey Aldrich and George W. Peck, finally was limited. The tale had been situated after all in a time a generation before the reading of it took place, and in a frontier which by 1885 had many years before disappeared into nostalgia. It was a crucial difference for Alger's boys that they were in Lower Manhattan and that they were there at this moment, and were drawn from an actual population of children known everywhere to be much more independent of civility than ever was Huck, and known to be shrewd and tricksy and threatening.

Relationship certainly exists between Alger's fable and *Tom Sawyer*, as has been suggested by the historian Richard Slotkin: Tom at the end has rescued the judge's daughter from captivity, has rescued the lower-class friend from disreputability, has achieved unexpected wealth, and like an Alger boy has done it all through pluck and luck (504). Perhaps still more to the point of the comparison is the fact that in his most memorable moments Tom is a conniving trickster, as in the whitewashing of the fence and the accumulation of the tickets which will enable him to win the Sunday School Bible. But it was certainly the case also that, at least while Tom remained in his own book, prior to *Huck Finn*, he was to be known to be a rapscallion, primarily and merely, while as for the novel which honored him, in Twain's own estimation, it was a "hymn."

When, at the end of *Huck*, Tom tortures Jim and does so just for the appalling fun of it, then Mark Twain perhaps did contemplate pure evil, as never did Horatio Alger. Alger never went so far, nor by likely intention very far at all. Alger, for all of the ruthless didacticism and the tireless homiletics and the indefatigable moralizing, was no moralist.

But he did offer interesting information. Both the numbers of the readers and the persistence of the myth so testify. Persons were indeed interested. For all of the fact that Alger's characters never actually developed morally, and that their individual adventures were so episodic as typically to seem to be without direction or plot, and that such triumphs as they had were essentially the gifts of plain dumb luck rather than of any kind of effort or mettle—for all of that, they proposed perception which might well have liberated the middle-class young boys of America who read the books, which perception remains.

The fact that Alger's novels really did not go anywhere was itself a probable disclosure. Alger's boys were outlaws by origin and definition—or, if they happened to be other, then Alger typically arranged a kidnapping and transportation to the city slums for their souls' sake. They were prowlers in the city. If they themselves, in the books, did not lie, cheat, and steal, even within the books they were in touch with those who did, and therefore by association were glamorous. They spoke a different language, which Alger quite unnecessarily was at pains to translate—when Alger interrupted a narrative to say what was meant when somebody was called a "brick," or a "swell," really he was talking about the discongruity between speaker and reader, as also between the speaker and the "brick." The street language, moreover, was joshing, evasive, highly metaphorical, hyperbolic, and indirect and teasing. Most of all, it set its own separating terms. "All I know about readin'," says Ragged Dick, insouciantly, "you could put in a nutshell, and there'd be room left for a small family." A customer asks Ben Gibson why he is blacking boots, and with more than impertinence he will reply, " 'Cause I can't make up my mind whether I'd rather be a lawyer or a banker. While I'm decidin' I may as well black boots."

These boys were outside of the civil community, linguistically and otherwise, and were adamantly so, and if at the end of the tale the hero was declared to be Respectable, that development always was absolutely unconvincing. Abruptly, usually in the penultimate chapter, the boys do begin to speak the common language. Sometimes they put themselves to learning French. They equip themselves with savings accounts and other such investments. They take on a job of work of the sort that anyone else might have, in a store or a counting house, and they rehearse the good-employee pieties for which Horatio Alger was to become famous. And all of this was an instructive and fetching lie.

The most frequent signal of advancement for an Alger boy is a new suit of clothes, often second-hand from a rich boy who is his envious double, in exchange for his rags. Dressed in the new pants, coat, and vest, the little Arab becomes a young swell. Fantastically, he has been so completely transformed that no one recognizes him. Dressed in his new second-hand suit, Ragged Dick greets his old and good friend Johnny Nolan, who asks, blankly, "Who be you?" The possession of two suits of clothes, the old and the new, brings Dick as close to ontological *Angst* as any Alger hero can come; there are times when he doesn't know which to wear because he doesn't know who he wants to be this time. Ben Barclay, of *The Store Boy*, returning for a visit to the village whence he came, decides strategically that he had better wear his old suit rather than the "new and stylish suit of clothes" which he also owns. And there was a lesson here, to the effect that the "swell," young or old, was a tailor's creation.

Far from being prescriptive of the proper behaviors for ascending from Rags to Respectability, the essential action in these novels amounted to chilling parody of the American Dream as commonly understood. The novels asked the question, How might a young man, or sometimes a girl, emerge from the Poverty and Obscurity in which one might have been born and bred, like Benjamin Franklin in the olden days, so as to enter a state of Affluence and Reputation? And in their typifying action the novels answered, Put on a new second-hand suit of clothes. if anything more was to be required for success, that more was more of the same: a different, and blander, mannerism of language, a bit of useless learning, a change in the venue of one's gambling, and so forth. Knowing well that the signs of Respectability really were not merely the signs at all but were the thing in itself, Alger's children were adepts of the signs.

"Respectability," moreover, was enterprising American society itself, by definition, and so it followed that the object of the parody was no such small thing as a local unfairness or excess of cupidity or a quirk in the system, but was, radically, the whole of the thing. And it was to the point that not much money was involved. One could do better as a bootblack. "Success," such as it is, and such as it was thought to be, was a dress-up, so the message went. Morally, "Success" and hence "Respectability" were the equivalent of the drop-game and the mock auctions and check operating and bunco steering, in the knowledge of all of which enterprises for ambition Alger's youngsters were already wonderfully expert. They were not only knowledgeable but knowing, and cynical, by definition given the content of their knowledge, and by their actions they were subversive, and altogether they were sinister young people.

This fabled Horatio Alger early in his career as a minister had tried to corrupt children. In his great career as a maker of fictions he undermined the literature of childhood, and he endured.

# PART II

## Westerns

"My real object was to visit some of the
principal cities, to study into Eastern ways
and customs."
—Deadwood Dick in Philadelphia

# 4    Royalty

I N eighteen months, 1868 to 1869, Buffalo Bill, a meat
supplier for the crew of the Kansas Pacific Railroad,
killed 4,280 buffaloes, by his own careful count. "It
was at this time that the very appropriate name of 'Buffalo Bill,' was
conferred upon me by the road-hands," so he said in his autobiography,
written when he was thirty-four years old, adding, perhaps oddly, "I have
never been ashamed of it." He called his book *The Life of Hon. Wm. F.
Cody, Known as Buffalo Bill.* But on the other hand he knew very well,
for he was a witty man, that it was not for his commissary activities
that suddenly he was famous. He was, in fact, already a legend, to the
terms of which he was trying to adapt himself by the act of writing
this book. The true beginning had come about in 1869 just after the
period of the great hunting. It was then that Edward (or "Elmo") Zane
Carroll Judson, known as "Ned Buntline," had visited Fort McPherson,
Nebraska, perhaps in search of materials for his fictions. Happening
upon William Cody, Buntline had written the story called *Buffalo Bill,
the King of the Border Men.* And Buffalo Bill had then been grateful. When
his wife gave birth to their first son, he had wanted to name the boy
Elmo Judson, in honor of the man who certainly Cody knew then had
been his own true father, but had been talked out of it. (They named
the boy Kit Carson.)

That was the beginning. The first installment of *The King of the
Border Men* would be published in December, 1869, in the *New York
Weekly,* subsequently as a short novel, and then produced as a play, its
popularity having been demonstrated.

When the play came to the Bowery Theater in New York, in 1872,
Bill attended the opening, a private box having been reserved for him.
Among his hosts even in this early time were such dignitaries as James
Gordon Bennett, editor of the *New York Herald,* and the financier August

Belmont. "The theater was packed," so Cody recalled in the autobiography, "every seat being occupied as well as the standing-room." And then, "the audience, upon learning that the real 'Buffalo Bill' was present, gave several cheers between the acts, and I was called on to come out on the stage and make a speech"—presumably not only to lend flesh to the fiction of the *King of the Border Men* but by way of extending it, for it was he who was the King. There had been an episode in the fiction when Bill had rescued a maiden (from the insults of drunken soldiers, a Buntline touch). Both in life and at the end of the story Bill would marry the girl (Louisa La Valliere in the fiction, Louisa Frederici in the life), but in the fiction not without his first settling questions of status. "If I see her any more, I shall love her," so he had said to her father, "and love above my station would be madness and folly," but then it had been revealed that in fact, in the fiction, and originally, Bill had been her superior in social rank, having been born to gentility. And then, on stage, that trope would have been extended beyond anything when the King himself appeared, replacing the J. B. Studley who had been playing the part. The manager of the theater, a Mr. Freleigh, had promptly offered Bill five hundred dollars a week in order, as it were, to play himself, apparently recognizing the value of a complex dramatic irony. And Bill himself would apparently soon recognize the same, although in this instance he refused the offer.

In his biography of Buffalo Bill, Don Russell says that in *The King of the Border Men* Ned Buntline actually had been writing about Wild Bill Hickok and had used Buffalo Bill's name probably for no better reason than that it alliterated. The story Buntline wrote had to do with raids and kidnappings along the Mexican border during the Civil War. The older Wild Bill really had been there, and not Buffalo Bill. But no matter. The act of genius was not the less for having been perhaps inadvertent. Ned Buntline, for all of the shallowness of his imagination and his proneness to cliché, had caught the essence of Buffalo Bill, if he did not in fact create it, although probably the former is the case.

Russell says as well that Buffalo Bill never really took himself seriously. But then even so, the joke by which the career and the legend might be said to have been principally defined would have had its own rich and not unserious meanings.

The legend was created by dime fiction and on the stage, and then most wonderfully of all in the circus to be called "Buffalo Bill's Wild West," and the joke was that he was the king. Buffalo Bill was royalty come to visit—or, since in obvious fact when he came to visit he was just putting on a show, the irony was in the fact that he so consistently and fluently played his part. Apparently he loved the fraudulence of royalty and was a virtuoso of just that. In the beginning apparently it had been the somewhat similar talents of Ned Buntline that had attracted Bill's own attention, even prior to the writing of the first tale. That is the implication of the passage in the autobiography in which Bill recorded his first meeting with the writer, indicating that it was the something at once regal and tawdry in the appearance of Buntline that had attracted him, namely, exactly, the regalia: "Just then I noticed a gentleman, who was rather stoutly built," Bill recalled, "and who wore a blue military coat, on the left breast of which were pinned about twenty gold medals and badges of secret societies." His left breast would have made a good mark to shoot at, said Bill to Major Brown, scoffing—but then after all he would spend his own subsequent lifetime in the deliberate costuming and gorgeous bedecking of himself. He would present himself precisely so as to secure wonder for the look of him.

In 1872, when he was twenty-six years old, he appeared in his first show, *The Scouts of the Plains*, written by Buntline and produced first in Chicago. After that for the rest of his life he was primarily a showman, primarily of himself. For all of his gratitude, he would drop Buntline within a year of the *Scouts* spectacle in order to be his own author and producer. In the autobiography he suggests that it was first of all a financial consideration that had led him to sever the connection, but there would seem to have been other considerations as well. By 1873 he was writing and organizing his own show, and obviously by the time of the autobiography knew that he was himself a superior maker of the fiction. Buntline's *The Scouts of the Plains* had been an "Indian drama," so he recalled, in which he, Bill, along with "Texas Jack" Omohundro, would blaze away, killing forty or fifty Indians in the first act only to have them reappear for the second. It had been a foolish business, so he now clearly thought. The Chicago reviews had said as much. Buntline had written the play in four hours. The *Chicago Times* had said that if Buntline had actually spent four hours in writing the play, it was difficult for anyone to see what he had been doing all the time, so Bill now recalled, not gratuitously. Buntline himself had played the part of the villain "Cale Durg," who was killed in the second act, after a long temperance speech, and the *Inter-Ocean* had said that it was to be regretted that he had not been killed in the first act.

Not so "Buffalo Bill's Wild West." Bill produced it himself and directed it and acted in it, finally for a period of more than thirty years, and, according to all recollection, made of it something glorious. He was the Master of the Ceremonies. He presided. He dispensed, his every gesture, in recollection, constituting an act of noblesse oblige. It was only a circus, and as plotless as had been *The Scouts of the Plains*, but plentiful testimony says that the pretense was wonderful, seemingly even inspirational.

Col. W. F. "Buffalo Bill" Cody. Poster Portrait 1908, Printer: Strobridge Lithographic Co., Cincinnati, Ohio. Collection: Buffalo Bill Historical Center, Cody, Wyoming.

The show settled into formula, as has been reconstructed by Sarah J. Blackstone. First there was a playing of "The Star Spangled Banner," then some announcements by a deep-voiced orator. Then came the Grand Entry of performers, on horseback, who galloped around the ring and then lined up in front of the grandstand. Then came "Colonel W. F. (Buffalo Bill) Cody," introduced in just that way, riding a white horse decked out in a breastband with gold pieces and with its tail and mane unbraided and rippling. Buffalo Bill wore his trademark leather shirt with fringes and beads, with hip-high leather boots, and on his head he wore his great white ten-gallon Stetson, and his long hair flowed, while in any event anyone would have known him anywhere by his moustache and goatee, both carefully trimmed. He would sweep off his hat and bow deeply, and his horse would bow, too, for it was a trick horse, and Buffalo Bill would say graciously, courteously, formally, "Ladies and gentlemen, allow me to present to you a Congress of Rough Riders of the World"—this latter after the show had become international.

He would have been not exactly aloof. He was a performer as well as the master of the ceremonies, but in that, too, apparently, the mastery was the message. He would shoot clay pigeons from horseback. "Buffalo Bill's/defunct," e. e. cummings was to say, meaning that the days of glory had passed, but remembering that Buffalo Bill would "ride a watersmooth-silver/stallion/and break onetwothreefourfive pigeons just like that."

And if he was not a figure quite to defeat death, as cummings's poem goes on to say, he did impose upon much more than his circus. (The Messiah when he comes will look just like Buffalo Bill, said Michael Gold in his 1930 novel *Jews Without Money*, which probably was to overstate the case.)

When they played "The Star Spangled Banner" by way of introducing "Buffalo Bill's Wild West," it was not yet the American national anthem. It became the national anthem following upon its being Buffalo Bill's anthem. As a matter of parallel significance, it was Bill who invented that ten-gallon Stetson he wore, thereby to contribute to the costuming of the Old West, not of course as it had been but as in story and legend it was to be. Meanwhile, he was iconic. In 1911 the Supreme Court of New York would rule that "Buffalo Bill has a sort of copyright on goatees of the peculiar form and color that adorn his chin."

And of all of the numberless tributes accorded him, one of nicest pertinence would seem to have been a poem by Marie, Queen of Rumania. She was after all an appropriate singer of the praises of Buffalo Bill, if a little deaf to American ways. She hailed Buffalo Bill as "master of the hunt." The phrase without doubt implied a status rather than a skill and meant something different from being a masterful hunter, but the allusion, to pastime of the nobility, had a rightness after all. "Buffalo Bill," she did say, was "a master of picturesque beauty and grandeur" and was "a link between the old world and the new." As he was, granted Queen Marie's idea of the old world.

Still out west, early in 1872, prior to New York and Chicago, at Fort McPherson, he had been appointed host to the visit of the Grand Duke Alexis, of Russia, who had wanted to kill some buffaloes. He had showed the grand duke how to do it, and had helped him, lending him his rifle, and the grand duke afterward had given Bill some valuable presents and cordially had invited him to visit should he ever be in Russia. And later that year, in the fall, out to Fort McPherson would come the earl of Dunraven, on a second visit, similarly inclined and similarly to be the guest of Buffalo Bill, for the second time. In 1887, in London, visitors to the campsite which had been set up for "Buffalo Bill's Wild West" included Albert Edward, Prince of Wales, with the Princess, Alexandra, and their children, the Princesses Victoria Louise, Maude, and Louise; Crown Prince Frederick of Denmark; the comtesse de Paris; and the marquis of Lorne. Then Queen Victoria herself, who never went anywhere, went to the show itself, thereafter requesting a command performance at Windsor Castle. That was in May. On a day in June of the same year, still in London, in the audience for the show were the kings of Denmark, Greece, Belgium, and Saxony, along with the crown prince (later Kaiser Wilhelm II) and the princess of Germany, and Crown Prince Rudolph of Austria, the crown prince of Sweden and Norway, Prince George of Greece, the hereditary prince and princess of Saxe-Meiningen, Prince Louis of Baden, Princesses Victoria, Sophie, and Margaret of Prussia, Prince Albert Victor, Prince George of Wales (later King George V), along again with Albert Edward and his wife and, again, the children. At Buffalo Bill's invitation, the kings of Denmark, Greece, Belgium, and Saxony, along with the prince of Wales, rode round the circus in the stagecoach, Bill himself driving, while Indians attacked. The prince of Wales said to Buffalo Bill, "Colonel, you never held four kings like these before," and Buffalo Bill said, "I've held four kings, but four kings and the prince of Wales makes a royal flush."[1]

Hobnobbing, he actualized pretension.

But then on the other hand, Buffalo Bill himself along with most of the personnel of the "Wild West," and much of the equipage, happened to be the real thing, which made ultimately for a more sober kind of irony.

Buffalo Bill himself, as not much more than a boy, growing up in Kansas, had indeed ridden the Pony Express, and not much later had indeed proved himself to be a remarkably skilled hunter, and, according to repeated testimonials, actually he had been an excellent scout and was continuously employed by the U. S. Army. In the autobiography he claimed to have killed many Indians, his first at the age of eleven. That was probably a lie, but, according to his biographer Don Russell, he had for a certainty killed at least one Indian, the Cheyenne Yellow Hand, which would be to indicate that there was real blood on his hands, human as well as animal.

Among the principals of "Buffalo Bill's Wild West," meanwhile, as the years went by, were such other authentic westerners as Bill's fellow scout John Burwell Omohundro, known as "Texas Jack," and William Levi "Buck" Taylor, and "The Cowboy Kid" Johnny Baker, and James Butler "Wild Bill" Hickok, a friend of the Cody family from the days of Buffalo Bill's childhood, and others. Among the stars of the show only Annie Oakley was not a true child of the Plains. She was Phoebe Ann Moses from a farm near Cincinnati, daughter of Jacob and Susan Moses, but she really could shoot. And the Indians, too, were authentic, including for a season Sitting Bull himself. (Sitting Bull wanted that bowing horse. He took it as partial payment for services and was sitting the horse when he was murdered. As the bullets flew, the horse went through its tricks.) For a season in the 1890s, among the Indian troupe there were a number of prisoners of war, captured following upon the massacre of Wounded Knee and recruited for the show by arrangement with the Commissioner of Indian Affairs. Except for those prisoners, all of these other performers, were also already dime novel subjects, like Buffalo Bill himself, and, all of them at the same time, like Buffalo Bill, represented an actual and a problematic history, and contributed to the same irony.

Buffalo Bill and his entourage were the comedy of conquest. They exaggerated outrageously. They were glamorous—and it was their glamour, in this version of the Winning of the West, that in effect was offered as legitimacy, or as a circus pretense to the same.

The historical event of the winning of the West moreover did obviously and directly involve a question having to do with rule and legitimacy, and then in the decades at the end of the nineteenth century that question had ramifications quite beyond the conquest only of the American West. Here was a time and a place where the question of proper authority was critical. In the kind and the associations of their gorgeousness, Buffalo Bill and entourage presented an answer, not without irony.

The story of the Wild West is so infused with post–Civil-War American history that it becomes misleading to stress its origins going back to James Fenimore Cooper, as do historians and critics beginning with Henry Nash Smith, in his seminal *Virgin Land.* The questions of proper authority to rule and of title to the land, however, would in fact seem to have been there from the beginning.

So indeed it was in 1823 in the first of the Leatherstocking Tales, *The Pioneers.* Old Judge Marmaduke Temple was not actually the owner of the village of Templeton, as everyone had supposed. With all good grace, he has in fact been suffering bad conscience, because by right of patrimony the place really has belonged to young Oliver Edwards, who is suspected of having Indian blood. Then it was, so it might be said, that the crucial problematic of the tale of the Wild West was invented. Cooper, moreover, would seem to have followed the indicated logic, at least within the pages of this first novel of the series. While the village of Templeton has been promised to Oliver Edwards, who as it turns out is not an Indian after all but is the grandson of the British Major Effingham who was "the rightful proprietor of this very soil," the novel in its wisdom goes over first to Chingachgook, who had been a king, and then to Natty Bumppo, the white man who dresses and thinks like an Indian, causing Fenimore Cooper, the son of Squire Cooper, to lament the unresolvable issue. Thus *The Pioneers* came to its one moment of undoubted eloquence, with the death of Chingachgook, and thus also it discovered its crucial problem, when Judge Temple and Natty discuss the laws which have been newly imposed for the purpose of preserving game. Natty will go to prison and to the stocks for shooting a deer out of season, which is to say for his daring to assert his good and prior title to the land. He has begun life in the novel as a minor character and ends as an infinitely suggestive victim; and it was Cooper's genius that having admitted Natty, he could not hereafter let him go.

The question from the beginning would seem to have been one of primogeniture—in the "West" wherever that was from moment to moment but as well with every implication for the East. When the Buffalo Bill of Ned Buntline's original story, *The King of the Border Men,* is revealed to be of gentle and therefore superior birth, that was to confirm the question. Buffalo Bill had rights, by birthright. And so it was earlier, in 1860, in the first and one of the most popular of the dime novels to have a western theme, Edward Ellis's *Seth Jones.*

*Seth Jones* was novel number eight in a list of more than five thousand to be published by the house of Beadle and Adams. It was "the perfect Dime Novel," said the Beadle's editor Orville Victor, and was reissued repeatedly well into the time of the subsequent dime-novel westerners. With obvious debt to Cooper (it was set in western New York just after the Revolution), it too carried forth the essential tale of birthright: it will be revealed in the novel that "Seth Jones" is not the grizzled hunter and Indian fighter he has pretended to be, but is the gentle-bred Eugene Morton, eligible for the hand of Mary Haverland, whose land he will have, in addition to her hand. "I'm Seth Jones from New Hampshire," he says repeatedly, but he isn't. And it was that irony that shaped the novel. "Seth Jones" speaks in grizzled dialect but knows the King's English very well, and, as Morton, is fluent in it. The given reason for Morton's pretending to be "Seth Jones" is in the first place entirely flimsy. He has been checking up on Mary, having heard that she had married someone else. It was all a bald-faced trope— composed by Ellis, who was a schoolteacher in Red Bank, New Jersey. But then not everything is explained by saying, as does for instance, the historian Henry Nash Smith, that Ellis employed the "persona" for its own sake and merely as an amusement. The irony in the fact itself of the "persona" is active in the tale. Seth Jones controls everything because he is not really just a Seth Jones. No Seth Jones without the authorizing Morton. Morton has the right to be Jones, not certainly vice versa in such a tale as this.

Obviously the trope, here and in Cooper as well, borrowed from romance going back before Shakespeare, which might indicate nothing beyond its conventionality even within the terms of the democratic nation, except that the trope did persist in literature of the Wild West high and low, both fictive and scholarly, and as spectacle and as theory.

The motif of birthright (of title, of high estate, of nobility, of the rights and the true identities of lords and kings) was in fact perfectly appropriate to the story of the Wild West considering particularly that the story was invented almost entirely by easterners, for their own purposes and justifications. As has been said by the historian G. Edward White, the West of the final decades of the nineteenth century was created in great part by such easterners as Owen Wister, Frederic Remington, and Theodore Roosevelt, and was intricate with the emergence of what was plausibly an American version of a nobility or in any event a wealthy, upper-class "Eastern Establishment," identifiable by its boarding schools and metropolitan men's clubs, among other institutions, and by the *Social Register* (first published in 1887). And if this West was not invented in its entirety by the members of an elite social class, the story did anyway almost invariably encounter the question of proper, rightful social authority.

That encounter in fact occurred nowhere more forthrightly than in the absolutely serious novel which was to turn out to be both the most popular Western of them all and the principal archetype for all of the stories and movies and television dramas to come, namely Owen Wister's *The Virginian*, of 1902. It established the scenes and personnel: the card game, the saloon, the cowboy with a gun (rather than the scout or the hunter), the schoolmarm, the pard, at the end of the action the duel in the dusty street of the western town. In its time, for a period of a decade and a half, it was the best-selling novel in America. More than a million copies of it had been sold by 1920. There was a stage version, followed by a musical version, and then the novel would be made into a movie several times over, and, if in very loose adaptation, in the 1960s was the basis for a television series.

Most of all it was its hero that the novel offered, tall and taciturn and skilled and drawlingly ironic. "The Virginian" might have a name. It could be "Jeff." That's what his friend Steve calls him, once in the present action of the novel, "because I was Southern, I reckon," says The Virginian. But that is all. Nor on the other hand is he usually actually anonymous, but rather is presented in a series of tableaux in which the main point is not identity in any depth, but rather his generic superiority. The one constant irony of the novel consists of the fact that this supposed roughneck of a cowhand is a better man than any others, westerners and easterners alike, and not only or even saliently as a matter of skill or as a matter of honor but just naturally. The character called by the epical and generic name of The Virginian confirms himself and demonstrates status, and that is his story. Sometimes he does so by playing practical jokes, as it were just for the fun of it. In Medicine Bow he frightens a "drummer" from the East: hotel beds are in short supply; the drummer has offered to share his bed; The Virginian frightens him away by pretending that he has violent nightmares—and that is a good joke on the drummer. Later The Virginian frightens a fundamentalist preacher by pretending to be overwrought by sin. In the lengthiest and most substantial episode of this episodic novel, he makes a fool of the villain Trampas; he tells Trampas that fortunes are to be made in frogs' legs, for easterners think that they are a delicacy, and then when Trampas takes the bait and becomes eager, he is told by The Virginian that no, he is too late, the fad has passed.

Wryly, The Virginian humiliates these gullible others. It cannot be said that he is arrogant, for, simply and in all nonchalance, he is better, as some men are naturally better than others, and the novel moves forward by offering lessons to that effect.

To follow the implications of this hero might have been to discover principles for social organization generally and for the United States in particular, and Wister did indeed do that. *The Virginian* is a surprisingly didactic, even a hectoring novel. The episode of the frogs' legs is preceded by an essay of a duration of three chapters in which Wister speculated on aristocracy in America, saying:

> It was through the Declaration of Independence that we Americans acknowledged the *eternal inequality* of man. For by it we abolished a cut-and-dried aristocracy. We had seen little men artificially held up in high places, and great men artificially held down in low places, and our own justice-loving hearts abhorred this violence to human nature. Therefore, we decreed that every man should thenceforth have equal liberty to find his own level. By this very decree we acknowledged and gave freedom to true aristocracy, saying, "Let the best man win, whoever he is." Let the best man win! That is America's word. That is true democracy. And true democracy and true aristocracy are one and the same thing.

"If anybody cannot see this," Wister added, "so much the worse for his eyesight," for Wister often was crusty. Apparently, however, a great many Americans did see eye to eye with him. Else they would not have loved his hero so. But then it still remained a question as to who this best man was, who was to win.

# 5    Roosevelt

IMPERIALISM was a principle. In his Foreword to the 1900 edition of his *The Winning of the West*, Theodore Roosevelt would justify the invasion of Cuba in 1898 as an extension, to the east, of the western continental expansion which in turn, he said, "has been the central and all-important feature of our history" (1:x–xi). In the four large volumes of the book itself, 1889–1896, he had elaborated the theme of the inevitability of "race expansion," the most striking instance of which in all of time had been that of the English-speaking peoples. "It is, indeed," he had said, "a warped, perverse, and silly morality which would forbid a course of conquest that has turned whole continents into the seats of mighty and flourishing civilized nations. . . . In its results, and viewed from the standpoint of applied ethics, the conquest and settlement by the whites of the Indian lands was necessary to the greatness of the race and to the well-being of civilized mankind" (3:4; 3:174). "This great continent," he had said, "could not have been kept as nothing but a game-preserve for squalid savages" (1:90). In 1860 the author of *Seth Jones* had paused in his narrative to observe that "when the Anglo-Saxon's body is pitted against that of the North American Indian, it sometimes yields; but when his mind takes the place of contestant, it *never* loses," but Roosevelt would be less moping. "The warlike borderers who thronged across the Alleghenies," he reflected, and "the restless and reckless hunters, the hard, dogged, frontier farmers, by dint of grim tenacity, overcame and displaced Indians, French, and Spaniards alike, exactly as, fourteen hundred years before, Saxon and Angle had overcome and displaced the Cymric and Gaelic Celts" (1:26).

And if Roosevelt with his "abnormal energy" (in Henry Adams's phrase) brought a special forcefulness to the argument, his views here were not unique. Eventually he himself would discard the term "Anglo-Saxon race," but prior to the turn of the century he was speaking for respected and advanced theory, which brought science (with German university pedigree) to Manifest Destiny, and which had impressive supporters. Roosevelt, says the historian Thomas G. Dyer, had absorbed ideas of Anglo-Saxon and/or Teutonic superiority from his teachers including Nathaniel Southgate Shaler, at Harvard, and John Burgess, at Columbia. Shaler was a geologist, historian, and naturalist who, in Dyer's words, "enthusiastically accepted notions of white supremacy, innate black immorality, and the desirability of slavery as an instrument of necessary racial 'adjustment' " (6). Roosevelt the historian corresponded regularly with such other Anglo-Saxonists as Henry Fairfield Osborn, director of the Museum of Natural History in New York, David Starr Jordan of Stanford, Senator Henry Cabot Lodge, Rudyard Kipling, Sir George Trevelyan, and Edward Alsworth Ross (who had invented the term "race suicide"), and advanced his own refinements. Like Shaler, he was a Lamarckian and therefore in particular he was able to entertain the idea of not only an "Anglo-Saxon race" but a distinct "American race". And it followed from observation, for both Nathaniel Shaler and Roosevelt that, again in Dyer's words, Americans were "quicker witted and more adaptable to change than the other white 'races' " (7).

It followed that in the story of the winning of the west, the idea of an "American race" discovered its seemingly inevitable expression, while in Teddy Roosevelt the idea found not only its most energetic proponent but its natural bard. No matter indeed where he might have come upon the idea for itself, first or later, Roosevelt knew that idea both for itself and in its poetry, the latter especially, and for the particular reason that he had lived it, or almost had.

The period covered by *The Winning of the West* was for the most part the late eighteenth century, only. At the end of volume 4 Roosevelt had not got much beyond the Louisiana Purchase. But if obviously it was homework that gave him the basic narrative, nonetheless and with whatever seeming whimsy, perhaps impudence, he tended to confirm history by reference to personal experience. He knew the *type* of the frontiersman, so he said, and the type did not change. In the footnotes, where he might have claimed scholarly authority, as often as not he cited personal acquaintance. Did Daniel Boone once remain alone in the wilderness for three months? Such endurance was to be expected of the type, for "in 1880, two men whom I knew wintered to the west of the Bighorns, 150 miles from any human beings," going nine months without seeing a white face, and "last winter (1887–88) an old trapper, a friend of mine in the days when he hunted buffalo, spent five months

entirely alone in the mountains north of the Flathead country" (1:142).
Did Daniel Boone refer once to *Gulliver's Travels?* Frontiersmen were
*likely* to be readers, and "the better men among them appreciate really
good literature quite as much as any other class of people. In the
long winter evenings they study to good purpose books as varied as
Dante, Josephus, Macaulay, Longfellow, Parton's 'Life of Jackson,' and
the Rollo stories—to mention only volumes that have been especial
favorites with my own cowboys and hunters" (1:144).

He had gone to the West in September of 1883, at the age of
twenty-six, for personal reasons, following upon personal tragedy. His
mother and his wife had died, within twelve hours of each other. He
owned two ranches in the Dakota Territories. Like many of his wealthy
young friends, he had invested in western land. He went now to his
ranches needing time and distance, but he stayed on, living on one or
the other of the ranches for a period of almost three years, actually
working as a ranch owner and cattle boss; later, therefore, when he
referred to the authority of his personal experience, he had it.

At the time of this first trip to the West he was also already a
recognized historian, and therefore had his additional authority, while
still in his twenties. His first historical work, *The Naval War of 1812*,
had been published in 1882. Also while yet in his twenties he was a
recognized naturalist and "ethnologist," and as well, further, was already
something of a political leader. He was a rising star in the New York
State Assembly.

On the other hand, and just because of who he was and probably
inevitably, his discovery of the West, both in the first instance and later,
was directed by concerns other than discovery just for itself. Now and
later when TR spoke of the West, he spoke to the East, and for the
sake of the East. By birth, upbringing, milieu, as well as by his several
careers, he was as eastern a person as one could be, for all of the
western costuming early and late. He addressed himself to that Eastern
Establishment to which he himself belonged more certainly than almost
anybody. He was an eighth-generation New Yorker on his father's side.
Had he happened to have been born in Georgia, on his mother's side
he would have been a sixth-generation Georgian. He was heir to very
substantial if not extravagant old money. His natural habitat was old
family. Of Teddy's first wife's father, his friend Owen Wister was to
say, in his biography of Roosevelt, "Henry Lee was one of those fine
Americans with Colonial traditions who knew how to be rich," and while
the statement was not appropriate to TR himself, it suggested a state
of mind with which certainly he would have been very familiar. At the
time he went West he was already the apostle for the strenuous life, but

the quarrel with luxury reasonably was addressed to his own class and was within the family. When he famously said, "A life of slothful ease, a life of that peace which springs merely from lack either of desire or of power to strive after great things, is as little worthy of a nation as of an individual. . . . When men fear work or fear righteous war, when women fear motherhood, they tremble on the brink of doom"—it was to the men of the Hamilton Club of Chicago that he was speaking. Inevitably it was as an easterner in excellent social standing that he discovered the West, as it was as an easterner whose expectation as well as destiny it was to rule, that he created his version of the West and the westerner.

His friend Wister would later say, in the biography, that Roosevelt had been the pioneer in taking the cowboy seriously. Whether or not so, and no matter how much or little the cowboy whom Roosevelt put into print and whom for the rest of his life he valorized resembled any actual cowboy, he did discover in this livestock attendant an emblem of national importance and did compose a remarkably complex, seductive, and durable figure.

Whatever his intentions and presumptions, nonetheless there can be no doubting the immediacy of Roosevelt's response to the West. He wrote two books about his experience in the Dakotas, *Hunting Trips of a Ranchman*, published 1885, and *Ranch Life and the Hunting Trail*, published 1888. As a writer Roosevelt was more fluent than he was eloquent, but there were moments in those books when the composition was quite wonderfully fresh, vital, and engaged. Given the personal circumstances, perhaps the West was at this point dogmatically redemptive for him. In any event, he thrilled to the sight of the animals he hunted—the water-fowl, the grouse, white-tail and black-tail deer, antelope, mountain sheep—and described them with the talents and enthusiasm of the naturalist he was. He could take the life of the West to himself so intimately as to find it tasty: "Elk tongues are most delicious eating," he would advise, in the first of the two books, "being juicy, tender, and well flavored; they are excellent to take out as a lunch on a long hunting trip" (282). He found to his great delight that the Bad Lands, for all that they deserved to be called such, as he thought, were open and in many places still untouched. He was as delighted by that fact as had been Mark Twain coming upon a virgin shore of Lake Tahoe.

Nor was it as a frontiersman or conquering Anglo Saxon that he himself arrived in the West. The West was for Roosevelt what it was for others particularly of his class: a pastoral, a garden, a picnic. For Roosevelt as for others, the West of the 1880s was already a fatally established refuge for status. In the seventies and eighties the trip to the Far West had become something of an acceptable alternative to the

Grand Tour, except that it might be more expensive. "The number of Harvard graduates alone that appeared on the cattle frontier is ample testimony," says the historian Gene M. Gressley, "to the fact that long hours were spent in the Hasty Pudding Club by scions of wealthy families romanticizing the West as a place for adventure."[1] By the time Roosevelt went to the West, in 1883, two transcontinental railroads had already been completed. The Pullmans were in service, as were the grand resorts in the West where wealthy men played polo on mustangs. The West in this aspect was an interlude between an immediate past and an immediate future, rather than being a frontier, and rapidly was becoming only a locale for imagination.

Obviously the West was doomed, despite the fact that some areas of it were still untouched. Moreover, and more potentially perturbing, the specific agent of doom was eastern money in the possession of eastern family and power, carrying with it eastern ideas of order and polity and history, which was to say everything that Teddy Roosevelt himself represented. He himself was the agent of the destruction of the West, even in fact according to his own speculations about the future of the West.

Therefore seemingly, and after such knowledge, with great wit Roosevelt altered the tense and mood of his immediate observations of the West. That which was before him he regarded in future perfect. For all of the apparent immediacy of his delight, from the very first, in 1885, the West in his perception became a locale where displacement was natural law. His was a storied West, doom becoming a part of the story. The white hunters and trappers had expelled the Indians, so Roosevelt observed, who themselves had driven out the game. Now the cattle ranchers were displacing the hunters but would in their turn soon be forced from the land by new settlers. In *Hunting Trips* he reflected, "For we ourselves and the life that we lead will shortly pass away from the plains as completely as the red and white hunters who have vanished from before our herds." The buffalo had already disappeared, and the elk were at the point of extinction. "The free, open-air life of the ranchman," he said, "the pleasantest and healthiest life in America, is from its very nature ephemeral. The broad and boundless prairies have already been bounded and will soon be made narrow." He was not against fencing but, he said, at age twenty-seven, he hoped against hope that he himself would not live to see it (19, 31).

The West was by this much a locale for high melancholy. No doubt that the West had its aggressive reality, but at the same time it was also a kind of confirming fiction, and was one very much like the reigning fiction of the antebellum South, as indeed Roosevelt perceived. His fellow ranchers, he said in *Hunting Trips of a Ranchman*, were men who had a stake in the country having invested their wealth in it. They constituted "a class whose members were in many respects closely akin to the old Southern planters" (28–29). They had the manners and the moral authority of the old Southern planters, and that was to imply that his fellow ranchers as well shared their poignancy, that namely of a defeated aristocracy.

Cowboys, too, Roosevelt observed in *Ranch Life and the Hunting Trail*, although they came from anywhere, prevailingly were southerners (2), as might be considered to be appropriate beyond the mere fact of the matter, because southerners were better candidates than other Americans for a role of proud and sure defeat. If Roosevelt was serious about cowboys, no doubt he was so because he discovered in them an image of something he wanted to discover. Clearly he considered that they were the knights errant of the West. They were the personnel of a lost cause, miraculously surviving to carry on for a while and to be an emblem for a blighted age, about to be swept up into the dominating theme of disappearances, but meanwhile constituting a revelation. They were cause for joy and sorrow, being reminders of the line of the heroes. They had displaced the plainsman and the mountain man of an earlier era. "In the place of these heroes of a bygone age, the men who were clad in buckskin and who carried long rifles, stands," said Roosevelt, in *Hunting Trips*, "or rather rides, the bronzed and sinewy cowboy, as picturesque and self-reliant, as dashing and resolute as the saturnine Indian fighters whose place he has taken; and, alas that it should be written! he in his turn must at no distant time share the fate of the men he has displaced. The ground over which he so gallantly rides his small, wiry horse will soon know him no more, and in his stead there will be the plodding grangers and husbandmen" (31).

The glamour of the figure was intricate with knowledge of defeat near at hand. The cowboy was a temporary staving-off of what one knew, according to the lessons of contemporary events in the East, and in the North, to be the likely death of the tradition of the heroes. The cowboy was that which was imperilled by modern times and by the East, which two quantities were synonymous.

The cowboy was an antique hero, equipped to be just that with the necessary and complex qualifications of looks, manner, vigor, race, and silence. "They are mostly of native birth," Roosevelt discovered, in *Hunting Trips*,

> and although there are among them wild spirits from every land, yet the latter soon become undistinguishable from their American companions,

for these plainsmen are far from being so heterogeneous a people as is commonly supposed. On the contrary, all have a certain curious similarity to each other; existence in the west seems to put the same stamp upon each and every one of them. Sinewy, hardy, self-reliant, their life forces them to be both daring and adventurous, and the passing over their heads of a few years leaves printed on their faces certain lines which tell of dangers quietly fronted and hardships uncomplainingly endured. They are far from being as lawless as they are described; though they sometimes cut queer antics when, after many months of lonely life, they come into a frontier town in which drinking and gambling are the only recognized forms of amusement, and where pleasure and vice are considered synonymous terms. On the round-ups, or when a number get together, there is much boisterous, often foul-mouthed mirth; but they are rather silent, self-contained men when with strangers.

Also, they wore a costume which was "both picturesque and serviceable," consisting of a broad felt hat, a flannel shirt with a bright silk handkerchief loosely knotted around the neck," trousers tucked into high-heeled boots, "shaps," and a large-calibre revolver (6–8), which had further implications. Such figures might excite wonder in New York, or even Chicago, as in fact they would do. They were distinctive, and somewhat flaunting (the handkerchief), and not a little ominous (the revolver), but finally they were a race apart.

They also, in fact, had a bad reputation, which in some ways Roosevelt reinforced. A few years earlier no lesser than the president of the United States, Chester A. Arthur, had also taken cowboys seriously; in 1881 in one of his addresses to the Congress he had referred to the numbers of "armed desperadoes known as 'Cowboys' " who were terrorizing Arizona. Now in Roosevelt's version they were still a company of armed men who, if rather silent and self-contained when with strangers, by that same bearing discouraged friendship, but for Roosevelt they seemed to be also alluring even when wicked. In any event he presented the wicked with attributes which would prove to be the basic enduring stuff of legend. In *Ranch Life* he would say that he had known " 'bad men,' or professional fighters and man-killers [who] are, of course, used to brawling, and are not only sure shots, but, what is equally important, able to 'draw' their weapons with marvelous quickness. . . . These desperadoes always try to 'get the drop' on a foe—that is, to take him at a disadvantage before he can use his own weapon" (13).

The cowboys were incongruous except in their own habitat, but then the place itself was less exotic than it was admonishing. The West might be a rapidly passing fancy, but it was also a demonstration of an ultimate truth of things containing implications for true social organization and evolution. "The whole existence [of ranch life] is patriarchal in character," said Roosevelt in *Ranch Life*, and was "the life of men who live in the open, who tend their herds on horseback, who go armed and ready to guard their lives by their own prowess, whose wants are very simple, and who call no man master." "Ranching," he said, "is an occupation like those of vigorous, primitive pastoral peoples, having little in common with the humdrum, workaday business world of the nineteenth century; and the free ranchman in his manner of life shows more kinship to an Arab sheik than to a sleek city merchant or tradesman." And: "The struggle for existence is very keen in the far West," he would say, "and it is no place for men who lack the ruder, coarser virtues and physical qualities" (6, 13). In the West law, too, was crude but was emphatic, and it too apparently was attractive to the ex-legislator from the state of New York. He took it upon himself to serve for a time as an under-sheriff in the Dakotas. Together with a couple of his cowboys, he had once captured a trio of horse thieves and had had his picture taken with them—but it is to be noted as well that he had taken care to preserve his station. His own morals certainly were better than those of the horse thieves, but just as importantly so were his tastes. He made note of his horse thieves' reading habits. They owned dime novels and "the inevitable 'History of the James Brothers'" and, surprisingly, "a large number of more or less drearily silly 'society' novels, ranging from Ouida's to those of The Duchess and Augusta J. Evans," while he at this moment, on the trail, was reading *Anna Karenina* (126).

No doubt Roosevelt discovered in his cowboys such qualities as he wanted to discover for his own sake for this moment, but in so doing he also did create a figure which for the whole of his public life would be a symbol of not only personal but national recuperation. His own astonishing popularity would in the future go quite beyond politics. "'Great-heart!' Roosevelt! Father of men!" would cry out Vachel Lindsay; similarly, no other president of the United States could have inspired anything like "Teddy Bears." Not that it was only his association with cowboys, early and continued, that made him to be tonic for a nation, but the cowboy connection undoubtedly added another quantity to the heartiness.

The cowboy was health and restoration.

Thus the regiment of Roosevelt's "Rough Riders" in 1898 would be popularly known to be a meeting of East, in a Rooseveltian version, with West, also in a Roosveltian version, issuing in the legend of San Juan Hill. The regiment was made up of a number of eastern "swells" together with a greater number of actual cowboys from the Southwest,

Theodore Roosevelt in hunting costume. From Theodore Roosevelt, *Hunting Trips of a Ranchman* (New York: G. P. Putnam's Sons, 1885), frontispiece.

in a proportion of approximately one to two, and it was remarked on all sides that they got along very well together. The explicit lesson in that was that this fellowship was both right and was fertile for heroism. They were brothers after all, long lost from each other. The cowboy had returned. The cowboy was the measure of these certain easterners, who did now measure up to family obligation. It was pointed out that while the easterners were students and clubmen, they were also athletes and trained sportsmen and finally therefore were entitled to the company they kept.[2]

Thus during the years of the presidency, Roosevelt repeatedly confronted eastern propriety with western virtue. In his *Autobiography* he recalled the day at the White House when an old friend from the cow camps had happened to drop by just before lunch while he was entertaining Lord Bryce, and he had said to his friend, "Remember, Jim, that if you shoot at the feet of the British Ambassador to make him dance, it would be likely to cause international complications" (121). Thus, just as his distant predecessor James K. Polk had installed Nathaniel Hawthorne in the Custom House at Salem, so Roosevelt appointed Pat Garrett collector of the customs at El Paso. Pat Garrett was an old friend who had shot Billy the Kid, and patronage in a high sense was still in order. In the late summer of 1903 Roosevelt went to Colorado. There, once, caparisoned presidentially in top hat and frock coat, so he wrote to John Hay, he ate his grub at the tail end of a chuck wagon, and relished the joke of it.[3]

That the cowboy virtues were also proper political virtues, he well knew from particular experience. In *Ranch Life and the Hunting Trail* he recalled the occasion in 1886 when the cowboys on his ranches had volunteered to join the ranch owners in a private cavalry to fight off the Indians in the neighborhood, proving that in the West *comitatus* endured. Or the model was feudal and chivalric. It was decided ultimately that the task of the defense fell to the owners, but nevertheless the sentiments of the cowboys were much appreciated. Nor were his cowboys isolated from events in the republic at large. To the contrary, they followed events with a passion. Roosevelt recalled that they had been eager to obtain reports of the riot in Haymarket Square in Chicago in 1886, and that they followed the trials of the Anarchists. "The day that the Anarchists were hung in Chicago," he remembered, "my men joined with the rest of the neighborhood in burning them in effigy" (109).

There was a lesson here for a time of misrule, written into an entertainment.

# 6     The Lessons of Deadwood Dick

EVEN the exorbitant Ned Buntline had convictions. Buntline was "the great rascal," in the words of his principal biographer, Jay Monaghan. He was as well his own fiction. Once (prior to his joining the United States Navy at age fourteen) he had saved some persons from drowning, heroically, so he said and allowed others to say. It was said, too, that once he had captured a pair of murderers, for a reward, and that he had fought a duel over a woman and had been lynched when he killed his opponent—someone had cut the rope just in time. Along similar lines, it was said by his fellow hack writer Prentiss Ingraham that he could write sixty thousand words a week. (His completing the script of the first of the Buffalo Bill shows, *Scouts of the Prairie*, might have been his personal best.) He would publish some four hundred novels and perhaps more before he was done. In 1869, when he wrote *The King of the Border Men*, he was, it is said, the best-paid writer in America; he had made some of his literary money while editing a newspaper dedicated to several crusades for the public good, by blackmailing gamblers, threatening to print their names for wives and children to see. He would be married six times, overlappingly.

But there was another side to him. He was devoted to Temperance, for one thing. (Buffalo Bill, who toped, was annoyed when Buntline interrupted the second act of that first performance of *The Scouts of the Prairie*, in Chicago, to deliver his lengthy lecture on Temperance, just as the Indians were about to torture a captive.) Moreover, Buntline was a civic-minded person who did things. In either 1847 or 1848, while he was writing a study of low life in New York, in five volumes, he had organized the "United Sons of America," subsequently the "Patriotic

Ned Buntline. Collection: Buffalo Bill Historical Center, Cody, Wyoming.

Order of Sons of America," which in its guiding principle was anti-British. In 1849 he had been a prime mover in the fomenting of the "Astor Place Riot" in New York, directed against the British actor William C. Macready, in which 34 people were killed and 141 wounded. For that he had been sentenced to a year on Blackwell's Island, and when he was released, he had been treated as a returned hero. A torchlight parade had escorted him home, and patriots had banqueted him. "Workingmen," said the invitation to the Astor Place Riot, probably composed by Buntline, "shall Americans or English rule in this city?"[1] Unbiased in his nativism, in 1852 in St. Louis during that city's elections he had led a mob which aimed to save local government from the Germans. The same year back in New York, where his base was, he was raising funds for the "American Party" (or "Sons of '76," or "The Native American Party") to which he attached his "United Sons of America." It is said that he wrote the American Party's ritual, introduced a secret way for calling the members together with instructions as to whether or not they were to be armed, and himself gave it the name "Know-Nothings," by which it came to be known.

He contributed at least significantly to the definition of Know-Nothingism that is to say, as well as to the definition of Buffalo Bill, which two were not incongruous with each other. In both of those projections there was an appeal to some supposed purity of Americanism and an appeal therefore from a current depraved, heterogenous state of things. Buffalo Bill was manifestly a Son of America and a Son of '76, and was in fact a miraculous atavism, and, in the higher sense, knew nothing. Know-Nothingism and Buffalo Bill had been precipitated from the same justification.

Buntline, with his unusual energies, had come along early. He was born probably in 1823, and died in 1886, just at the time of the great proliferation of the dime-novel Westerns, in the 1880s and 1890s. The hacks who now wrote the dime-novel Westerns and the half-dime-novel Westerns were so tremendously productive that it cannot be said that they had any distinct ideas at all, but the underlying attitudes and experience they brought to the fiction were not very different. With some informative frequency, their apparent chief concern within the Westerns was for the contemporary condition of the urban East, wherefore the hero of the West became, again, the essential American whose services now were needed by way of a recuperation, or, perhaps, redemption.

Although hacks, the writers of the dime-novel Westerns were not necessarily anonymous.[2] With few exceptions they were in fact easterners, and were confirmed easterners.

There was Edward L. Wheeler (1854?–1885?), author of *Fritz, the Bound-Boy Detective; or, Dot Leetle Game Mit Rebecca,* who also invented Deadwood Dick. Wheeler was born in upstate New York and lived most of his short life in and around Philadelphia. It was said of him that he had never been farther west than Jersey City, but this was untrue

Edward Wheeler, ca. 1854–1885. From *The House of Beadle and Adams and Its Dime and Nickel Novels*, Volume 2, by Albert Johannsen. Copyright © 1950 by the University of Oklahoma Press.

because as a boy for several years he had lived in Titusville, Pennsylvania, near Erie. ("Buffalo Bill's Wild West" had played Titusville in 1873 and perhaps had inspired him.) There was Jesse C. Cowdrick (1859–99), sometimes known as "Arizona Cy," who was born in Tom's River, New Jersey, died in Ogdensburg, New Jersey, and recorded no significant

Jesse C. Cowdrick, 1859–1899. From *The House of Beadle and Adams and Its Dime and Nickel Novels*, Volume 2, by Albert Johannsen. Copyright © 1950 by the University of Oklahoma Press.

travel any time in between. When he died the writer of his obituary said of him, "Though he wrote of the Wild West, he was delicate and refined, and would have been taken for a clerk or book-keeper." Charles Morris (1833–1922), author of *Dick Dashaway; or, A Dakota Boy in Chicago* (1882), lived out his long life in Philadelphia where for a time he was a

Col. Prentiss Ingraham. *The House of Beadle and Adams and Its Dime and Nickel Novels*, Volume 2, by Albert Johannsen. Copyright © 1950 by the University of Oklahoma Press.

professor in an Academy of Ancient and Modern Languages. He wrote a biography of Queen Victoria and a biography of William McKinley. Albert W. Aiken (1846?–1894), author of the Dick Talbot series, was an actor in a family of actors. (He also wrote the most popular of the "Tom" shows, loosely derived from Stowe's novel.) Dick Talbot's locale for exploitation was southern Arizona and northern Mexico; Aiken had been born in Boston, seems to have lived most of his life in Brooklyn, and died in New Jersey.

Prentiss Ingraham (1843–1904), who wrote many of the Buffalo Bill novels, was exceptional. He had had adventures and actually had gone to the West. The son of a minister, and a Mississippian by birth, he had been a professional soldier in several armies prior to becoming a hack— he had been with the Army of the Confederacy, with Juarez in Mexico, then in Austria, and then in Crete fighting the Turks, and in Egypt, and later would go to Cuba to fight against Spain. He made at least two trips to the Far West, not counting his soldiering. As a writer, however, he was so stunningly productive as to argue that what his soldiering had taught him above all else was discipline. He was the author of books about Texas Jack Omohundro and Wild Bill Hickok as well as the Buffalo Bill novels. An admirer of Ned Buntline, in the years approximately 1870 to his death in 1904 he wrote between six hundred and a thousand novels—thirty-five thousand to seventy thousand words a month for thirty-four years. During the many years when he was primarily a writer he lived in New York City, in Easton, Maryland, and in Chicago.

"Exterminationist fever" had burned itself out shortly after Little Big Horn in 1876, the historian Richard Slotkin has said (480). In any event, in the eighties and nineties and into the early twentieth century, among all of the multitudes of the authors of the fiction of the West, low and high, there were few who discovered that the Indians presented even a significant presence. There was TR, but in *The Winning of the West* he was writing of an earlier time. There were former scouts who wrote their books, including Buffalo Bill Cody and Tom Horn. Horn actually as a child had lived among Apaches, but despite that, for neither of these, either, did Indians become singular personages. (The critic Jane Tompkins observes the same of movie Westerns, granting an exception or two.) In the dime novels the Indians were not the antagonists, or if so then only secondarily and at a remove. But on the other hand neither did "bad men, or professional fighters and man-killers," in TR's phrase, actually figure very prominently for their evil. To the contrary, the heroes of the West in these tales were usually ex- or temporary desperadoes—and not merely in the tradition of the rogue tale but repeatedly, explicitly, because law nowadays, which was to say the law of the decadent East as it was threatening to corrupt the West, was no longer a scheme for justice, wherefore potential heroes were likely to become desperadoes. The Westerns were written by easterners for easterners, and the villains of the tales were eastern types, instantly recognizable as such, and were such as were thought to be the enemies of the East, from a certain point of view.

*Dick Talbot, the Ranch King, or The Double Foe,* by Albert Aiken, published 9 November 1892, might be taken to stand for some others. Dick Talbot had figured in a series of novels. He had been a desperado and was now a ranch king with a wife and employees, and was doing

Albert W. Aiken, 1846–1894. From *The House of Beadle and Adams and Its Dime and Nickel Novels*, Volume 2, by Albert Johannsen. Copyright © 1950 by the University of Oklahoma Press.

well. He now has two foes—not exactly one "double foe" because the two in fact occupy different plots, but they are related thematically. One of the foes is the ne'er-do-well son of fine British aristocracy who has been sent to the West by his disgusted relatives. He is a gambler, a cheat, a whiner, and cowardly backshooter. Dick Talbot in fact boots him from the country and the tale within a few paragraphs, but he does have his role, namely and precisely to be a disgrace, for true aristocracy is what this tale is about. The other foe is a Mexican bandit chief who is everything the Britisher is not. He is forceful, shrewd, eloquently gallant, and also from fine family, albeit he is a bandit. He has been unjustly robbed of his wealth and, more important, his rank in Mexican society, by the machinations of some jealous persons, and knows that his role as western bandit is to present lessons in right behavior. He is a Robin Hood figure, not because he gives to the poor, which he does not do, but because his place is in an old story about dispossessed nobility.

This novel nonetheless, and for all of the usual slack stereotyping, becomes strikingly, indeed disturbingly contemporary. The bandit chief has been forced to become a merchant haggler. He has kidnapped Dick Talbot's wife, for money. It goes without saying that he will not harm her, for he is not that kind of a bandit, but then much of what there is of a plot has to do with the kinds of his negotiations. Business is not his style, as it is not Dick Talbot's, either. Therefore the bandit chief delegates business to those to whom business comes naturally, presumably in the manner of his forebears. He will direct Dick Talbot to a shopkeeper, one Aaron Mosenstein, who keeps shop in the village of Cobota in Mexico. Talbot has a companion, Mud Turtle, formerly a chief of the Blackfoot Tribe. Talbot says to Mud Turtle: " 'to judge by the name, the Cobota man is a Jew, and although in my time I have met with a great many Jews who were every bit as good as any Gentiles that I ever ran across yet as a rule, these gentle Jews don't flourish in a climate like this, so I am probably safe in setting down this Aaron Mosenstein for a cunning rascal.' " And Mud Turtle agrees. Later, Mud Turtle will lasso Aaron Mosenstein, thereby offering a lesson from the West to the Jewish chaffering which in the 1890s was of course a fact not of the streets of Cobota in Mexico but of Albert Aiken's Brooklyn. Aaron Mosenstein when we meet him is "a short, fat man, with bushy red hair and a beard of the same hue; his eyes were small, pig-like in their appearance, and his nose was enormous in size." When he speaks he says, " 'Goot-evening—goot evening, my tear sir! v'at can I do for you, my fr'ent, dis evening?' "

Dick Talbot, meanwhile, is a composite of rhetorical formality and high caste. In an episode which has nothing whatsoever to do with whatever plot there is, except that the Ranch King has an emblematic role to play, Talbot confronts a cowardly officer in the Mexican army. It is Dick Talbot's task to define distinction—why after all so many "Kings"? the word meant what it meant. The two are to fight a duel. The officer, like the Britisher before him, is an example of degraded aristocracy. He swears that he will kill Dick Talbot, and Dick replies:

> "I do not want to kill you; you have not harmed me in any way. You are arrogant and inclined to be insolent, but that is no reason why you should be killed. If I simply wing you, so as to show that I could wipe you out if I felt disposed, it will teach you to be more civil in the future."

And this is not after all a superfluous development. It is to be expected that kidnapping might be exonerable, as will be theft and murder, but never insolence.

It has sometimes been said about the dime Westerns, that although most of the male characters are presented as "nature's noblemen," the term does not mean anything other than that the character is strong, healthy, and vigorous.[3] But the Dick Talbots (and the Buffalo Bills and Buck Taylors and Deadwood Dicks, et al.) tend to nobility quite in the old sense, thereby as often as not quite specifically to challenge this democracy and what it has currently wrought. They are guardians of the higher law, namely protocol, and they act in behalf of a society which when it is returned to its purity will be orderly and, properly, observantly hierarchical. Like that Mexican officer, those who are of fallen estate are to be taught above all to be civil, and are to be taught so with a certain measured, skilled, and graceful violence.

This story, of *Dick Talbot, the Ranch King, or, The Double Foe,* happened to have been published two years after the Bureau of the Census declared the closing of the frontier, not that it needed that confirmation to prove that Dick Talbot belonged to an older, better order of things. Dick Talbot is an anachronism of a hero who has been fitted to current usage. He was like others who had been anachronisms earlier on. As was the case with his fellow heroes, the very language by which supposedly he engages the present day, in fact sets him apart. He cannot possibly haggle with Aaron Mosenstein. Aaron Mosenstein speaks Yiddish, in the time of the floodtide of Eastern-European immigration; Injun Dick speaks the language of the late-medieval pages of Sir Walter Scott.

And even when heroes such as these talked in a supposed western dialect, the drawl and the irony of the talk removed them just as effectively from ordinary contemporary discourse. The style of that dialect, carrying forth to John Wayne, was likely to involve either ironic circumlocution or an irony of self-deprecating understatement, in either case implying distance and a forbidding composure, and denial of a relevance for discourse. With considerable frequency these heroes were soliloquizers, by that much objecting the more eloquently to transactions in real history. "I'm a young greenhorn Texan, who knows little more than herding, riding and shooting, with a little experience of Injun trailing," says Buck Taylor, in *Buck Taylor, or, The Raiders and Rangers: A Story of the Wild and Thrilling Life of William L. Taylor,* by Col. Prentiss Ingraham, 1887. He says that to no one. He is not being modest in any usual sense. But certainly he suggests that he knows what greatness is, and that those readers out there who will overhear his musing, lead lives that are far more distant from his than is his from greatness. He bows only before the ineffable. Thus his fine humor: when Buck is surrounded by twenty-seven Indians he mutters to no one, " 'Just twenty-seven more Injuns than I want to see.' "

The villains in the romance of the West were Mosensteins, not Indians or "bad men," or they were other foreigners, or radicals, or bankers, or Eastern politicians, or some several others who, similarly, were the natural enemies of the older and better scheme of things.

The Deadwood Dick novels were perfect of the type, especially those published between 1877 and 1885 composed probably by Edward L. Wheeler.

Wheeler himself was a witty, sophisticated man, apparently nicely aware both of his provisional place in letters and of public response. He brought to the genre a considerable amount of playfulness and evidently a clear realization of the nature of the genre. He knew who he was and what he was writing. The letterhead originating from his studio in Philadelphia read: "Studio of Edward L. Wheeler, Sensational Novelist." In his writing he alluded to and thereby measured himself against other popular writers, and he managed to imply that—like Mark Twain, for instance—he was not merely a writer for juveniles. In the first few lines of the first of the Deadwood Dick series (*Deadwood Dick, The Prince of the Road; or, The Black Rider of the Black Hills*), presenting a dramatis personae grouped around a camp fire, Wheeler would observe of them, "only one is specially noticeable, for, as Mark Twain remarks, 'the average of gold-diggers look alike,' " which was to say that he shared a territory with Mark Twain who had just published *The Adventures of Tom Sawyer*. In a Deadwood Dick novel of 1878 improbably entitled *Wild Ivan, the Boy Claude Duval; or, The Brotherhood of Death*, a hairy old trapper, Josiah W. Hogg, composes minstrel doggerel—

> Jim Crow shot a man,
> An' shot him all ter pieces,
> An' all thar was left o' him
> War a cupple little greasers.
> So Hop along, skip along,
> Do just so—

—and is " 'poet o' Powder River Range, an' own cousin to Wawkeen Miller an' sech shinin', flickerin' lights o' ther poetical profession as Bill Tweed, Moar, Shakespear, an' Oakey Hall,' " which was matter for reflection. Joaquin Miller, "The Poet of the Sierras," was appropriate. "Bill Tweed" was Boss Tweed of Tammany Hall, back in New York, who had been a member of the poetical profession only in an extended whimsical sense. (Tweed had just died, in April of 1878, in jail, and was in the news.) "Moar" perhaps was the young George Du Maurier, although there would be other candidates—a "Henry Morford" was one of the Tammany poets; perhaps a "Moore." "Oakey Hall" was A. Oakey Hall, who was very much alive. He was "The Elegant Oakey," former mayor of New York, said to be a tool of Tammany, who was in fact a much-published poet and playwright, and an inveterate punster frequently in Latin.

As Hogg soliloquizes, an Indian maiden steps forth from the forest to say, " 'I am Sue,' " to which the relentlessly literary Hogg responds, " 'Sue, eh? Any relation ter Eugene Sue?' "—"Sioux," he might have said, but, once again, Indians really did not figure as such.

Wheeler was a man of donnish wit uttered in vernacular. Reflexively patronizing of his own materials, he said in effect that he knew true states of affairs and that his romance after all was not naive. He was no moralizing Oliver Optic. He presented westerners who were real men with real eastern information, often comical but on the slant. Thus in the same tale of Wild Ivan: a gang of robbers which calls itself "The Brotherhood of Death" is led by Colonel Bill Blood, who prepares his men for the morrow's labor. "It's an overland wagon train coming into the hills," he tells them. "There is five families, and all are fixed in the world's goods. Three families are Jews, and have upwards of five thousan's worth of treasure aboard" (2). And in this case, in a way to indicate that the intention of the fiction was authenticity first of all, Wheeler himself came forward to say authorially, "Of the Jews there were ten in number, but as our story has comparatively little to do with them, we will not tarry for a description."

In *Deadwood Dick on Deck, or Calamity Jane, the Heroine of Whoop-Up,* of 1878, evil consisted of Mormonism, the government in Washington, the betrayal of women, but mostly was a matter of Capital in the Gilded Age, although Labor too was to be examined. The hero of the tale is a mine owner, named Sandy, not Deadwood Dick himself. As mine owner, Sandy is an employer of miners and is the wealthiest man in Whoop-Up. The villain of the piece is the Honorable Cecil Grosvenor, and he is identified initially and primarily as an apologist for eastern speculators besides being a salesman for that new invention, the corporation. Sandy has maintained a properly personal, protective relationship with his employees. To Sandy's pard, grizzled Joe Tubbs, Honorable Cecil Grosvenor says, "One first-class corporation would have paid you more for your entire claim, by three-fold, than you received from the poor cusses you leased it to," but Tubbs replies:

"Mebbe yer purty nigh right, stranger; but we pilgrims ain't generally hogs, an' we divide up ekal wi' ther boys. D'ye remember et, sir, I'd ruther 'a' not got a cent out o' ther hull business, than to have sold et ter men who'd hev hed et all under three or four piratical pairs o' fists, an' w'ile hoarding up their pile, ground ther workin' men down ter Chinamen's wages—'washee shirtee for fivee cents!' Mebbe ye cum frum out in Pennsylvania, whar they do thet kind o' playin', stranger, but et's most orful sure thet ye ken't play sech a trick out hyar among ther horny-fisted galoots o' this delectable Black Hills kentry—no sir-e-e-e!"

Honorable Cecil Grosvenor happens not to come from Pennsylvania, but Wheeler, who was living and writing in Philadelphia, did, and therefore Joe Tubbs's mistake was understandable.

And Sandy himself (later revealed to be not a plain "Sandy," but "Earl Beverly") shared Wheeler's sentiments. Addressing his dog, he says:

"No, I will not sell out; would you, Buffalo? . . . I am realizing a handsome thing out of the mine, and, better than all, am giving a gang of honest, industrious men of families employment at paying wages. No doubt there are capitalists who would like to step down into the little city of Whoop-Up, and grasp the tyrant's reins in their hands; but they'll be mightily disappointed when they find that very few poor men are so poor but what they can stand firm for their rights."

"Sandy was an enthusiast on the labor question," so Wheeler assured his readers, stepping forth from the tale, "and," he added, "if the country to-day had more of his make and resolute mind, there would, undoubtedly, be a change for the better, when every man would, in a greater or lesser degree, have an independence, and not be ground down under the heel of the master of money."

In the last chapter of this tale we will learn that Sandy is originally, mysteriously, from the East, as was to be anticipated. Back East he had been falsely accused of forgery and murder, and in this respect too he is emblematic. In the West to which he has flown, all who have known Sandy have known very well that he is an upright, not to say a noble fellow, but in the East these matters have become confused. In the East, as is well known generally and is known according to the laws of the Western, law has been undermined.

To be outside of what "law" now was, was the only way in which to be truly lawful, as is the message of the great Deadwood Dick himself. At the beginning of a life which will extend over thirty-three novels, Deadwood Dick is a road-agent who has turned to a career as a leading outlaw because of corruption in the East: a wicked uncle, his guardian, had tried to kill him for his inheritance. "I appealed to our neighbors," says Dick, in *Deadwood Dick, The Prince of the Road*, in October of 1877, "and even to the courts for protection, but my enemy was a man of great influence, and after many vain attempts I found that I could not obtain a hearing; that nothing remained for me to do but to fight my own way." And as with Deadwood Dick, so with his successor Deadwood Dick, Jr. At the beginning of a life extending over some ninety-seven novels, in *Deadwood Dick, Jr., or, The Sign of the Crimson Crescent*, in 1886, the second but no lesser a Dick is a refugee from the authority of a wicked stepfather, who at this point has already migrated to the Middle West.

None of these were wild westerners although all of them were men with guns. They offered not freedom, but its opposite. They were fatally civil. Their motives were so prominent, indeed so resolved into stereotype, and their appeal to simple, antique ideas of justice was so clear, that it had to be seen that the new assertion of old law, with its manners and courtesy and chivalry, quite beyond the demands of justice, was the chief reason for their being in the stories.

And so too, reasonably, with the women.

In his classic essay "The Westerner," in 1954, Robert Warshow would observe that in the myth of the Wild West women are an irrelevance at best and at a usual worst are a restriction, because the idea of the West in its purity will allow no civil structure. And it is a commonplace that the true enemy of the cowboy is the schoolmarm, although, saying so, Warshow himself was undoubtedly taking and extending information from D. H. Lawrence's reading of the Leatherstocking Novels. ("Whatever would poor Mabel have done, had she been Mrs. Bumppo? Natty had no business marrying. His mission was elsewhere.") But in fact the better kind of schoolmarm—and there was never any other kind—would become pupil to the westerner, who himself stood for tradition and avenged lapses from good order, which is to say that he represented exactly what the schoolmarm herself was supposed to represent. And indeed the women of the Westerns, too, were likely to be armed and were likely also to be self-appointed agents of good order. With some considerable frequency, women were the protagonists of these fictions, and were in fact the more likely to be cast into roles of general retaliation just because they were the more likely to have suffered from the degradation of the true law.

The dime-novel West was in any event well-populated with buckskinned belles. It is probable that the great Edward L. Wheeler began his career in dime fiction, in 1877, with, first, *Hurricane Nell, the Girl Dead Shot, or, The Queen of the Saddle and Lasso*, and then *Old Avalanche, the Great Injun Annihilator; or, Wild Edna, the Girl Bandit.* Beginning in 1882, while composing Deadwood Dick, he wrote a series of novels about "Denver Doll. " In a novel of 1886, *Old Tom Rattler,* the writer known as Oll Coomes invented "Captain Rachel, the Female Outlaw." Wheeler, again, in 1885 invented "Sante Fe Sal," in a novel of the same name. Philip S. Warne created both "Colorado Kate" and "Lariat Lil," in 1886 and 1888 respectively. And so on innumerably. "Calamity Jane" was everywhere, in part aided by a genuine original, Martha Jane Cannary (of whom it was said, "she was a good woman only she drinked").[4] And if there was covert sexual meaning in all of this, perhaps it was confirmed by the would-be lover of Colorado Kate, named "Limpy Dick."

These were punishing women, and although without doubt there was a designed amount of titillation in that, as in the underside of much Victorian fiction, the women were also merely plausible exaggerations of the male protagonists. The men were doing women's work, and the women the same. In the case of each of these women the codes by which females in traditional society should be protected, had been violated. In every case these females mete out discipline, with gun and rope. And then, not infrequently, they marry and have children, thereby to restore the social order which had been betrayed.

Thus with Wheeler's Calamity Jane, who had been present as a major character in the Deadwood Dick novels from the beginning. In *Deadwood Dick, the Prince of the Road,* the first of them, she had been a hoyden with a Winchester, without further explanation. In *Deadwood Dick on Deck,* in the second year of the series, all was revealed. Calamity Jane was really Jane Forrest, "foully robbed. . . of her maiden name, but *never* of her honor," by Alf Kennedy, known as "Arkansas Alf," a Danite. Flight from legal injustice, and also presumably from the cultural insult of Mormonism, has caused her to take up arms. Nor was it the case that she was compelled to sacrifice her role as a domestic heroine. Her influence is womanly. In Deadwood and environs her major occupation is tidying up, albeit violently and on an ad hoc basis. And like others to follow, of her history, costume, and tendency—like, for instance, "California Kit," who will marry Injun Dick Talbot—she does marry the hero. Then, in good order, in *Deadwood Dick's Big Deal; or, The Gold Brick of Oregon,* in 1883, she bears a child, little Deadwood Dick, Jr.

Perhaps the birth of the child prompted Wheeler to new sensitivities. (Or prompted whoever succeeded him. Until long after his death, perhaps in 1885, his name was regularly attached to stories by other writers.) The series of "Deadwood Dick, Jr." novels followed— not the original babe, however, and provided with other parents. The eastern meaning of the western material in any event now became still more explicit. In *Deadwood Dick, Jr., or The Sign of the Crimson Crescent,* the first of the new series, the principal disturber of the peace—or not even that, but an intruder on the peace—is a "Dutchman," which was to say a German, who is an intruder categorically, for the reason that he is a "Dutchman," therefore socially discrepant. He is the owner of Dutch Duff's Daisy Saloon in Bummer's Bay, Nevada Territory. They call him "Limburger," and he is ripe for ostracism as soon as he is allowed into the story because he talks like the recent immigrant he is, or a vaudeville version of the same: "Ve all go deadt, und den ve go—vere der tyfel ve go, anyhow? Oh! how I vish I was pack in Yermany, vere der vas no Deadwood Dicks!" And in the last line of the tale he is sent back to Yermany by an amused author in league with an outraged citizenry.

In eighteen months between 6 March 1888 and 12 November 1889, in eight novels, serially, Deadwood Dick, Jr., was sent off on visits to "Gotham," Boston, Philadelphia, Chicago, Coney Island, Detroit, Cincinnati, and Buffalo. The detective had become a new staple of dime fiction. Deadwood Dick was altered for the market, becoming a detective from the West. As a detective he needed urban locales. Travel books were also popular. Dick's excursions allowed the author or authors of these tales to confirm such observations as that Detroit was interesting in being close to Canada, that Cincinnati had fine hotels, that there were many respectable Germans in Buffalo. Dick finds Coney Island, in *Deadwood Dick Jr. in Coney Island, or, The "Piping" of Polly Pilgrim,* with its "myriads of dazzling electric lights," to be as gaudy as the Bowery, "only more so." Withal, these novels significantly clarified some latent assumptions. The law was to be delivered not to, but from the Wild West. An allegory of sorts having been played out in Deadwood, the lessons were to be brought back to New York, or Philadelphia, to which they had been addressed in the first place. On his way to Gotham in the first novel of this series, Dick will say to a stranger on the train, " 'My business in the East is simply a pleasure trip—to see this new world to me.' " It will not be a pleasure trip, of course, but the idea, for eastern readers, that it was the East that was the new world was in itself a tonic irony. By the time Dick gets to Philadelphia (in *Deadwood Dick, Jr. in Philadelphia or, The Wild West Detective Among the Crooks*), he is more anthropological in his ambitions. To the chief of police he says, "My real object in coming was to visit some of the principal cities, to study Eastern ways and customs as contrasted with Western life and people."

In all cases Dick discovers crooks and crookedness of a distinctly eastern and urban kind: embezzlement, blackmail, and insurance fraud with peculiar frequency. Deadwood Dick by virtue of basic identity, as westerner and as former highwayman (by virtue of his namesake), had carried with him implication of straightforward violence: robbery, for instance, rather than burglary. The urban crimes which young Deadwood Dick now discovers are insidious and alien and oblique, as are the perpetrators.

His adventure in Gotham (in *Deadwood Dick Jr. in Gotham or Unraveling a Twisted Skein*) consists primarily of his rescuing a rich girl who has been kidnapped by Italians, who want to sell her into white slavery. Such things happen in Gotham, where the Italians are, as we have known and as is confirmed by the fact that it is a real American named Dick, from the West, who prevents the crime. (In this case something else that one well might have suspected is confirmed by the fact that the rich girl has just graduated from Vassar, and so it is likely that she is equally a victim of her own misguided liberalism.) In Boston (in *Deadwood Dick in Boston or, The Cool Case*), Dick's main adventure consists of his tracking down a faithless, thieving wife. She herself is of no particular ethnic persuasion, but it will make a difference to the tale that this Boston—Boston, no less!—is filled with Jews. Dick's introduction to the place will be provided by one Moses Mumb, who with wonderful candor will tell him that, " 'while I am a Hebrew, and a pawnbroker, I always conduct my dealings with honor and integrity, and no one in Boston can say that Moses Mumb is guilty of extortion, trickery or dishonesty.' " But this Moses supposes erroneously, for within the space of another three columns of print he will turn blackmailer and be referred to as that "wily son of Israel." Deceit, moreover, is in the nature of the race. When Dick has need for a good disguise, he goes to Nathan Lazarus, who is doubly qualified because he speaks in impenetrable dialect.

As Cincinnati had fine hotels and as Gotham had malevolent Italians, so Chicago had Anarchy, mostly of German descent, as Dick discovers in 1888 just a few months after the execution of the Haymarket conspirators, in *Deadwood Dick Jr. in Chicago, or, The Anarchist's Daughter*. In some ways, in this instance he had come upon the fundamental definition of his task. Dick will rescue Dolly Drew from the life of drudgery imposed by her Anarchist father, Doc Drew, owner of "a dingy little lager beer saloon on Lake Street." Dolly is in her own way an enthusiast on the labor question. She does not subscribe entirely to her father's position because, as she says, " 'I do not believe either in the overthrow of the Government nor in violence or murder to right even a great wrong.' " On the other hand, so she will say:

> I do know that the working people, who have but small advantages of education, are kept down and treated as an inferior class, wholly subject to the rich and educated; I do see that the rich are made so by the incessant

toil, small wages, great privation and debarment from the pleasures of life of the workers; and I do realize, how in their forlorn condition, it is utterly impossible for the workers to educate their children, who, like themselves, must therefore remain the slaves of toil—the mere serfs of the men of money.

This is stern stuff which might well make an impression, and Deadwood Dick is impressed. In the moment of his listening to this speech, he is strapped to the floor in a room behind the dingy lager beer saloon. But the impression he receives will be qualified by immediate revelation that Dolly Drew is not really the Anarchist's daughter but was a foundling, and is actually "of good birth" and comes "of good English family," namely that of Sir Jay and Lady Compton. Genealogy here is unmistakably an argument, and is sufficient. The plot within the pedantry of the tale will unravel so as to reveal that Dolly is also the niece of the great Chicago mill-owner who is chief enemy to organized Anarchy but who really is not only ultimately fair but utterly wise. This is a tale once again in which anarchy—this time in the convenient metaphor of "Anarchy"—is suppressed by the upper classes, who have not disappeared after all but merely were misplaced.

No doubt that the contemporary facts of social stratification were totally enunciated as soon as Dick was placed in the dingy little lager beer saloon, now just following upon the Haymarket affair. The matter is nonetheless elaborated. These Anarchists are not to be confused with American workers. At table, Dick talks to the seated Anarchists about Haymarket:

> "We Americans don't believe in that sort of cowardly and barbarous thing. It is only the foreign element, who can't get along in their own country, that come over here with the idea they can run and regulate matters pretty much as they please. By the time a few more of them are cared for by the sheriff, perhaps they'll know enough to stay at home, or else conduct themselves as peaceable citizens!"

Whereupon one Jacob Steinmetz hits him on the head with an empty beer bottle.

But that was not the end of the story. Deadwood Dick, Jr., will of course rescue Dolly Drew along with all of her genealogy, and in that, in his being the western redeemer of a corrupted America, he was prophetic.

He was prophetic also with special regard to Chicago, as it happened.

After the Haymarket trials, in Chicago, there was the Pullman Strike, in 1894, and it too would be cast into terms of an allegory of the Wild West, at the level of serious journalism. The "reversible analogy between workers and savages is the most significant new term in the language of American mythology after the [Civil] war," Richard Slotkin has said (311). Certainly in this episode of labor history, the striking workers became unruly savages who were to be tamed by distinctly western heroes who, equally with Deadwood Dick, Jr., disliked the foreign element, had simple and strict ideas of order, had had some experience with Indians, and knew how to shoot.

President Grover Cleveland had sent federal troops to Chicago in order "to restore obedience to law." Many of the approximately two thousand federal troops had in fact fought in the Indian wars, and their commander, the ambitious Major General Nelson Miles, was making political capital for himself on the basis of his role in those wars, while many of the strikers were immigrants from Eastern Europe. The governor of Illinois, John B. Altgeld, had opposed the sending of the federal troops. Two years earlier he had pardoned the surviving Haymarket Anarchists. As a German by birth, he was himself one of the foreign element. In the opinion of *Harper's Weekly*, Altgeld was "essentially a European anarchist," while General Miles had rendered fine service to Americans. In an editorial entitled "Men in Evidence," with intended accent on the first word, *Harper's* welcomed General Miles to Chicago:

> [General Miles] has subdued the warlike Sioux under Sitting Bull and Crazy Horse, subdued the Nez-Perces under Chief Joseph, brought the Bannocks within their lawful reservation, and finally—the most difficult, splendid, and skillful of all his work—he hunted down Geronimo and the Apaches of Arizona, the best and most stubborn Indian fighter of the continent, freed the whole Southwestern territory of all Indian dangers, and left the way to civilization clear to the Pacific. And this work he has done not merely with indomitable courage and energy and skill, but with a broad, just, and humane consideration for all the rights of the Indians, so that the race can be said to have no firmer or more faithful friend than the conqueror of their warriors. (678–79)

Moreover, he was conducting himself like a true westerner, perhaps a cowboy: "Amid the most intense excitement General Miles has been cool, quiet, self-possessed, and cheerful, making no threats, employing no angry or boastful language, but making all understand that his duty would be done as completely in the streets of Chicago as in the face of

Chicago strikes—U.S. cavalry in the stock-yards. From Frederic Remington, "Chicago Under the Mob," *Harper's Weekly* (21 July 1894): 680.

the Indian foe" (679). And the style of the man, so surely it would have been seen, was exactly pertinent to the new situation; General Miles was competent, cool, threatening, and anachronistic.

Accordingly, it was appropriate that the editors of *Harper's* should call upon a Wild West expert, Frederic Remington, to write an account of "Chicago Under the Mob." When Remington went to Chicago, he would, and did, see a version of the West he knew. His illustrations for the article he wrote conveyed only the slightest suggestion that the milieu of this strife was metropolitan and dense—the backdrops for his soldiers and horses were only and occasionally some faintly sketched low storefronts, and some telegraph poles, while the prose (of this upstate New Yorker) was a western plain speaking, made threatening by a western drawl. "Well," said Remington, observing Chicago, "it is a great change of air for the Seventh Cavalry. . . . The regiment was born on the Platte River, pretty far up stream. . . . it has fifty copper cylinders in its belt, and its old campaign hat on, and there are things in Chicago it doesn't like, and if you want the recreated spirit of Homer

"Giving the Butt"—the way the "regular" infantry tackles a mob. From Frederic Remington, "Chicago Under the Mob," *Harper's Weekly* (21 July 1894): 680.

you ought to hear a Seventh Cavalry trooper tell what he thinks of Chicago's mob" (680). The cavalry had briefly charged a group of strikers,
and Remington reported: "After the malodorous crowd of anarchistic
foreign trash had run as far as its breath would hold out and the cavalry
halted, a real workman came out on a window-landing of a big factory,
and shook his fist at the flying mob. 'Kill 'em,' he says, 'kill every one
of 'em, you soldiers.' . . . Whereat Uncle Sam's troopers felt refreshed
morally" (681). And Remington would reflect that:

> When infantry must walk through a seething mass of smells, stale beer,
> and bad language, . . . they don't at all understand. The soldier idea
> would be to create about eleven cords of compost out of the material at
> hand. And, again, the soldier mind doesn't understand this Hungarian
> or Polack, or whatever the stuff is; he will talk to a real American striker
> in an undertone, and tell him it is best to go home and not get shot,
> but he tells me in his simple way, "Say, do you know them things ain't
> human?—before God I don't think they are men." (681)

—Which in near approximation was what Deadwood Dick, Jr., had been
trying to say before Jacob Steinmetz hit him on the head with that beer
bottle.

# 7    Wister

IN his biography of his friend Teddy Roosevelt, to whom he had dedicated *The Virginian* in 1902, Owen Wister would reflect on early White House days when he had considered himself to be one of the small group of the "Familiars," as he called them. Some of the others were Oliver Wendell Holmes, Jr., the jovial William Howard Taft, Henry Adams, Henry Cabot Lodge, Elihu Root, General Leonard Wood, and the witty French Ambassador Jules Jusserand. Unlike the "Unfamiliars," who were to be dreaded and who had to be entertained, and who were likely to stand for something—"a tropical Commonwealth, a seat of learning in Nish, a medical mission to the hook-worm belt, the street railways in Kansas City, votes for women, the war against cigarettes"—the inner group was distinguished by its clubbability. They understood. Said Wister, writing in 1930 as the Great Depression was becoming generally noticeable, and just before the second Roosevelt was to change many things, "Never in our history at any other time has such a company as these Familiars gathered in the White House. To the society of the present day, they seem to bear the same relation that Gobelin tapestry bears to linoleum." And he added with a wistfulness that was almost audible: "After all, good society is the best invention of mankind" (125ff).

That was a sentiment to which he had been faithful from the beginning. He had inherited it. He had confirmed it in training and by aesthetic preference. It was a sentiment become principle by which, sometimes knowingly although sometimes not, he had discovered the subjects of his writing, including the West in particular and including more particularly the contents of *The Virginian*. The hero of that tale had been created by an author whose every instinct bespoke a feeling for "good society," which was to say for privilege and manners, for nuanced sensitivity, and for the inner circle. There was some irony

therefore in the fact that the novel was to become so huge a popular success.

Wister was a man equipped with genealogy. One of his great-great
grandfathers on his mother's side, Pierce Butler, had been the delegate
to the Constitutional Convention from South Carolina. Wister himself
had been born in the Germantown suburb of Philadelphia, in 1860,
in circumstances where the old colonial tradition was palpably present.
His boyhood home, which eventually he inherited, was "Butler Place," a
country estate located six miles north of Philadelphia's City Hall. In the
entranceway to Butler Place, as Wister's daughter, Fanny Kemble Wister,
was to recall, were hung two framed letters from George Washington
addressed to the first Pierce Butler. In the dining room there were
ancestral portraits, two by Sir Thomas Lawrence and one by Sir Joshua
Reynolds.[1] There was tradition here, which Wister certainly wanted to
feel that he was carrying forward, albeit against odds. In the Roosevelt
biography he would recall that when with his wife (great-granddaughter
of William Ellery Channing) he was a guest at the White House,

> It filled me with a certain pride to reflect that I was the fourth generation
> of my family that had stayed there. My great-great aunt, Miss Isabel Mease,
> went there when Dolly Madison presided over it; my grandfather Pierce
> Butler when General Pierce was President; my mother during the same
> administration; and now here were we, the guests of Colonel and Mrs.
> Roosevelt. None of us had ever been invited for political reasons, but
> merely because of personal friendship; which seemed a better sort of
> welcome. (106–7)

He also liked a southern style of recollected aristocracy, to which
he himself did have family claim. There was nothing in the plot of *The
Virginian* to require that his Westerner be a Southerner. The actual
most likely inspiration for the character, one George West, was a New
Englander, come to Wyoming from Boston. When in 1901 Wister was
performing the collecting and editing of the tales from which *The
Virginian* largely was pieced together, he was living in Charleston, which
he had first visited on his honeymoon and which he could reasonably
take to be his other ancestral home. His most ambitious if not most
memorable novel, *Lady Baltimore*, published in 1906, would be a study
of the manners of Charleston. (The "Lady Baltimore" of the title was
not a lady but a cake; the tasting of the cake provoked the fiction,
as in Proust but some years before Proust.) Wister, said his mother's
very good friend Henry James, in the latter's *The American Scene*, was "a
Northerner of Southern descent (as well as still more immediately, on

another side, of English)". Wister was explicit, in any event, in finding a relationship between the South which he had in a measure inherited, and the Wild West which had been a good part of his career. "I had found in Charleston," he would later say, in the Roosevelt biography,

> and wherever I had gone in the South, many more people whether urban or rustic, who were the sort of people I was, with feelings and thoughts and general philosophy and humor and faith and attitude toward life like my own: Americans; with whom I felt just as direct a national kinship as I felt with the Western cowpunchers, and which I feel less and less in places like New York, Boston, and Philadelphia, that are affected by too many people of differing traditions. (247)

Virtually his every association and published attitude indeed intimated an American *ancien regime*, with, frequently, appeal for confirmation to the capitals of Europe.

He had attended boarding schools in both Europe and the United States. At Harvard—where he had been a distinguished student, graduating *summa cum laude*—he had met Roosevelt and many of the others of the future "Familiars," and he had been a member of the inner circles of the clubs and the theatricals. (In 1930, in the Roosevelt biography, he would recall: "Ellis Island had not yet diluted Harvard and imported Broadway into the college spirit of the shows" [13].) He had had his connections. He had studied music, intending to become a composer. Back in Europe one afternoon in 1882, in Bayreuth, in Wagner's house, he played one of his piano compositions for Franz Liszt, who was a friend of his maternal grandmother, Fanny Kemble. Fanny Kemble herself was the celebrated writer and famous actress, and was the daughter of a famous British theatrical family, and was therefore likely to know anyone of any distinction who composed or painted or wrote, on two continents. Deriving from his mother's side Wister was therefore the son of a family which in addition to much else had its secure place within a socially defined international community of the arts, and Franz Liszt invited him to Paris for further study. He had returned to Harvard, instead, to study law, but certainly he was conscious of his title to this other inner circle. Even the physician who sent him off on his first trip to the West, in 1885, was the right one. Dr. S. Weir Mitchell was not yet the immensely popular novelist he would become in the late 1890s, but in Philadelphia society he was already well known for both his fiction and his cultivation, and he was a relative.

And if it was ironic that "The Virginian" should have been created by such a man, the irony was doubled by the fact that Wister felt that his proper audience was not those tremendous numbers who bought the book, but an elite. In two years, from 1902 to 1904, *The Virginian* went through fourteen editions and sold more than three hundred thousand copies. In 1907, in the Preface to a reissue of his *Lin McLean*, Wister was complaining that he had not been appreciated, because "matters of craftsmanship do not fall into the light of critical attention here as they do in Europe, where the writer is held as much accountable for his manner of saying a thing as for the thing he says" (vii–viii). A few years earlier, in 1900, by way of Preface to his collection of western tales *The Jimmyjohn Boss*, he had written an irregular sonnet, concluding:

> Stranger, do you write books? I ask the question,
> Because I'm told that everybody writes;
>    That what with scribbling, eating, and digestion,
>    And proper slumber, all our days and nights
>    Are wholly filled. It seems an odd suggestion—
>    But if you do write, stop it, leave the masses,
>    Read me, and join the small selected classes.

Henry James was a reigning presence for him. He submitted work to James, and while in private he would express ambivalence about James's advice, eventually he would go well beyond the master, in the sense of scrupulous discriminations of civilized manners and in a fond grasping of intricacies and quaintnesses of social organization, where society was antique and fragile. Wister's *Lady Baltimore* is one of the most refined novels ever written by anyone, and was refined beyond the point of civilization. Charleston, called "Kings Port" in the novel, in the words of Wister's narrator was "the most lovely, the most wistful town in America; whose visible sadness and distinction seem also to speak audibly, speak in the sound of the quiet waves that ripple round her Southern front, speak in the church-bells on Sunday morning, and breathe not only in the soft salt air, but in the perfume of every gentle, old-fashioned rose that blooms behind the high garden walls of falling mellow-tinted plaster." "Kings Port the retrospective, " he said, "Kings Port the belated, who from her pensive porticoes looks over her two rivers to the marshes and the trees beyond, the live-oaks, veiled in gray moss, brooding with memories!" And it followed that Kings Port was one other of the rare refuges of good society:

> This Kings Port, this little city of oblivion, held, shut in with its lavender and pressed-rose memories, a handful of people who were like that great society of the world, the high society of distinguished men and

women who exist no more, but who touched history with a light hand, and left their mark upon it in a host of memoirs and letters that we read to-day with a starved and homesick longing in the midst of our sullen welter of democracy.

While his views on democracy were not uncomplicated, Wister was forthright and had been constant in his opinion of the contemporary "sullen welter" of the United States. He had for a long time known that the so-called servants of democratic government in these days were inept at best. Early, in the Preface to his first collection of western tales, *Red Men and White*, in 1896, he had observed: "It is sorrowful to see our fatal complacence, our as yet undisciplined folly, in sending to our State Legislatures and to that general business office of ours at Washington a herd of mismanagers that seems each year to grow more inefficient and contemptible, whether branded Republican or Democrat" (v). That was the best case, while at somewhat worse he was as aware as his friend Remington of not only the danger but also the offensiveness of radicalized labor in America. Remington had written his account of the Pullman Strike for *Harper's Weekly* in July 1894. In September of 1894 in *Harper's Weekly* Wister wrote an account of the National Guard of Pennsylvania, of which he approved. The single virtue to be credited to organized labor, he said, was that it resulted in the creation of a good soldiery. As a consequence of the railroad strikes of 1877 when "the public enemy" had burned freight cars in Pittsburgh, the National Guard of Pennsylvania had acquired some vigor. In 1892 the National Guard had received an approximation of the respect which was its due when it had confronted the strikers at Homestead: "In July 1892 the rats came out of their holes again," he said. "During the ensuing days the rats, by threats, incendiary pamphlets, and all methods clearly showed the sort of rats that they were. Up till now they had driven owners from their property, maltreated prisoners, shot those sent to disperse them, and established an advisory committee superior to the civil law, violating personal liberty, and providing a censorship of the press. They now undertook assassination." One poor fool of a guardsman had called for three cheers for the would-be assassin Sasha Berkman, but that episode had turned out not badly because it had provided opportunity for exemplary discipline. The guardsman had had half his head shaved and had been drummed out of the service, and also had lost his lawsuit for assault and battery (824).

And he warned: "It remains to be seen if, like Pennsylvania in a small way, the United States in a large way has had a sufficiently severe

lesson to place a correct value upon the soldier. If not, may we have
one soon—before, what with the Debses, the Waites, the Altgelds, the
Pennoyers, and the Markhams, we are become altogether rotten" (826).

But clearly, along with Remington, Wister did believe that a redemption was actually and materially available, from the West, as was
to be seen in contemplation of the events in Chicago:

> Two Chicago rioters who had their opinion of militia were busy at un-
> hindered destruction of other men's property some weeks ago, when a
> sudden and novel stillness in the air caught their attention, and they
> turned round. They saw some dingy objects moving up the street. These
> were United States troops, just come from fighting Indians. They were
> dirty and dogged, and looked straight ahead. The rioters gazed at them
> a moment. "Let's you and me get out," said one of them to the other;
> "them fellers don't carry bokays in their guns." (824)

And, explicitly, again it was the fact that these soldiers were from
the West that particularly, miraculously qualified them. Similarly, in a
journal entry the following year Wister would remark about cowboys in
the West that they were "our hope in the future" because they were
manly, simple, humorous, "and," most to the point, "they don't go
on strikes."[2] (That was a belief that he shared belief with Roosevelt.
Several years earlier, at the time of the Haymarket Riots, Roosevelt had
been writing to a friend about his Dakota cowboys, "The men here are
hardworking, labouring men, who work longer hours for no greater
wages than many of the strikers; but they are Americans through and
through; I believe nothing would give them greater pleasure than a
chance with their rifles at one of the mobs.")[3]

If, on the other hand, organized labor contributed to the sullen
welter, along with Anarchists and contemptible politicians Democrats
and Republicans alike—so no less did corporations and trusts. The
visiting northerner who is the protagonist of *Lady Baltimore* says to his
southern hosts:

> "Oh, hang slavery! Hang the war! . . . Of course, we had a family quarrel.
> But we were a family once, and a fine one, too! We knew each other, we
> visited each other, we wrote letters, sent presents, kept up relations; we,
> in short, coherently joined hands from one generation to another. . . .
> It's all gone, all done, all over. You have to be a small, well-knit country
> for that sort of exquisite personal unitedness. There's nothing united
> about these States any more, except Standard Oil and discontent. We're
> no longer a small people living and dying for a great idea; we're a big
> people living and dying for money."

It was also Wister's idea that essentially and properly the nation was old family, and apparently the idea stayed with him. His 1911 collection of western tales would be entitled *Members of the Family*. In the Preface to that collection, harkening to the same danger, he would observe: "In the West, where the heart of our country has been this long while, and where the head may be pretty soon, the citizens are awakening to the fact that our first century of 'self' government merely substituted the divine right of corporations for the divine right of Kings." They, moreover, might be expected to realize that in this Progressive Era the several devices of Reform would not be adequate to true American purposes. "Surprising it is not," said Wister, "that a people whose genius for machinery has always been paramount should expect more from constitutions and institutions than these mere mechanisms of government can of themselves perform; the initiative, referendum, and recall are excellent inventions, but if left to run alone, as all our other patent devices have been, they will grind out nothing for us: By his very creed is the American dedicated to eternal vigilance" (12).

Paramountly—and better than Frederic Remington, Deadwood Dick, Jr., Ned Buntline, and Injun Dick Talbot, and with greater personal authority, although lacking Teddy Roosevelt's scholarship—Wister knew that the sullen welter of contemporary democracy was a welter of foreigners tolerated by a liberalism which disregarded all distinctions. Thus in an amusing little closet drama on the subject of Prohibition, in 1923, *Watch Your Thirst* (in which he wrote about Juno, who was a great prude, and Ganymede, who succeeded in bringing back the cups), in the important part he would have Choregos sing: "Are we not coming to be ruled by a horde of Barbarians that infest ill-fated Greece? They know not our ancient faith nor our language, but speak many outlandish jargons. And crazy societies of male women and female men and all of the neuter gender, rule us through a Congress that listens but never leads, and is intimidated by that old hag Juno—" so to nominate a general mongrelization of the American polity, as well, incidentally, as loss of gender specifics.

Thus in 1901, as he was assembling *The Virginian*, Wister would pause to write a fondly joshing memoir of old Harvard days, *Philosophy 4*. Billy and Bertie, having skipped classes all semester, cram for their philosophy exam. They hire a tutor, as the fine old practice was, but they are irrepressibly spirited lads and go on an outing rather than attend to their lessons—and yet when the grades come in they have done better than the tutor himself, because: "Bertie and Billy had colonial names (Rogers, I think, and Schuyler), but the tutor's name was Oscar Maironi, and he was charging his pupils five dollars an hour each for his instruction." Moreover: "Bertie's and Billy's parents owned town and country houses in New York. The parents of Oscar had come over in the steerage. Money filled the pockets of Bertie and Billy; therefore were their heads empty of money and full of less cramping thoughts. Oscar had fallen upon the reverse of this fate. Calculation was his second nature." As Wister approached the climax of this tale he noted: "The final examination had begun. Oscar could lay his hand upon his studious heart and await the Day of Judgment like—I had nearly said a Christian!" Late in life Wister would nominate *Philosophy 4* as one of his few favorites among his works, along with a couple of the western tales.

All of this had been there from the beginning and was crucial to his encounter with the West.

He had gone to the West for the first time at age twenty-five, in the summer of 1885, on doctor's orders. He was about to enter Harvard Law School on his way to becoming a gentleman lawyer, apparently against his deepest wishes. The spaces between the lines of the biography assembled by his daughter suggest that he needed to get away from family pressures, although in fact he was accompanied by two of his mother's female friends. A later biographer, Ben Merchant Vorpahl, suggests that Wister was quite seriously ill, suffering nightmares, attacks of vertigo, and hallucinations (*Dear Wister* 17). Wister's most substantial biographer, Darwin Payne, disputes that, but says that for certain Wister was disillusioned and dispirited (75–77). In any event, as was the case with his friend Roosevelt, and at the same time, Wister went to the West seeking recuperation, and, as did Roosevelt, he converted a complex of his own emotional needs into observations on history and public policy.

He kept a journal. On 8 July, at a ranch in Wyoming, he wrote, "I'm beginning to be able to feel I'm something of an animal and not a stinking brain alone." On 10 July he wrote: "Americans! There are very few of them so far in our history. Every man, woman, and cowboy I see comes from the East—and generally from New England, thank goodness. . . . I feel more certainly than ever that no matter how completely the East may be the headwaters from which the West has flown [sic] and is flowing, it won't be a century before the West is simply the true America, with thought, type, and life of its own kind." On 16 July, in abrupt despair, he wrote: "[The West has] a life as strange as any the country has seen, and it will slowly make room for Cheyennes, Chicagos, and ultimately inland New Yorks—everything reduced to the same flat prairie-like level of utilitarian civilization." He had come across some colorful squatters named Branan and Beech, and could not help reflecting: "Branans and Beeches will give way to Tweeds and Jay Goulds—and the ticker will replace the rifle."[4]

Owen Wister. From an advertisement for a "Saturday Daily Reading" course.

Certainly there was a self-consciousness in these jottings, that of a young man beginning to write a journal and therefore attempting some large thoughts and imposing opinions, but there was clarification here for him nonetheless, which then in turn he offered to his friends at home as he became a teller of western tales. There were lessons to be learned having to do entirely with life in the East, how it had decayed and how it might be restored. He would go back to the West repeatedly. By 1900 he had made fifteen trips to various locales in the West. What he wrote was in one major aspect travel literature, consisting of first-hand observations together with collected anecdotes. Almost all of his western tales were told in first person by a gentrified easterner traveling in the West. For all of his writing about cowboys, he had little interest in the cattle industry and seldom bothered to record cowboys doing their work, perhaps because he had seldom actually seen cowboys at their work. Nor for all that he wrote about men with guns, did he usually trade in violence. The characteristic tone of the telling of the tales was droll, mannered, sardonic, that of a gentleman traveler, and the tone of the telling had exclusionary implications. These tales evidently were addressed in the first instance to a select audience of the people Wister knew, while for all that, the tales came to be vastly popular among the vulgar.

In the West he satirized cultural climbers, not of course from the bottom and jealously, but good-humoredly, whimsically, with candid superciliousness. In a tale called "Sharon's Choice," typical of many, Wister the traveler is called upon to judge the annual elocution contest in Sharon, New Mexico. The tale goes forward from there, but the main thing is to point to the incongruity of there being such a contest in such a place. Of course no one in Sharon actually either knows or cares anything about true principles of elocution, certainly not the mothers of the place, who seem to be in charge of culture. By spontaneous acclamation the prize goes to an urchin who has recently been orphaned, has lost two fingers in an accident, and is full of spunk.

And in the West in like vein he satirized sob-sisterism. In "The Serenade at Siskiyou," the Ladies' Reform and Literary Lyceum, chaired by the wife of the judge, comforts a pair of rapscallions who have robbed a stagecoach and murdered the guard. The men of the town are prevailed upon to allow a trial, but at the end and with the vigor of common sense they lynch the two brothers, thereby to rescue law from reform-minded ladies, with Wister's authorial approval.

Wister would naturally have opposed Populist rabble-rousing, especially since 1890s Populism in its own way was mythicizing the West. Populism for him was a brew consisting of equal parts of sentimentality and greed. The immediate occasion for a long story collected in *Red Men and White*, "A Pilgrim on the Gila," was the Populist agitation in 1893 for granting statehood to Arizona. William Jennings Bryan figures in the tale as, here, "The Boy Orator of the Rio Grande." The tale begins in Washington where, before starting out for Arizona, Wister visits the Senate. There he listens to the politicians who talk about the good order and prosperity which prevail in the Arizona Territory, but he knows better, and knows as well something about base motives. Arriving in Arizona, Wister finds little evidence of good order. The chief incident reported by the story has to do with the robbery of a government payroll, which Wister himself had happened to have witnessed. At the trial the other witnesses either perjure themselves or are poorly represented by the government's attorney. "The scales had many hours ago dropped from my eyes," he says, "and I saw Arizona clear." But, he adds, "[I] felt no repining for roses and jasmine. They had been a politician's way of foisting one more silver State upon our Senate, and I willingly renounced them for the real thing I was getting!" (229).

On the other hand, neither here nor anywhere else did Wister valorize untrammeled human nature. To the contrary, a strictness of law was called for, but—such was the issue—law was not to be entrusted to politicians of the current type. "The unthinking sons of the sagebrush ill tolerate a thing which stands for discipline, good order, and obedience," he said, "and the man who lets another command him they despise. . . . I can think of no threat more evil for our democracy, for it is a fine thing diseased and perverted—namely, independence gone drunk" (269), thus to condemn democratic politics and the demos itself both at once.

The attitude was explicitly aristocratic and, in this Wild West, was traditional to the point of being archaic. In the first of his western tales, "Hank's Woman," completed in early 1892, Wister the visiting tenderfoot listens to a cowboy who tells him the story of Hank's woman. She was an Austrian maid-servant who had been abandoned in Wyoming by her employers and who in desperation had married Hank. It had been a mismatch, which leads the cowboy to reflect not on marriage, but on the finenesses of Austria in the old days, here sprawled by a pool in the shadow of the Tetons. "But I reckon Austrians have good religion," he says.

> Better'n what I've saw any Americans have. Of course I am not judging a whole nation by one citizen, and especially her a woman. And of course in them big Austrian towns the folks has shook their virtuous sayin's

loose from their daily doin's, same as we have. I expect selling yourself
brings the quickest returns to man or woman all the world over. But I
am speakin', not of towns, but of the back country, where folks don't
just merely arrive on the cyars, but come into the world the natural way,
and grow up slow. Onced a week anyway they see the bunch of old grave-
stones that marks their fam'ly. Their blood and name are knowed about
in the neighborhood, and it's not often one of such will sell themselves.

Wister was concerned for the failings of old family much as were
Teddy Roosevelt and Albert W. Aiken, and like them he found in the
West a fleeting hope for renewal, or a restorative reminder, for those
who would listen. In "The Right Honorable the Strawberries," which
was another of his own few favorites among his works, he told the story
of a young Briton, "a beautiful, consummate product, a thousand years
in the making," who has fallen in character, is a card cheat, and has
been exiled by his family to Drybones, Wyoming. The cowboy Chalkeye
admires him despite his fall. When the local chief gambler tries to kill
Strawberries, Chalkeye jumps in front of him and receives the fatal
bullet. And that is the end of the action, but there is a moral here, expressed explicitly. At the end of the tale the narrator, a "Philadelphian,"
is approached by Strawberries:

> "I say," he called.
> I turned. There he stood, and into his face came a something that
> recalled the old smile like a pressed flower.
> "Chalkeye was a good fellow, you know."
> "Yes."
> "I suppose you're thinking he was a better fellow than me?"
> "Yes."
> "Right."

There were Indians in the West. Wister had met a few. He also
knew soldiers at the western forts. His first collection would be called
*Red Men and White.* His opinions about the Indian wars might have had
some authority, had he offered any. He had been a near witness to
signal events: the Ghost Dance, the Apache War of 1886, the Battle
of Wounded Knee in 1890. But he saw Indians too in the perspective
of his usual concerns, when he did see them. (The Indian attack in
*The Virginian* would take place offstage.) The Indians he saw tended
to be good because they were noble, and they were noble not in a
Rousseauvian but in a genealogical sense. In a tale entitled "The Gift
Horse," Wister recalled: "Old Washakie, chief of the Shoshone tribe,
did me the honor to dine with me at the military post which bore his

name. Words cannot describe the face and presence of that old man; ragged clothes abated nothing of his dignity. A past like the world's beginning looked from his eyes; his jaw and long white hair made you silent as tall mountains make you silent." But much like Americans, as it were, Indians were spoiled by mongrelization. "I know most any Injun's better'n most any white man till he meets the white man," says Scipio LeMoyne, one of Wister's repeated cowboy characters, in a tale called "Happy-Teeth." "Not smarter, y'u know, but better." In a tale called "A Kinsman of Red Cloud," Wister offered up a half-breed for pure Indian judgment. Toussaint, a villain who cheats at poker and has killed two white men, is described in kennel terms: "He was by a French trapper from Canada out of a Sioux squaw." Chief Red Cloud is technically his uncle. Red Cloud goes to the fort to save him from the white man's justice, but finally will not:

> Then the mongrel strain of blood told, and the half-breed poured out a chattering appeal, while Red Cloud by the bedside waited till it had spent itself. Then he grunted, and left the room. He had not spoken and his crest of long feathers as it turned the corner was the last vision of him that the card-players had. Red Cloud came back to the officers, and in their presence formally spoke to his interpreter, who delivered the message: "Red Cloud says Toussain heap no good. No Injun, anyhow. He not want him."

In another mood Wister thought it amusing that some people believed that American Indians were descended from one of the lost tribes of Israel, for that would make them Jews, and one knew about Jews. In "Absalom and Moulting Pelican," the theory is pleasantly disproved when at a western fort an Indian is put upon the stage to act the part of a Jewish pawnbroker. "Nize gentleman," says Moulting Pelican, "what you want for that nize hair? I gif you ten dollars."

In these tonalities of dealing with race Wister was indeed different from both Roosevelt and Remington. Wister was every inch the patrician. Moulting Pelican speaks to a patrician sort of humor. Red Cloud confirms what was for Wister a patrician idea of bloodline. But Wister was different in tonalities only.

For the three of these who made the fiction of the West, there was an appeal backward, reaching in each case finally to a primitive Anglo-Saxonism, alternately martial and melancholy, which obviously was serviceable primarily in confrontation with the East. After all of the civilities and manners and codes of the western hero, there was fundamentally and astonishingly the preserved purity of the blood, given which the rest would follow.

Roosevelt the politician wrote about the winning of the west as an episode in the inevitable spread of the English-speaking peoples, at a time when, in his own words, he perceived that the United States was in danger of becoming a "polyglot boardinghouse."

Remington, who had Mayflower antecedents although he was neither wealthy enough nor gentle enough to be genteel, was nothing if not forthright in his "vehement opposition," in the mild words of one of his biographers, "to immigration, populism, and social change." Both publicly and privately. "You cant glorify a Jew—coin 'loving puds'— nasty humans," he observed in a letter to a colleague. "I've got some Winchesters and when the massacreing [sic] begins which you speak of, I can get my share of 'em and whats more I will. Jews—inguns [sic]— chinamen—Italians—Huns, the rubish [sic] of the earth I hate—Our race is full of sentiment and we invite the 'rinsins—the scourins and the devils lavins' to come to us and be men—something they haven't been, most of them—these hundreds of years."[5]

In his novel *John Ermine of the Yellowstone*, published in 1902 just a few months after *The Virginian*, Remington did in fact propose a further term to the argument, according to which Indians and Germanic tribesmen of a dim historical past alike became victims of modern times. Remington was a choleric man who liked horses better than people, but he seems also quite genuinely to have sympathized with Indians and with blacks, and to have had some knowledge. He rode with and wrote about the "Buffalo Soldiers" in the West, praising them for many virtues while, significantly, scarcely bothering to mention race at all. Moreover, he disliked the "cracker cowboys" whom he discovered on a trip to Florida, in part, explicitly, because of their "*ante bellum* theories" of race. He sketched Indians in their camps. In articles and fiction he presented considerable detail about daily Indian life in various of the western tribes. Certainly he was sympathetic to the plight of the Indians and blamed the government, or, more particularly, "certain political circles backed by public apathy and a lot of theoretical Indian regenerators," for, in his words, "oppressing a conquered people."[6]

In *John Ermine*, in any event, he resolved whatever there was of a contradiction in his attitudes by inventing a white boy who has been raised as a Crow Indian and therefore is an Indian except that in the crucial moment his underlying identity asserts itself. Far from representing a rupture, however, this event reveals the common bond, namely that the white boy, too, with his yellow hair, is basically a savage. Savagery is the theme. It is nature's way. "The wolves, the ravens, and the Indians were brothers in blood," said Remington, "and all followed the buffalo herds together . . . A lame or loose pony or a crippled Indian often went the way of the wolves, and many wolves' hides passed over the trader's counter. They always got along together, with the raven last at the feast." When little Indian boys play, their ideas of play are "founded on the way of things about them, they are warriors, wild animals, horses, and the hunters, and the hunted by turns." And as for John Ermine the white boy, he reenters white life as a scout for the army and is respected for his skills and his bravery, but will be confounded by civilization. In the second approximately half of the novel, the daughter of the major will come from the East to visit. John Ermine, known also by his Indian name, White Weasel, falls in love with her, is rejected by her in horror, shoots her other suitor, a soldier from the East, wounds him, and then, having lusted and tried to kill, he runs. And here was a moral: "The mountain boy had brought little to the soldier camp but the qualities of mind which distinguished his remote ancestors of the north of Europe, who came out of the dark forests clad in skins, and bearing the first and final law of man, a naked sword on a knotted arm. . . . Now he was fleeing for life because he had done two of the most natural things which a man can do." In fact it will be another Indian who will kill him, but for reason of a fancied insult having to do with the impossible courtship.

But John Ermine had been fated to die because for Remington as well as for everybody else the true West was essentially provisional and precarious, in motion toward disappearance even as it was discovered. Remington would recall that on his very first trip to the West, in 1881, somewhere in Montana he had come across a wagon-freighter who had told him, "Now there is no more West." The major action of *John Ermine* takes place from 1876 to 1877, following the Battle of Little Big Horn, when already the end is in sight. John Ermine the scout sees a Sioux Indian a mile off seated on a horse, and reflects, "If all these white men were dead, it would make no difference; if that Indian on the far-off hill was dead, he could never be replaced."

And so for Wister in a slightly different tonality. In 1894 in Arizona, less than a decade after his first trip to the West, Wister was writing to his mother: "The frontier has yielded to a merely commonplace society which lacks at once picturesqueness and civilization. When I heard that the Apache squaws now give their babies condensed milk, my sympathy for them chilled. The survivors of Tombstone sit there and dwell on how things used to be . . . and all over the adjacent hills stand silent silver mines—the machinery rusty, falling to pieces, and a good deal of it burned."[7] In the first sentence of the Preface to his first collection of western tales, *Red Men and White*, in 1896, he would reflect: "These eight stories are made from our Western Frontier as it was in a past as

near as yesterday and almost as by-gone as the Revolution" (v), while
the earliest of the tales in the collection, "Hank's Woman," implicitly
mourned the passing of another prior past. *The Virginian*, in 1902, was
to be read as a "historical novel," said Wister in his first preface to the
novel. The novel was said to present "a vanished world, " presumably a
pristine world, namely Wyoming in the years between 1874 and 1890,
but then in fact when in the novel itself the narrator first rides off "deep
into cattle land," in the author's recollection it is the contemporaneous
littering of the landscape that is most of all to be noted: as memento of
the day of the cowboy, it is written, "the empty sardine box lies rusting
over the face of the Western earth." Wister's collection of interlaced
tales, *Lin McLean*, in 1897, had begun: "In the old days, the happy days,
when Wyoming was a Territory with a future instead of a State with a
past. . . ," and so on.

Motives leading to discovery of both the West and its heroes had
been revealed with extraordinary clarity in a lengthy essay of 1895
called "The Evolution of the Cow-Puncher," written by Wister, illustrated by Remington, and conceived in concert by the two of them.
The essay presented some data on cow-punching, but emphatically the
subject was, rather, "evolution," from Anglo-Saxons to buckaroos, with
the miraculous survival of the one in the other. In the essay Wister told
the tale of an English duke who had gone off to Texas and who, contrary
to what some might have expected, had become a cattle millionaire.
Many perhaps would suppose that British nobility by this decadent
time had become too effete for Texas life, but: "Directly the English
nobleman smelt Texas, the slumbering untamed Saxon awoke in him,
and mindful of the tournament, mindful of the hunting field, galloped
howling after the wild cattle, a born horseman, a perfect athlete, and in
spite of the peerage and gule and argent, fundamentally kin with the
drifting vagabonds who swore and galloped by his side." "The man's
outcome," Wister said, "typifies the way of his race from the beginning,"
and constituted a reprimand.

> No rood of modern ground is more debased and mongrel [than
> ours] with its hordes of encroaching alien vermin, that turn our cities to
> Babels and our citizenship to a hybrid farce, who degrade our common-
> wealth from a nation into something half pawnshop, half broker's office.
> But to survive in the clean cattle country requires spirit of adventure,
> courage, and self-sufficiency; you will not find many Poles or Huns or
> Russian Jews in that district; it stands as yet untainted by the benevolence
> of Baron Hirsch. Even in the cattle country the respectable Swedes settle
> chiefly to farming, and are seldom horsemen. The community of which

the aristocrat appropriately made one speaks English. The Frenchman
to-day is seen at his best inside a house; he can paint and he can play
comedy, but he seldom climbs a new mountain. The Italian has forgotten
Columbus, and sells fruit. Among the Spaniards and the Portuguese, no
Cortez or Magellan is around to-day. Except in Prussia, the Teuton is
too often a tame, slippered animal, with his pedantic mind swaddled
in a dressing-gown. But the Anglo-Saxon is still forever homesick for
out-of-doors.[8]

*The Virginian*, that essential Western, followed. The Virginian did
not howl when he galloped. He did not gallop very much at all, in fact.
For the most part he was poised for action rather than being involved
in any action, for performance of labor would have been superfluous.
Wister was not interested in the cattle industry. Nor was The Virginian
a peer from Britain, but he was a Virginian hardly by accident, and, like
the English duke, was there in the West to repossess his heritage. He
was an aristocrat, whose heritage and status comprised his task. Against
some odds, and also mindful of some hints of the encroaching alien
vermin, he was there to reinvigorate and to reassert a tradition. His nonchalance was itself his labor, along with the exclusionary implications
of his manners and bearing.

The Virginian when we meet him is a master of obliquenesses and
long silences. He understates. He drawls. His discourse is habitually
indirect, suggesting at once his perfect ease among those who already
understand him, and his facility in estranging others. Virtually the first
thing we are to know about him is that he makes the author uneasy,
although indeed there will be other implications to the author's unease.
In one of their first exchanges Owen Wister observes, politely, "You're
from old Virginia, I take it?" and The Virginian answers slowly, "Then
you have taken it correct, seh," and Wister reports that he felt the chill
in that response. "This handsome, ungrammatical son of the soil had set
between us the bar of his cold and perfect civility," he says. "No polished
person could have done it better." Moreover, Wister, who previously
had told almost all of his western tales in the guise of a traveler and
participant, in fact progressively loses his part in this story. The point
of view in the novel slips from first person to third. That was seemingly
a technical problem, of which Wister was aware. He wrestled with it and
ended by writing to his mother, who disliked the novel, that in *Madame
Bovary* too the first person "simply dissolved away into the third." But
the problem was more than technical, given this chilling protagonist.
As a matter of the inherency of the character of the protagonist, the
narrator simply was ruled out.

This protagonist was provided with a sense of the proprieties which astonishes the narrator for its being at once so subtle and so ominously determinative. In the novel's single most memorable incident, the issue between The Virginian and Trampas is an insult merely, or hardly even that but a bit of passing irritability, while the energy of the incident is created by the startling disproportion of The Virginian's response. Trampas, at poker, says, "Your bet, you son-of-a——," whereat:

> The Virginian's pistol came out, and his hand lay on the table, holding it unaimed. And with a voice as gentle as ever, the voice that sounded almost like a caress, but drawling a very little more than usual, so that there was almost a space between each word, he issued his order to the man Trampas:—
> "When you call me that, *smile!*"

Just a few paragraphs earlier The Virginian's friend Steve had also called him "You old son-of-a——!" affectionately, and The Virginian had not minded. Wister as narrator wonders about this. "The same words, identical to the letter," he reflects. "But this time they had produced a pistol. 'When you call me that, *smile!*' So I perceived a new example of the old truth, that the letter means nothing until the spirit gives it life"—but this was beside the point because it is neither the words nor the spirit that create the incident. What is to be known is that The Virginian is a man who will brook no affront to his dignity no matter how slight. And one more thing: it is to be realized according to the authority of his example, that death is the appropriate punishment for insolence.

In the matter of the respect due him, The Virginian is a virtuoso from the beginning, much more than he is demonstrably competent in such other cowboy matters as shooting, roping, riding swiftly, and hunting down rustlers, although he can do those things as well. A very great quantity of such action as there is in the novel is attached to questions of propriety. So when at the beginning of the novel The Virginian plays his practical joke upon the "drummer" in Medicine Bow, frightening the man from his bed, the victim of the joke seems to have deserved what he gets because he has breached some rules of conduct, which he does not know. He is in the West for the wrong reason, first of all, in order to sell something, with the wrong company— "two Jews handling cigars, one American with consumption killer, and a Dutchman with jew'lry." He errs secondly by the strategies of his affability. He says to The Virginian, "you turn in when you feel inclined, old man!" and Wister observes, "The drummer had struck a slightly false note in these last remarks. He should not have said 'old man.' . . . It had a hateful taint of his profession; the being too soon with everybody, the celluloid good-fellowship that passes for ivory with nine in ten of the city crowd. But not so with the sons of the sage-brush. They live nearer nature and they know better." And so The Virginian in effect threatens to murder him, pretending to having a "fit." On the other side of the matter, in the lengthiest and most substantial episode of the novel, when The Virginian makes a fool of Trampas by convincing him that fortunes are to be made in frogs' legs, the joke works because Trampas, villain that he is, is still sufficiently sensitive to ploys of status that he can be embarrassed. He is a villain in the first place because he has been disloyal to the ranch owner, Judge Henry, who in effect in the scheme of things in this West is the ruler of a Duchy, if not quite a Kingdom, which is to say that Trampas is a villain because he has not been content with his place in an antique and arbitrary scheme of things. There is direct allusion here to Arthurian romance. In the present instance he loses the respect of his own followers, who of course also understand status. It is that loss that spells Trampas's downfall. When some pages later The Virginian kills him in a gun duel, that is merely confirmation.

There is little good humor here, nor is there much real suspense or other overt excitement, either. Throughout, discursively and by exempla, *The Virginian* insists upon status and privilege, and because of the enormous popularity of the novel, it must follow that an appeal back from democratic institutions was welcome in the East where the readers were. It is to be presumed that, for instance, when Wister stepped forth from the novel in order to defend lynching, his readers not only accepted his argument, but appreciated his impatience. "Forgive my asking you to use your mind," said Wister. "It is a thing which no novelist should expect of his reader," and presumably his reader was not offended.

The argument follows upon The Virginian's lynching of his (former, late) best friend, Steve, who had succumbed to rustling. Wise Judge Henry has been brought into the novel's pages to say: (a) that lynching in Wyoming is different from the lynching of blacks in the South because in Wyoming it happens more swiftly and does not involve torture, (b) that all justice is people's justice, and so there was no reason to wait for a court of law, for the outcome would not have been any different, and (c) that anyway, here in Wyoming there was no court of law reasonably at hand. It is to be noted that if the judge's argument is itself tortured (as Wister the lawyer certainly must have suspected), at least Wister the novelist did not flinch from the appalling implications of the event. The Virginian himself sees ghosts. In a scene following upon the event, Wister had little children playing a game of lynching, five little boys and three little girls.

But the persuasion was elsewhere, not in the words of the Judge but resting still and again upon the categorical authority of The Virginian, while that authority itself was unargued but was repeatedly demonstrated.

Acceptance of The Virginian's authority in fact amounts frequently to submission, and is sexualized. Therein indeed was the plotting of the novel, otherwise missing, proceeding by innuendo and displacement and surrogation, as also apparently beyond Wister's own authorial recognitions. The Virginian is not only the man with the gun, but he is *The Man*. The first chapter of the novel is entitled "Enter The Man." Although action in the novel begins with the entrance of the author-narrator into Medicine Bow, clearly it is The Virginian and not the narrator who is The Man. Wister is struck immediately by the manly grace of The Man. Still on the train and looking through the window, he sees a sight. A cow pony is to be roped. "Then for the first time," says Wister, "I noticed a man who sat on the high gate of the corral, looking on. For he now climbed down with the undulations of a tiger, smooth and easy, as if his muscles flowed beneath his skin." And just afterwards, after detraining, he observes: "Lounging there at ease against the wall was a slim young giant, more beautiful than pictures. . . . In his eye, in his face, in his step, in the whole man, there dominated a something potent to be felt, I should think, by man or woman." In that first chapter there is a play with the funny old geezer Uncle Hughey who is on his way to finding a bride. "Had I been the bride," says Wister, "I should have taken the giant, dust and all."

So the tale begins, with a narrator who is not only impressed but, as it were, smitten. The action just thereafter then is complicated by the attempts at ingratiation on the part of Wister the narrator. He flirts, and is rebuffed. He competes for the attentions of The Man, with best friend Steve who can affectionately call The Virginian a son-of-a-bitch, with the "good-looker" Mrs. Glen who owns the saloon ("no woman's eyes ever said more plainly, 'I am one of your possessions,' " it is said), and competes with some success against the drummer whom The Virginian forces from his bed. And as then the tale goes forward, implicitly the terms of a relationship are negotiated with the tenderfoot Wister taking on a feminized, passive, not infrequently rather comic role. Arrived at Judge Henry's ranch, Wister needs be escorted by The Virginian on brief hunting trips, because he gets lost. In the set-piece chapter "Em'ly," Wister clearly sympathizes with the crazed mother hen Em'ly, driven mad by her inability to lay her own eggs, while it is significant

that in the first place, in the distribution of the duties of the ranch, he
has been put to tending the chickens, becoming "an object of mirth,"
as he says. The other men are cow-punchers.

The first-person narrator does progressively succumb to a third-
person telling, but the character Wister—as admiring, baffled, smitten,
naive, would-be companion to The Virginian—is replaced.

Enters The Woman, who first of all and obviously is a more likely
agent of courtship but who also otherwise provides for a fulfillment of
the logic of this tale better than might even the Philadelphia Mainliner
Owen Wister.

The novel finally is wonderfully resolute in the pursuit of its own
logic. The Virginian does marry the schoolmarm, shortly after she
has been educated in the occasional necessities of lynchings and duels. Other matings thereby take place: brawn with booklearning, West
with East, also South with North, and, most emphatically, blood with
blood. Miss Molly Stark Wood is the one and appropriate mate for
The Virginian. She is extraordinary, explicitly: "First," it is said, "there
was her descent," and second her character—but it is the first datum
that secures expatiation, from which the second follows. "Had she so
wished," we are to know, "she could have belonged to any number
of those patriotic societies of which our American ears have grown
accustomed to hear so much. She could have been enrolled in the
Boston Tea Party, the Ethan Allen Ticonderogas, the Green Mountain
Daughters, the Saratoga Sacred Circle, and the Confederated Colonial
Chatelaines." She is one of the New Hampshire and Vermont Starks, of
Revolutionary days, of the line of the great soldier John Stark of the
Battle of Bennington. "She traced direct descent from the historic lady
whose name she bore, that Molly Stark who was not a widow after the
battle where her lord, her Captain John, battled so bravely as to send his
name thrilling down through the blood of generations of schoolboys."
(Wister's reader was to recall that at the Battle of Bennington Stark was
said to have exclaimed to his troops, "There, my boys, are your enemies,
the red-coats and tories; you must beat them or my wife sleeps a widow
tonight.") Molly's most treasured possession is a miniature portrait of
that first Molly Stark. Nothing gives her greater pleasure than to be
told each summer by a certain great-aunt that she herself has come
more and more to look like the original. "There can be no doubt of
this—" says Wister, on his way to telling the anecdote of the frogs' legs:
"All America is divided into two classes—the quality and the equality.
The latter will always recognize the former when mistaken for it. Both
will be with us until our women bear nothing but kings." And, that
last being impossible, there was no doubt that Molly was one among

the few, and was perhaps unique. Along with her husband, the cowboy from Virginia, she was entirely aloof from the equality.

The novel concludes not at all with the melancholy cowboy riding off into a receding West. The Virginian has a savings account. He has made wise investments. He has good holdings in land and coal. Epilogue to the actions assures us that when the cattle business was forced out of Wyoming by the knaveries of the politicians (so Wister accounted for the cattle wars in Johnson County), The Virginian had done business with the railroad. He is important and rich, and his wife has borne a son. The last scene of this Western takes place in a house in Dunbarton (formerly actually Starkstown), New Hampshire, where the surviving Starks forgather annually. Molly's great-aunt, a vigorous and wise lady who has done her part to forward the mating of her niece, recognizes The Virginian as kin. "Then," it is said, "she showed him old things that she was proud of, 'because,' she said, 'we, too, had something to do with making our country.' "

Henry James read this novel by the son of his friend Sally Wister, grandson of his friend Fanny Kemble, and was very kind, but he did object to the ending with its "prosperity" and the union with "the little Vermont person." Had he himself written the novel, he said in a letter to Wister, he would have doled out "all sorts of poetic justice" to the hero. "I," he said, "should have made him perish in his flower & in some splendid sombre way."[9] But James was guilty here of vulgar realism. Western heroes had been perishing all along. By 1902, moreover, all of that high tradition which the western hero had been made to represent and protect was, if not gone, something already beyond being imperilled. And Wister had doled out poetic justice exactly. By recognizing the prerogatives of a displaced aristocracy, by bringing his westerner back east and presenting him with the power which was his due, he wrote the proper end-term of the romance, so that forever afterward the conventional ironies would be recognized and translated instantly: when in all of the versions of the Western to come the hero would ride to the sunset, it would be really to the East that he was traveling, ominous and armed.

# PART III

## Private Eyes

I'm a detective—I know everything.
—The Continental Op

# 8    McParlan

CROSSING the Atlantic sometime early in 1914 aboard the SS *Olympic,* sister ship of the *Titanic,* traveling to New York despite the submarines, in the smoking room, William Pinkerton had a talk with his friend Arthur Conan Doyle. He was the son of Allan Pinkerton, founder of The Pinkerton National Detective Agency, and was now himself a co-director of the Agency along with his brother Robert. They called him "Big Eye." He had tales to tell, of crime and detection. That day he told Conan Doyle about the case that had made his father famous.

It had been in the 1870s during the time of the troubles in the hard-coal fields of Pennsylvania, instigated, so it was said, by a secret organization known as the Mollie Maguires. The civil government had been inoperative if not totally nonexistent. In Schuylkill County in the dozen years prior to 1875, 142 persons had been murdered, without any of the perpetrators having been convicted. Foremen and other bosses in the mines had been the primary targets of assassination, but many other and ordinary civilians also had been killed, by accident of being bystanders or in private acts of vengeance. The Pinkerton Agency had been called in, in 1873, hired by the Philadelphia Coal and Iron Company, which owned most of the mines along with much else, including the houses in which the miners worked and the stores from which they bought, and which in turn was owned by the Philadelphia and Reading Railroad, which had an interest in identifying the trouble-makers. Pinkerton had selected one certain young detective for work in the fields, James McParlan. McParlan then would live in the coal region for two and half years, playing the part of a roistering, hot-headed, and hard-drinking young radical, and as the event would prove, he would be very successful. He had been invited to join the Mollies and had risen in their ranks. Finally he had returned from the coal fields, early in the spring of 1876, with evidence sufficient for the hanging of twenty men, ten of them on one day, 21 June, 1877, some three weeks not so incidentally before the first shots were fired in that summer's great and bloody railroad strike.

Allan Pinkerton himself had written an immensely popular book about the case, *The Molly Maguires and the Detectives*. It had been published in 1877, quickly following upon the first ten of the executions, one of eighteen of his books about his and the Agency's various cases.

And Conan Doyle evidently was interested, and with good reason for here was nothing less than a brand new archetype for detective stories, albeit with unsettling implications, as evidently he almost realized. Not for the first time he was intrigued by the possibilities in the exotica of American conspiracies. "A Study in Scarlet," the very first of the Sherlock Holmes stories, had had Mormons. "The Five Orange Pips" had the Ku Klux Klan. But in the instance of Pinkerton's true account, it must have occurred to Conan Doyle that the given central character himself, the detective, was something new. Not only was he not aloof, elegant, and slightly decadent, after the amusing manner of his Holmes, but also he was not untainted. More broadly, a range of social and moral assumptions might be questioned. In this adventure of McParlan's it was not so certain what was and what was not crime, nor who was the criminal, nor what was the justification for the work of a detective hired by capital investors in a business which controlled a population, the members of which were killing each other not necessarily for high principle. America was brutal, probably hopeless modern history. As evidently Conan Doyle's sympathies dictated, it was most important that this detective be saved both from American and from modern history, so far as possible. The result of the endeavor, then, would indicate not only a difference in the styles of detective stories, but radical difference in opinion between the British and the Americans as to what constituted civilization.

He wrote *The Valley of Fear*, a novel-length Sherlock Holmes tale, quickly following upon the conversation with the younger Pinkerton. It would be published in 1915. The unusual length of the tale, for a Sherlock Holmes story, might have indicated that Conan Doyle had something particularly serious in mind, perhaps an essay in historical understanding. (Within the whole of the corpus, only four of the tales of Sherlock Holmes are carried to novel length.) In any event, *The Valley of Fear* was a fictional version of the adventures of James McParlan, based very closely on the book of the elder Pinkerton, although some other accounts also would have been available. There would have been an irony in the fact that Pinkerton's book in the first place had been something of a fiction in the senses both of technique and of whole-cloth invention. ("[The author] is aware," said the author in his Preface, "that, in many places, the relation reads much like fiction, and that it will be accepted as romance by very many"—while in fact the "author" probably was one of the many ghostwriters who worked for Pinkerton and who in all likelihood considered romance to be his primary trade.) Nonetheless, *The Valley of Fear* certainly was ambitious to be fiction beyond itself, for all that it was another detective story. It was to be suffused with history and truth and public presence. From his source or sources Conan Doyle took rituals and passwords and alleged secrets of the Mollies (to be called "Scowrers" in the novel, old Scottish for "scarers," as is pointed out), and particular adventures of the original McParlan, and even some of the real names of both the murdered and the accused.

*The Valley of Fear* consists of two parts plus epilogue. In part 1 Holmes learns of the murder, as supposed, of one John Douglas, a wealthy and well-respected country gentleman, master of ancient, moated Birlstone Manor in Sussex—who, however, as Holmes will soon know, really has not been murdered at all but, rather, has killed some-one else; Douglas had blown off the other man's head using an Ameri-can-style shotgun, hence the confusion. Particularly, he had killed Ted Baldwin, a Scowrer from Pennsylvania bent on revenge, for (as will be revealed in part 2, which is a flashback to Pennsylvania) John Douglas really is, or had been, an American, named Birdy Edwards, and had been a Pinkerton detective, and it is he now rather than Holmes who will be central to the tale. In the coal fields he had called himself John McMurdo. (McParlan's alias had been James McKenna.) There in the coal fields he had pretended to having a criminal past, as a murderer and a counterfeiter in Chicago and Buffalo, serially. As had McParlan.

But there were differences, none so salient first of all as what followed in the aftermath. After the trials and the revelations leading to the hangings, the original McParlan had gone off to be superin-tendent of Pinkerton's Denver office, where he would be in charge of cases involving train robbery and the infiltration of other miners' organizations. (McParlan was still alive and active at the time of the publication of Conan Doyle's novel. He would die in 1919, peacefully.) Birdy Edwards, on the other hand, now five years after Pennsylvania, al-though lacking heritage actually to be a real British country gentleman, nonetheless occupies the position of one, and in a number of ways is an improvement: he has a great deal of money, and he is much loved by the villagers for the reason that in his peculiar American way he is friendly to his inferiors. In the epilogue he will drown, abruptly, along with his wife. They had been on their way to South Africa to escape their troubles and perhaps had been swept overboard during a gale at sea, or perhaps, as Holmes suspects, had been pushed by an agent of Professor Moriarty acting in behalf of the Scowrers. Little matter either way, however. Whether come to by accident or by mischief, their end did a service for civilization. Murder even in self-defense, with an American-style shotgun, is not to be sanctioned, and also, after all, a genealogical integrity, of British country gentlemen, is to be salvaged.

And that different sense of an ending is instructive. "Permeating the thought and language of Conan Doyle's stories," says Ross Mac-Donald, "is an air of blithe satisfaction with a social system based on privilege. . . . Nostalgia for a privileged society accounts for one of the prime attractions of the traditional English detective story" (298). And so it is here as well, with peculiar distinctness just because of Conan Doyle's exploitation of an American history. The original McParlan in his lengthy term in the coal fields had lived the life, forming friendships, which indeed he would betray, securing even a romantic attachment or two, one of them more than casual, also sacrificing health as the life demanded, while everything about John Douglas suggests that the Birdy Edwards of the coal fields had been the aberration. Doyle compressed the time in Pennsylvania to four months, February to May of 1875. No doubt he did so for purposes of narrative efficiency, but nevertheless this change also made the difference that the deceit was not his character's life. "Douglas was a remarkable man both in character and in person," so it is said, as might be expected, while the whole of the utility of McParlan in matter of looks and general demeanor had been in the fact that he was not remarkable at all but could be taken for a typical Irish immigrant—while Douglas is strong-jawed, has a rugged face, a grizzled moustache, keen grey eyes, youthful wiry vigor, is "cheery and genial to all," his democracy having been transformed, or (more properly, no doubt) having reverted, to perfect noblesse oblige.

Douglas moreover subscribes generously to all of the local Birlstone charities and attends the village concerts. He is a hero of Birlstone civilization which in turn is a metaphor for civilization itself, while crime is an antonym and is that which occurs elsewhere, in Pennsylvania. Birlstone "is a small and very ancient cluster of half-timbered cottages" which for centuries has remained unchanged although it is now on the point, ominously, of becoming a modern town. Birlstone Manor, half a mile from the village, dates back to the First Crusades, while as for the coal country, in part 2: "It had been a severe winter, and the snow lay deep in the gorges of the Gilmerton Mountains. . . . Desolate it was. . . . this gloomy land of black crag and tangled forest. Above the dark and often scarcely penetrable woods upon their sides, the high, bare crowns of the mountains, white snow and jagged rock, towered upon either flank, leaving a long, winding, tortuous valley in the centre. Up this the little train was slowly crawling." McParlan's base had been Shenandoah, a name which most likely had always begged for music, which becomes "Vermissa" in Conan Doyle's version, from *vermis*, worm, and which showed "a dead level of mean ugliness and squalor": "The broad street was churned up by the traffic into a horrible rutted paste of muddy snow. The sidewalks were narrow and uneven. The numerous gas-lamps served only to show more clearly a long line of wooden houses, each with its veranda facing the street, unkempt and dirty."

The remoteness in which John Douglas had passed a term is a locale for savages at night, a memory of the lurking primordial, the worm of distant racial memory before Birlstone. For the inhabitants of such a place, "this most desolate corner of the United States of America," terror will have been dogmatic with or without organized purveyors of terror, and it was Conan Doyle's strategy, then, briefly to insinuate one landscape into the other, perhaps as a warning, or perhaps just for the thrill of it, but that too would have been instructive. John Douglas has been to Pennsylvania and has known crime, which is to be recognized as such from the perspective of "a settled community where the readers' sympathies are on the side of law and order" wherein only, according to a statement attributed to Lord Hewart of Bury, late Lord Chief Justice of England, the detective story flourishes.[1]

McParlan meanwhile had occupied a position of perfect ambiguity, morally and socially, as no doubt Conan Doyle both knew and recoiled from knowing. Certainly in his reality he was not a candidate for Birlstone Manor. He had been a "detective," nominally and according to general usage, employed by a "Detective Agency," but he neither analyzed nor ratiocinated nor in fact detected. He was a spy. Reason was not his particular talent. ("Detection," Jacques Barzun has said, "is par excellence the romance of reason." We delight in the "spectacle of mind at work.") He was entirely an American detective of the new day, in no way a dandy after the manner of either Sherlock Holmes or the predecessor, Poe's C. Auguste Dupin. Both of those two typically were to be discovered to be apart from the action, at home in their apartments, defined by their taste in furnishings amidst which they sit and think, rather superciliously. Holmes in "A Study in Scarlet" speaks slightingly even of Dupin, as for that matter Dupin, in "Murders in the Rue Morgue," speaks slightingly of his direct forbear, the French detective Eugene François Vidocq. It is their style. McParlan, to the contrary, had been wonderfully successful in his work because the nominal criminals among whom he lived quickly and reasonably and beyond peradventure had recognized him to be one of their own.

He had done a job, which some might have thought a dirty job, for an employer, the Philadelphia and Reading Railroad, with offices in Philadelphia about a hundred miles away, which employed its own private constabulary, the so-called Coal and Iron Police, which effectively was the law in the anthracite region, and which was not Civilization, but was, rather, the law unchecked by law. No doubt indeed that McParlan had been engaged in a dirty job because, on the other side and on the other hand, the Mollies were of the blood. They were recent Irish immigrants, with roots and essential loyalties in the old country. Those who were called Mollies were themselves miners, or saloon-keepers, and were husbands and brothers and fathers, whose avowed purpose it was to defend their own kind against the tyranny of the exploiting Interests. But then things had got complicated, for it was also the case that the Mollies (or in any event persons identified as Mollies) had gone quite beyond the occasional assassination of a mine superintendent, proceeding to a killing here and there for money or for family or for love or high spirits. It followed that McParlan was the agent of a plausibly immoral authority, engaged by it to bring about the suppression, by execution, of some numbers of attractive assassins who were also murderers, and it was his skill to be so fluently adaptable as to be beyond all moral considerations.

And as such he was there at the beginning of a line which would extend forward to all of the stylized, morally neutral, entirely American tough-guy private eyes to come, appropriately and emblematically negotiating America after the Civil War and created in the particulars of a history.

If Schuylkill County in the 1870s was not exactly the same thing as the urban "mean streets" of the private eye to come, in Raymond Chandler's enchanted phrase, nonetheless it was a fatality with the same feeling tone, already quite beyond the loss of American innocence. If the Mollies were lawless, Law on the other hand was the same thing as Business, while Business was a thing which was naturally, inherently unregardful of private life except insofar as it affected Business, so that it followed that lawlessness, meaning violence and murder, on still another hand, was glamourous. It was self-expression. It was an impudence. Moreover, as in the mean streets to come, lawlessness had a distinct ethnic definition, with, by that much, implication for the fragility in modern times of the American experiment in civilization.

Business in the 1870s in America was Railroads, dominating the economy at large and not a little of the culture. Wall Street had its great railroad thieves in Jay Gould and Jim Fisk. The fine popular thieves and killers of the sixties through the eighties, "social bandits" like the Reno Gang and Jesse James and the Younger Brothers and the Wild Bunch, robbed trains. (And were themselves hunted by Pinkerton detectives hired by the railroads.) The chief stockholders in Schuylkill's Philadelphia and Reading, it happened, were some British financiers, who were thus the further removed from any interest other than financial in what the railroad did, but, like other owners, through their agents they controlled the miners' rates of pay, in the first instance, and then extracted further profit from them directly, prior to selling the coal, by selling the necessaries of tools and powder (in the particular instance at a reported two dollars a keg above cost), renting housing (at a rate calculated to return 12 percent on investment), and running the company stores from which either by contract or by intimidation miners were to purchase most necessities of life, while, by way of italicizing the intimidation, fresh labor was always available from the Irish immigrant markets in Philadelphia and New York.

The president of the Philadelphia and Reading was Franklin B. Gowen, soon to figure as a great villain in the history of American Labor. In the sixties, Gowen had been the district attorney for Schuylkill County; during the Mollie trials he would appear for the prosecution and in effect become chief prosecutor, supplanting the then district attorney, thus directly implying that Law and the Reading were one and the same, although indeed Gowen, who was said even by his enemies to be brilliant and who was famous for his mastery of periodic sentences, made the connection explicit. By way of summation to one of the juries he would say, as reported by Allan Pinkerton, "Many of you know that some years ago I was the District Attorney of this county. I am, therefore, not very much out of my old paths, and not very much away from my old moorings, when I am standing on behalf of the Commonwealth, in the Court of Pottsville, demanding the conviction of a guilty man." And then, warming up:

> It was when I was District Attorney of this county, a young man, charged with the prosecution of the pleas of the Commonwealth, that for the first time I made up my mind from what I had seen, in innumerable instances, that there then existed in this county a secret organization, banded together for the commission of crime, and for the purpose of securing the escape or acquittal of any of its members charged with the commission of an offense. . . . Murder, violence, and arson, committed without detection, and apparently without motive, attested the correctness of that belief, and when the time arrived that I became so much interested in the prosperity of this county, and in the development of its

mineral wealth, that I saw that it was a struggle between the good citizen and the bad citizen as to which should obtain the supremacy, I made up my mind that if human ingenuity, if long suffering and patient care, and toil that stopped at no obstacle, and would confront every danger, could succeed in exposing this secret organization to light of day, and bringing to well-earned justice the perpetrators of these awful crimes, I would undertake the task. (Pinkerton, *Molly* 511–12)

Wherefore he had hired Pinkerton, who thus in turn had become a tool of good government.

As for the Mollies, the undisputable facts in fact are few and brief. A number of Irish Catholic coal miners, having common membership in an Irish organization, were accused of constituting a secret criminal society. Acting as members of this society which was called "Mollie Maguires" by the community, they were said to have committed acts of violence including murders. When some of these were arrested, they admitted membership in a common society, and almost every man who was arrested was convicted.[2]—Given this paucity it might be said and has been said that everything else in the tale of the Mollie Maguires was a fiction, if ever indeed there was any such society, at least in the United States. Such was the opinion of Anthony Bimba, a labor historian writing in 1932 with fine contempt: "Although at least nineteen men died on the gallows as Mollies, there was no organization by that name. It was a fiction created in the course of a fierce class battle. Like many other similar fabrications it has been embalmed in bourgeois texts" (9). And so more recently say Richard O. Boyer and Herbert M. Morais, in *Labor's Untold Story*: "The spy [McParlan] in three years of effort had gathered in nothing but a certain amount of booze and pay. He had obtained no evidence" (53).

But the amount and detail of contemporary evidence suggest that some sort of secret confederation did in fact exist and flourish for a period of about fifteen years, from 1862 to 1877, with a membership of perhaps six hundred men throughout the coal region,[3] with a connection to the Ancient Order of Hibernians, a broad-based Irish benevolent association. The 142 murders did happen, the perpetrators of which, if and when apprehended, had alibis and were not convicted. According principally to the testimony of McParlan but confirmed by others, the murders were carried out by the operations of a kind of surrogate system in which members of one division of the loose confederation would solicit murderers from another in order to avoid local suspicion, and would stand ready to return the favor.

The Mollies moreover would have been the more likely to have been welcomed in the coal fields because they had a glamour of Irish history. Scarcely a generation earlier, in Ireland in the 1840s and 1850s, perhaps as early as 1835, "Mollie Maguires" so called had had their glory, distinguishing themselves from the other various groups of militant nationalists by their bravery and, by report, by their especial bloody-mindedness.[4] Now the old-country antagonisms were to be replicated in the new. In 1870 in Schuylkill County the "foreign" population numbered 30,856, among whom some 13,500 were Irish, some 9,000 were Welsh, and the remainder mostly English and German. It was the Irish who worked the mines, while the bosses tended to be Welsh and English, who had their own loose organizations and who, according to the perception, favored their own, so that violence perpetrated against the bosses had the dual justification of reprisal against privilege and retaliation for the ancient colonial wrongs. If high principles in fact suffered and if the Mollies sometimes fought merely for turf and as well did violence for purely personal reasons, nonetheless they were sustained by presumed approved motives.

That was from within. Meanwhile, the inheritance of the violence of approximately half a century of anti-Irish sentiment in the United States had come to be particularly concentrated in the coal fields, no doubt with some implication for the ethnic quantities of fictions to come. In contemporary commentary and in the trials themselves, everyone protested an understanding of the Irish, and, not infrequently, affection as well, but simultaneously everyone exploited well-established Know-Nothing prejudices.

The first full, book-length account of the Mollies, was written by Franklin P. Dewees, an attorney living in Pottsville. He wrote his book (entitled, comprehensively, *The Molly Maguires: The Origin, Growth, and Character of the Organization*) in 1876, remarkably even while the trials were going on and prior to any of the executions, and published it in 1877. Dewees said that he knew many of those who had a place in his account, and he acknowledged that therefore he might have given in to a disposition to extenuate but hoped, as he also said, that he had not "set down aught in malice." "It is sincerely believed," he said, "that the great majority of the miners and laborers of the anthracite coal regions will compare favorably with any large body of laboring men in the world, and that the great body of the Irish-American citizens residing there are well-disposed and law-abiding" (iv). Nor had he any intention of attacking the Irish people: "To do so would be in the face of the fact that Ireland is preeminently the land in which orators, poets, statesmen, and soldiers have claimed a birthplace or to which they trace their lineage. As a nation they are warm-hearted, generous, and impulsive to a fault; brave, romantic, and enthusiastic. Among no other people can be found examples of greater heroism or of more sublime self-sacrifice" (23)—with considerably more of the same. Nor was this merely unctuous, for it was Dewees's underlying effort to distinguish a bad element from an otherwise safe and dependable labor force and to declare the area safe for mining once again. He was not exactly hypocritical, but nonetheless the badness of the bad element had everything to do with the fact that its members were "Irish peasants," as he repeatedly also said. It was outrageous, he said, that this Irish peasant, coming here of his own free will and having been accorded all of the rights of the native-born citizen, should transfer his violence. "Whatever rights, real or fancied, he may have had to the Irish soil," he said, "he has not even the pretense of claim to any here. . . . That under these circumstances the turbulent spirit which created outrages in Ireland should develop itself here in repeated and aimless murders, for years undetected and unpunished, excites unmitigated horror and condemnation" (15). And: "With all their open-hearted enthusiasm and recklessness," so Dewees would point out, discussing the dimensions of James McParlan's task, "the Irish peasantry possess a low cunning that is proverbial, and a suspiciousness readily excited by a word spoken at random or a careless act meaning nothing" (78).

Franklin Gowen happened himself to have been a child of Irish immigrants, which fact he supposed to authorize his making of distinctions among Irish immigrants. (He happened to be Irish Protestant, but felt that that did not diminish his authority.) Thus he addressed the jury in another of the Mollie trials, as reported by Pinkerton:

> I shall say little about the Irish, except that I am myself the son of an Irishman, proud of my ancestry, and proud of my race, and never ashamed of it, except when I see that Ireland has given birth to wretches such as these! These men call themselves Irishmen! These men parade on St. Patrick's Day and claim to be good Catholics! Where are the honest Irishmen of this county? . . . Does an Irishman wonder why it is sometimes difficult to get a job in this county? Does he wonder why the boss at a colliery hesitates to employ him, when these people [Mollies] have been allowed to arrogate to themselves the Irish character and have been permitted to represent themselves to the people of this county as the proper representatives of Ireland? . . . The time has come when every honest Irishman in this county must separate himself from any suspicion of sympathy with this association. (Pinkerton, *Molly* 520–21)

On the other hand, Gowen was emphatic about the old-country connection of the Mollies. His appeal to every honest Irishman was uttered in June of 1876. In August, to still another jury in another trial,

Gowen was saying that the purpose of the Mollies of the coal country "was simply the same purpose which the same society in Ireland for so many years pursued with success. The purpose was to get the benefit of and use and enjoy the property of others without owning it, and without paying for it" (177). More generally, as would have been likely given Gowen's place in the prosecution, Gowen was primarily responsible for the emphasis placed upon the Irish ties of the Mollies in McParlan's testimony, as well as for repeated reference throughout the trials to what was described as the clannishness, belligerence, and undisciplined nature of the Irish miner in Pennsylvania.[5]

Dewees and Pinkerton between them inscribed the basic history of the Mollie Maguires. They were on the same side. Dewees would say of Franklin B. Gowen when the latter's turn came up in his narrative,

> By reason of previous business association and residence, combined with courage, honesty of purpose, comprehensive knowledge of the situation, and wonderful energy and executive ability, [Gowen] perhaps beyond any other living man, was adapted to carry out the ends in view,—to wit, the maintenance and increase of the power of his company; the regulation of trade; the establishment of law and order; and the protection of the rights of person and property throughout the coal regions. (71)

Also, Gowen was a man "of fine appearance and pleasant manners," who had "literary tastes, and is broad and comprehensive in his views" (292). As for Pinkerton, Gowen had hired him, and the two of them admired each other very much. "Allan Pinkerton, of Chicago," according to Gowen, as quoted by Pinkerton, was that "intelligent and broad-minded Scotchman" who with his National Detective Agency had already served (513), while Gowen for Pinkerton was that "brave, frank man" whose "boldness did much to reassure the depressed and suffering people of the coal region" (*Molly* 551, 508), and in his book Pinkerton gave to Gowen most of the lines which would indicate high idealism:

> . . . we want the laboring-men, of whatever creeds or nationalities, protected in their right to work to secure sustenance for their wives and little ones, unawed by outside influences. We want the miner to go forth cheerfully to the slope, or the shaft, for labor in the breast or in the gangway, wherever it may seem to him for the best, void of the fear in his heart when he parts from his wife at the cottage-gate in the morning, that it may be their last farewell on earth. . . . (Pinkerton, *Molly* 17)

—this in private conversation.

Dewees and Pinkerton inscribed the basic history of the American Mollies and there was no doubting which side they were on, but then even so, and even for them, the singular allegiance was neither entirely easy nor was it unqualified. Lawlessness in the coal fields was not to be abided, while it was also the case that Dewees and Pinkerton both relied upon and felt comfortable with an amount of bigotry. Nevertheless, sometimes, although infrequently, said Dewees, centralized capital had been wrong in its treatment of the Irish miners, and Pinkerton, who in his own youth in Scotland had been active in Chartist agitations and who indeed was proud of his working-class beginnings,[6] did recognize provocations. And by at least that much the authoritative history of the Mollies, in itself, was from the beginning qualified in the direction of a moral openness, as was the historical situation.

Pinkerton hired McParlan. No better operative was to be or could have been found for the job of infiltrating the Mollies, as eventually everyone agreed, notably including McParlan's victims. Pinkerton, according to Pinkerton, upon securing the commission from Gowen, had mentally reviewed the entire corps of his detectives searching for a "true Irishman" who would not be misled by the other Irishmen, before happening on McParlan, who at the moment was in Chicago posing as a streetcar conductor, engaged in catching pilferers. It was no ordinary man that was needed. He had to be Irish and Catholic, of course, and, said Pinkerton, it were best that he be hardy and tough and single-minded.

> I had to find a man who, once inside this, as I supposed, oath-bound brotherhood, would yet remain true to me; who could make almost a new man of himself, take his life in his hands, and enter upon a work which was apparently against those bound to him by close ties of nationality, if not of blood and kindred; and for months, perhaps for years, place himself in antagonism with and rebellion against the dictates of his church—the church which from his earliest breath he had been taught to revere. He would perforce obtain a reputation for evil conduct, from which it was doubtful that he could ever entirely extricate himself. Would the common run of men think such a position at all tenable? Would they consent to ostensibly degrade themselves that others might be saved? My man must become, really and truly, a Mollie of the hardest character, attend their meetings, and possibly be charged with direct participation in certain of their crimes. He must face the priest, and endure the bad opinion of his countrymen even until the end. For an indefinite period he was to be as one dead and buried in the grave—dead to his family and friends—sinking his individuality—and be published abroad as the companion and associate of assassins, murderers, incendiaries, thieves, and gamblers. (Pinkerton, *Molly* 20–21)

And said Dewees, who knew McParlan, it was further desirable that this Irish-Catholic detective "be imbued to some degree with the peculiarities and even the prejudices of his race," all the while remaining cool, wary, cautious, and methodical (78–79).

All of these things McParlan was and all of these traits he had, except probably for tough and hardy, nor does it seem to have been the case that it was necessary for him to be dead to family and friends because in none of the several accounts of his life is there any mention of current and present family or friends.

He was twenty-nine years old when he went to the coal fields and had been a Pinkerton detective for about a year, having previously for a couple of years before that been a detective for a rival agency in Chicago, and for several months a member of the Chicago city police. He was a native Irishman, born in 1844 in the province of Ulster, County Armagh, Parish of Mullabrack. He had immigrated to the United States in 1867 and had worked his way west from New York to Buffalo, finally to Chicago. He had been an up-and-coming, entrepreneurial young Irishman. For a few months in Chicago he had owned a successful saloon, but had been wiped out by the Chicago fire of 8 and 9 October 1871. As an employee, variously, he would seem to have been ingratiating. So the several accounts of his life indicate. As saloon-keeper he was likely to have been expert in bonhomie, as certainly he was when he went to Pennsylvania. And he looked and sounded Irish. "Of medium height," in Pinkerton's description, "a slim but wiry figure, well knit together; a clear hazel eye; hair of an auburn color, and bordering upon the style denominated as 'sandy;' a forehead high, full, and well rounded forward; florid complexion, regular features, with beard and mustache a little darker than his hair, there was no mistaking McParlan's place of nativity, even had not his slight accent betrayed his Celtic origin" (Pinkerton, *Molly* 24).

So likely a candidate was he for the job that when the time came for the trials, the chief argument of the defense was not that McParlan was wrong about his facts but that he had himself instigated the crimes of which the Mollies were accused, as to say that the others were betrayed because they had respected him so well. He had indeed been promoted within the Mollie ranks, to high office: he had been elected secretary of the Shenandoah lodge of the Ancient Order of Hibernians, by which development he had become a Mollie insider, or so he said, and since the leader, or "Bodymaster," of the lodge was both illiterate and frequently absent, McParlan had been the local leader in effect. Near the end of his residence he had, moreover, been the threatened target of vigilante action by the better citizens of the area, for his being one of the most prominent of Mollies.

And despite Pinkerton's confessed fear that his account might read like romance, what most of all the account suggests is, first, the ease with which McParlan infiltrated and was accepted, and, second, the unreflective fluency of his adaptation. Starting out, McParlan had dressed himself as a tramp and armed himself with a tale of a criminal past. He said that the police were after him because he had killed a man in Buffalo and that by trade he was a counterfeiter, he "shoved the queer," and he had provided himself with an alias, "James McKenna." But all the rest most seemingly was the man himself. He invited companionship. Taking the train from Philadelphia on the afternoon of a Monday, 27 October 1873, he had arrived in Port Clinton, seventy-eight miles away, at eight o'clock, and within hours had been taken in by a passing stranger. Then within days, now in Tremont, Pennsylvania, as they drank together, a presumed Mollie was testing him with coded messages, apparently believing that in McParlan he had found a brother. Within the month, now in Pottsville, McParlan had become a regular and a favorite in a saloon which served as a Mollie gathering place.

Pinkerton's title for the chapter in which this latter is recorded was "The Detective Sings, Fights, and Dances Himself into Popularity," which, with the addition of drinking fellowship, might be taken to indicate the basic technique of all of McParlan's detecting for the next two-and-a-half years. "All in the saloon were perfect strangers to McKenna," it is said,

> but that made no difference. He staggered about near the threshold for an instant, while he mentally measured the people in whose company he was, and made a hurried inventory of the immediate surroundings; then, appearing to gather inspiration from the lively squeak of the fiddle, he advanced to the middle of the floor, where remained a few square yards of vacant space, struck an attitude, and without further prelude, begun his best Irish break-down. The steps were nimble, well chosen, . . . (Pinkerton, *Molly* 75)

—and so forth, upon which the saloon-keeper, Pat Dormer, a giant of a man, and a "Sleeper," as the Mollies were also called, began to keep time, swaying his broad shoulders from side to side. "Very good! Very good!" he said. "Be the sowl of me great grandfather! I've niver seen such a jigger since the days of jolly Dan Carey! Walk up, stranger, an' have a sup of the best in the house" (Pinkerton, *Molly* 76). Then McKenna sang a ballad, the others joining in on the refrain, with that followed by another round of drinks, and then there was a card game, and a saloon brawl, and Pat Dormer and a man named Tom Hurley, later a fugitive and a probable multiple murderer, were pleased, and once again there were drinks all around.

McParlan sang at weddings. He managed chickens at cock fights, providentially having had some previous experience. Saloonkeepers, who in the time and place were an elite,[7] knew him to be "a wild boy wid the music an' dance" (Pinkerton, *Molly* 248), and he appeared to be, so Pinkerton said, "nearly always intoxicated, ready and willing to sing, shoot, dance, fight, gamble, face a man in a knock-down or a jig, stay out all night, sleep all day, tell a story, rob a hen-roost or a traveler" (Pinkerton, *Molly* 147).

Pinkerton qualified every instance with the reminder that all of this was a masquerade designed to suit those with whom McParlan came into daily contact and constituted a device for spying, but did so after reflection, as must have been the case, that this posing after all had an astonishing persistence and integrity. McParlan had lived this life for two and a half years. It had been his initial instructions to file daily reports with the Philadelphia office, by several various means, which schedule had he followed it might have reminded him daily of his presumed true identity, but (according to Wayne G. Broehl, Jr.'s history of the Mollies) company records indicate that actually he reported only every other week or so. Shenandoah, moreover, which was the site of most of his living, was in the 1870s a new mining town of about nine thousand inhabitants—one of the larger of the mining towns but a small town nonetheless, where people were likely to know one another very well, this beyond the fact that the Mollies whom he cultivated as his special friends constituted a small, closed, and elaborately secretive circle. The Shenandoah lodge of the Ancient Order of Hibernians had a total membership of eight. As part of his preparation for the job of detecting, McParlan had been required by Pinkerton to do some research on the Irish antecedents of the American Mollies and to write a report, which when delivered was not unsympathetic, if not partisan, either, and that fact of background along with his inevitable experiences in prejudice as a young Irish immigrant in America would as well have contributed to, as it were, giving the lie to his hypocrisy.

He had lived the life. By some various stratagems together with some lucky accidents, he had avoided having actually to work in the mines, but life in the mining towns nonetheless had its normal hardships. He might have pretended to being nearly always intoxicated. In the adventures as recorded he sometimes got out of a tight spot by passing out on the saloon floor, and sometimes was distrusted by the other Mollies because of what they thought to be his excessive drinking. Much of this might have been pretense, but he did drink enormous quantities of bad liquor, and this along with other hardships brought him to the point where his health was affected seriously. He suffered fevers. "He grew thin, cadaverous, and his strength perceptibly and rapidly failed," Pinkerton reported (Pinkerton, *Molly* 186). His hair fell out and he bought a wig, which was a couple of shades redder than his own hair had been and which he did not bother to keep clean, and he had lost his eyebrows as well. Also, he wore dark green glasses because his eyesight had been injured. Coming to the coal fields in the fall of 1873 he had dressed himself as a tramp ("his head covered by an old, dilapidated and dirt-colored slouch hat, . . . a grayish coat of coarse materials, which had, from appearances, seen service in a coal bin," and so on, with a faded vest and pants too large [Pinkerton, *Molly* 28])—and now what had been costume became ordinary daily apparel, at least in kind. He adapted to his clothing. Said Dewees, although intending a different implication: "Seeing him with a slouch hat on a bald pate, with green spectacles, rough shirt, and an old linen coat, swaggering along the streets, the last idea likely to present itself was that through his exertions a new era of peace, of law, and of order was about to dawn on the anthracite coal-fields" (96).

And McParlan had fallen in love, or something like that. Following a number of casual romantic adventures, he had formed an attachment with Mary Ann Higgins, who, one afternoon at a wedding, sportively, had kissed him. Mary Ann was the sister-in-law of James Kerrigan who was the Mollie Bodymaster of the lodge at nearby Tamaqua and who was to be implicated in a couple of the alleged Mollie murders. Perhaps, as McParlan was to say at one of the trials, he had "sparked" Mary Ann by way of establishing an alibi for spending time with Kerrigan in Tamaqua, or perhaps, as Pinkerton would indeed suggest, he really had been smitten: " 'She's a very fine girl,' " lamented McParlan to himself as reported by Pinkerton. " 'And to think that I must get her brother-in-law hanged! Oh, I never can hope to have "Miss Higgins" transformed into "Mrs. McParlan!" Brother-in-law to a murderer! No! Never!' " (Pinkerton, *Molly* 400). As it happened, Kerrigan turned state's evidence and was not hanged, and so that objection was removed, but still McParlan didn't marry the girl. Nonetheless, by this additional much, too, he had lived the life.

It then would not have been at all surprising, given the extent of his participation in the life of the community, that when the trials came McParlan would be accused of being *agent provocateur*. In the August 1876 trial, when McParlan testified against John Kehoe, the highest-ranking officer of all of the various Mollies, and who was subsequently hanged, defense counsel Martin L'Velle would advise the jury that prior to McParlan's arrival in 1873, "crimes of the higher grade," other than

James McParlan, 1907. Courtesy of the Library of Congress.

saloon killings, had been absent from Schuylkill County. "From 1865 until 1873 there was no such thing as a murder case in Schuylkill County, not until the emissary of death, James McParlan, made his advent into this county, and crime since then has been in the ascendant" (*Commonwealth v. Kehoe*, 193). "Of all the devils who have been in this county plotting against the peace and good order, . . . this man McParlan was the worst," so advised a second member of the defense, and a third said to the jury: "It is conclusive that after [McParlan's] coming into this county he worked up and proposed crimes, and after aiding and abetting the men who committed them, turned around and came here and testified against their authors" (207, 136).

There could have been little surprise in this at the time, nor, as the case of the Mollie Maguires drifted from history into the legends of Organized Labor, that McParlan would come to be a name for perfidy. He would be an object of contempt, a target for villification, sometimes florid. McParlan was in fact to have one more big case before he was done, in his role as the chief of Pinkerton's Denver office. In late 1905 the ex-governor of Idaho, Frank Steunenberg, was murdered. Largely by McParlan's doing, three members of the militant Western Federation of Miners were accused of plotting the murder and were arrested: the president, Charles Moyer; the secretary-treasurer, William (Big Bill) Haywood; and an ex-member of the executive board, George A. Pettibone. McParlan had secured a confession from the actual murderer, one Harry Orchard, who had implicated the others. The defense was to win this one, for Haywood immediately and for Moyer and Pettibone later, but meanwhile McParlan in effect stood accused by the defense counsel, the great Clarence Darrow, who, big and broad-shouldered, as described by Big Bill Haywood, dressed in a slouchy gray suit, a wisp of hair down across his forehead, his glasses in his hand, clasped by the nose-piece, addressed the jury:

> Here is a piece of work, gentlemen of the jury, that will last as long as the ages last—McParland's conversion of Orchard! [McParlan himself had now added the "d" to his name.] Don't you think this detective is wasting his time down in the Pinkerton office in the city of Denver? From the beginning of the world was ever any miracle like this performed before? Lo, and behold! A man who has spent his life as a Pinkerton— isn't a preacher—he has never been ordained except in the Pinkerton office. But here is [Harry Orchard] who has challenged the world...who has lived his life up to this time, and he has gotten over what religion he ever had, and meets this Pinkerton detective who never did anything in his life but lie and cheat and scheme (for the life of a detective is a living lie, that is his business; he lives one from the time he gets up in the morning to the time he goes to bed; he is deceiving people, and trapping people and lying to people and imposing on people; that is his trade), and Harry Orchard is caught, and he meets this famous detective, who speaks to him familiarly about David and St. Paul and Kelly the Bum, and a few more of his acquaintances...

—"Kelly the Bum" being soubriquet for one of the lesser figures of the old Mollie Maguire days.

Big Bill Haywood thought that this was one of Darrow's greatest speeches. So he said in his book *Big Bill Haywood's Book* (216). Not all of the eleven hours of the speech had been devoted to McParlan, to be sure, but what was said about McParlan along the way proposed and confirmed what was to be a trope.

James McParlan, still once again, was "the DEAN OF BLACK SLEUTHDOM" —this with its capitals in the phrase of a certain Morris Friedman who had been a stenographer in the Pinkerton office in Denver and who in 1907 while the trial was going on published an exposé entitled *The Pinkerton Labor Spy*. Friedman more than anything, in point of fact, was upset by McParlan's reputation for achievement in the line of work. McParlan had become a living legend, which datum in itself, according to Friedman, was the sole source of his authority. "Much has been said and written," wrote Friedman, "about Manager McParland and his wonderful achievements against the Molly Maguires."

> We merely wish to state that James McParland worked among the Molly Maguires for three or four years before he secured the evidence which resulted in conviction. It is well for us to remember this fact, as well as the fact that when Mr. McParland worked on this case he was young and vigorous, and free from the hallucinations sure to plague a conscience so dreadfully outraged as his has been, in the many years that he has served the Pinkerton Agency. . . . It may not perhaps be very decent, even for detectives, to keep on pointing to the gibbets which they erected thirty years ago. (200–201)

The years went by and McParlan indeed was remembered, appropriately in conflicting caricatures. For Friedman, just after the turn of the century, he was a dotard. For Louis Adamic in the 1930s, in *Dynamite*, a once-celebrated history of "Class Violence in America," McParlan at the time of the Idaho trial had the look of "an innocuous countryman" (144). A half-century later Richard O. Boyer and Herbert M. Morais, in their revisionist history of Organized Labor in America, *Labor's Untold Story*, looking back to the Mollie days recovered a Mc-Parlan who "seemed a merry fellow, ever ready for a fight or a frolic, until one looked into his eyes," for "they were as cold as a cobra's," and then later, for the record of the Denver days *circa* 1906, they recalled a McParlan who "old and crusty and embittered, had to use a cane now to get over the streets, and his insensate unblinking eyes were warmed when he spoke of the glory that had been his in the old days when he had been young and had hanged the nineteen [*sic*] miners of Pennsylvania" (51, 160).

Such attempts at virtually a poetry were significant, as were the numbers of endeavors, including Pinkerton's, to present McParlan with a distinctive voice and look and therefore personality, all of them vain, finally. McParlan in Pinkerton's version was given to speaking dialect: "An' what is it I'm here fur? Is that it? What should a dacent Irish lad want whose stomach is full of emptiness and ne'er a morsel of bread or mate in the wallet? What I want is worruk, and somethin' to relave my hunger!" (Pinkerton, *Molly* 34). (Pinkerton was aware of the comic possibilities in his tale of murders and betrayals. His book contained an amount of stage-German as well.) But the couple of stenographic reports of the trials, in which McParlan's language is transcribed with some presumable accuracy, indicate at most a colloquial ease. A 1907 photograph presents a McParlan with graying handlebar mustache, eyeglasses, sparse hair, rather a chubby face, wearing a formal coat, who is sitting for a photograph and who otherwise suggests nothing. He might be anything, even a detective.

And so it would seem to have been in May of 1876, at the time of the first of the Mollie trials at which McParlan testified and when thus, as it were, he was unmasked. It was here and now, in Pinkerton's fevered words, that McParlan "made his astonishing revelations, which, for interest and novelty, have startled the civilized world" (Pinkerton, *Molly* 508). He was in fact a surprise witness. No doubt the defendants and their friends were startled. But McParlan himself seems in no way to have been adequate to the drama of the moment, but only to the legalities. By all accounts he was a superb witness for the prosecution. His recollections were extensive and detailed, in this and in subsequent trials. Through four days of testimony and cross-examination by batteries of lawyers on both sides, he was factual and consistent, only occasionally more emphatic in his responses, when he was accused of not being a good Catholic. He was dressed nicely—"in the height of fashion," according to a newspaper reporter who was there (Broehl 297). His hair had begun to grow back. "He told his story in slow, measured sentences, without any manifestation of feeling or attempt at display," according to Dewees, who most likely was present at the trial. "Upon the witness-stand," so Dewees said, "his evidence is entirely devoid of passion, and although feeling proper pride in professional success, he never, for the sake of making a point, seeks to stretch the truth or give a false color to his recital of facts" (291, 79). McParlan demonstrated no animosity toward the persons among whom he had lived for the past two and a half years and whom he was incriminating, some among whom he was sending to the gallows.

Which is to say that he had turned out after all to be a loyal employee of the Pinkerton National Detective Agency, satisfying Pinkerton's original estimate, but at the same time it cannot be said that loyalty was principle for him. He had been hired to do a job and, in the spirit of the Continental Op to come, creature of the ex-Pinkerton Operative Dashiell Hammett, McParlan had done it, taking risks to body when necessary but investing no important judgments.

In fact there had been one occasion when he had objected. In a letter dated 10 December 1875, addressed to the Pinkerton field office in Philadelphia, recovered by James D. Horan, McParlan had threatened to resign because of the shooting of a Mrs. McAllister of Wiggans Patch, by vigilantes who had been organized by the Agency itself, as he supposed, for as of a certainty such things happened. "What had a woman to do in this case?" he asked. "Did the Sleepers [i.e., the Mollies] in their worst time shoot down women? If I was not here, the Vigilante committee would not know who was guilty. And when I find them shooting women in their thirst for blood, I hereby tender my resignation to take effect as soon as this message is received" (*Pinkertons* 226). But he did not resign after all, and outrage in him must even in the moment have been considered aberrant.

He had taken on a job, for twelve dollars a week. Not an Auguste Dupin nor a Sherlock Holmes, McParlan was a working man whose implicit, necessitated, no doubt unconscious realizations about crime and community, in the 1870s in America, were so complex that moral neutrality in him was genius, and evidently was fascinating.

That odd moment in late 1875 aside, he was adaptable and untroubled.

As for Mary Ann Higgins, when her brother-in-law turned informer, she was furious. Along with her sister, Kerrigan's wife, and with her father, she took part in concocting a plot to get "the little rat" (as her father called him, for Kerrigan was a small man) by pinning a couple of murders on him. Mary Ann's particular contribution was to suggest that they bring some of the bullets used in one of the murders into court, saying that they had been found in Kerrigan's bureau drawer. Kerrigan would be hanged and the actual murderers, whom the family knew, would be released. That was just before McParlan left the fields, and she told him about the idea. And here was a detective's dilemma, if he would acknowledge it. The girl he loved, or something, was engaged in a bloody conspiracy to hang an innocent man, her sister's husband, while protecting the guilty, which plan on the other hand was not without its ethical warrant, because no one likes an informer. But apparently McParlan did not discover any real dilemma here after all. He was again in touch with the Pinkerton office in Philadelphia, and he reported the girl.[8] "If they hang you I'll always remember you," he might have said but didn't. That would be Sam Spade.

# 9     The Detectives

TO know crime and criminals so well as to be a detective was to be suspect. It takes a thief to catch a thief, and therefore to catch a thief would be to be a thief, presumptively, in repeated paradox, while to inform would be worse, for nobody likes a snitch. On the other hand, now there were new opportunities for crime in the United States which in turn solicited new attitudes in thief-catching, and what particularly was provided was "professionalism"—which however was not a name for virtue and which did not imply a cynicism about human nature in general, necessarily, but did imply a presumption to the effect that, at least in the condition of post–Civil War American society, crime was integral, requiring a response in its own kind.

America was Business. To examine such texts as detectives' memoirs, and the curious "Rogues Galleries" of the 1870s and 1880s, and fiction derived from the memoirs is to notice the predominance of crimes indeed of the business sort, which would seem to have become the romance of the detectives. That rather than violence, of which there is not very much. The favored criminals are forgers, counterfeiters, and confidence men, or pickpockets and burglars, but even these, except in the case of bank burglars, do not have the cachet of the great fences and in any event tend to be regarded as small businessmen. Allan Pinkerton himself, initially a cooper by trade, had gained his first, local reputation for detecting when he had stumbled upon a counterfeiters' camp, in the late 1840s in Dundee, Illinois. Following up on that piece of luck he had solicited local businessmen who gave him some entrapment money, whereupon he had gone and entrapped, and subsequently thereafter in his great career he would serve business precisely by making the detective's work into a business.

And here was irony, for the bad reputation lingered even as this business was naturalized, with the consequence being an attachment to this business of a sense of truth and modern fatality.

From the time of the modern beginning, and reasonably given any amount of sophistication and indeed in the regard of all decent people acquainted with the ways of the law, detectives and most especially private detectives had been no better than the scoundrels whom supposedly they detected, if indeed they were not worse. And so they continued to be supposed, most especially by lawyers and judges and civic reformers, who would be presumed to know.

The beginning can be dated. It was in the 1840s, when New York City replaced a nightwatch and constabulary system of policing with a centrally administered, uniformed police force. The result of that was that the constables were retired, thereby creating a need because it had been they who had specialized in returning stolen property, usually for a fee. They were able to do that because, as was widely believed, they had connections with thieves. They were fences themselves, or so at least it was widely believed. It was in 1844 that New York City had its first police force. The first private detective agency in America followed immediately. The "Independent Police" of New York opened its doors in the early summer of 1845, founded by an out-of-work constable, one Gil Hays, who continued to retrieve stolen property for a fee.

The line founded thus in ignomy, detectives never would be respected by experts in justice. When Clarence Darrow in the 1905 Steunenberg trial advised the jury, with particular reference to McParlan, that "the life of a detective is a living lie," surely he counted on a long-standing and general informed opinion the validation for which was plentiful and had been so, continuously from the early beginning.

Frank Morn records the statement of a Judge John P. Vincent in 1867, at the trial of one John Van Daniker. Evidence having been presented by a Pinkerton Operative, Judge Vincent advised the jury that such evidence required especially strong corroboration because, "the character of the detective—and it is simply another word for spy—has always been, and always will be, an unpopular one. There is an element in human nature—and it is an element that humanity may be proud of and not ashamed—which looks with suspicion necessarily upon that calling in life and that kind of business, because there is necessarily connected with it more or less deception and deceit" (70).

It would be just a few years later, in 1872, that Edward Crapsey, a crusading New York reporter, in his exposé entitled *The Nether Side of New York; or, The Vice, Crime and Poverty of the Great Metropolis*, would report details first of all of "the pernicious detective system" which was

sponsored by the city government itself, and then would at greater
length reveal the especially evil practices of the private agencies. "The
word detective, taken by itself," he said, "implies one who must descend
to questionable shifts to attain justifiable ends; but with the prefix of
private, it means one using a machine permitted to the exigencies
of justice for the purpose of surreptitious personal gain. Thus used,
this agency, which even in honest hands and for lawful ends is one
of doubtful propriety, becomes essentially dangerous and demoralizing" (56). "The term of private detective," he said, especially and as
opposed to "public," was "a synonym for rogue" (61)—although here
in fact Crapsey was indulging local hyperbole because in discussing the
public detectives he had found no justifiable ends there either, but
rather a "corporation" which served to enrich certain officers ward by
ward. Victims of theft were a source of income for detectives and so
were the thieves themselves. "Obtaining conclusive evidence of guilt
against a thief," said Crapsey, "arresting him; wresting from him the
last possible dollar, and then turning him loose to repeat his crime and
again experience its condonment," was the usual practice. "There are
exceptions, of course," he said, "but this is the usual end and aim of
detective endeavor" (45).

And so again said Officer George S. McWatters, formerly a private
detective himself and more recently a member of the "Metropolitan
Police of New York".[1] He had published his memoirs in a lengthy book
entitled *Knots Untied: Ways and By-Ways in the Hidden Life of American
Detectives: A Narrative of Marvellous Experiences Among All Classes of Society,
—Criminals in High Life, Swindlers, Bank Robbers, Thieves, Lottery Agents,
Gamblers, Necromancers, Counterfeiters, Burglars, Etc., Etc., Etc.,* in 1871. In
the Publisher's Introduction, which on the basis of style would in fact
seem to have been written by another hand, it was said of McWatters
that "he has ever been greatly interested in social problems, having in
view the emancipation of the laboring classes from their more grievous
problems, and belongs, in his sympathies, to that class of humanitarians
who see in Association something like a realization of the teachings of
the Founder of Christianism" (29). Association being a synonym here
for Socialism. He would seem moreover to have had an audience for the
variety of his views, which would have been to say that he knew what a
substantial public wanted to hear. He had organized and administered
some public subscriptions, one in 1863 for the purchase of lemons to
be sent to wounded soldiers lying in Washington hospitals, and another
for the relief of organ-grinders, many of whom were war veterans. He
had as well had show-business connections, acting as an agent for the
actresses Laura Keene and the Countess of Lansfield, also known as

Lola Montez, and had been the lecturer who accompanied "a grand panorama of a 'Journey to California by Water and Back by Land.' " He was known as "the Literary Policeman," so it was said. He wrote for the journals. He was a frequenter of Pfaff's beer cellar, on Broadway near Bleeker Street, where literary and show-business people gathered. Most likely he would have been a member of the circle at Pfaff's which included editors and actresses and humorists and poets, most notably Walt Whitman.

Concerning his fellow detectives said McWatters:

> There are but two great classes in civilization, —the oppressed and the oppressors, the trampled upon and the tramplers. To the latter class belongs the detective. He is dishonest, crafty, unscrupulous, when necessary to be so. He tells black lies when he cannot avoid it; and white lying, at least, is his chief stock in trade. He is the outgrowth of a diseased and corrupted state of things, and is, consequently, morally diseased himself. His very existence is a satire upon society. He is a miserable snake, not in a paradise, but in the social hell. (648)

The detective "is a thief," he said, "and steals into men's confidences to ruin them. He makes friends in order to reap the profits of betraying them" (648–49).

In fact, however, this moralizing came very late in McWattters' memoirs, following upon many entertaining anecdotes concerning gamblers, burglars, forgers, "Genealogical Swindlers" (who offered to find properties left by European relatives), and so forth. Detectives surely were in bad odor, but on the other hand this thief of a detective clearly had enjoyed himself all the while that, as the "literary policeman," he had stocked stories, and clearly as well he was quite aware of the niceness of the irony of the life he was presenting, for McWatters was nothing if not ironic, and was particularly expressive. It was with complex, indeed literary apprehension and therefore authority, that he formulated and put into balanced tension the bad and the good of the matter, offering essential justification for, presumably, himself, and for other detectives. The detective's calling, he said, "is a very noble one, and a singularly blessed one, inasmuch as it is the only one which I call to mind, by which hypocrisy is elevated into a really useful and beneficent art," the results of which tended to be good, if, that is, "it be good to preserve the present order of things; for without the detective the laws, such as they are, could not well be enforced" (649–50). The very worst that could be said of the detective was that he was like everybody else these days, not that that wasn't bad enough. The detective, said McWatters, has the satisfaction of knowing that if he lies and cheats, he is no worse for this, in a business way, than his neighbors, and that his frauds are exercised to protect them in keeping whatever ill-gotten gains they may have in the shape of property, from being stolen from them by some of the rest of his (and their) neighbors; or in the discovery of criminals, such as murderers and assassins, in order that they may be punished, to satisfy the majesty of the law, made by the society which made the criminals. (649)

And in this sense the detective rightfully, Socrates-like, was to be regarded as "a public benefactor, and better entitled to the honors he wins in society than is, perhaps, any other useful citizen of the governing classes." "So cunning have the crafts of business made our unfortunate criminal classes," said McWatters,

that the ordinary officers of the law cannot surprise or entrap them; and, allowed to pursue their business uninterrupted, the pickpockets, counter-feiters, forgers, bank-robbers, and so forth, would soon monopolize the business of the country to the disparagement of the money brokers, grain and cotton exchangers, the land speculators, the usurers, the railroad robbers, the wholesale and retail merchants, the private bankers, etc., who, with less keen talent than the independent pickpocket proper, are obliged to have laws framed to help them in their iniquity, while he operates against the law. (649–50)

McWatters had his own special talents both for literary apprehen-sion and social fulminating, but the kind of his apologia for his own life, as must have been a part of his purpose, finally only borrowed from a mode of universalizing which was at least implied by all of his fellows, even though, like Allan Pinkerton, who was anxious to advertise his own unique integrity and thereby his business, they might occasionally say otherwise. They did a dirty business in a dirty time and place, not without some proffering of amusement, and indeed with some implication of special privilege.

There was Detective Phil Farley of the New York Police, author in 1876 of *Criminals of America; or, Tales of the Lives of Thieves, Enabling Every One To Be His Own Detective, With Portraits Making a Complete Rogues' Gallery.* It was Detective Farley's purpose, as he himself said, "to en-deavor to prevent crime; aid in the detection of criminals; show the young and inexperienced some of the pitfalls that await them along the route of life, if they should step aside from a straightforward course; and that there is no comfort, no happiness, no peace, no safety outside the

George S. McWatters. From George S. McWatters, *Knots Untied* (Hartford:
J. B. Burr and Hyde, 1871), frontispiece.

walks of honorable dealing," (xiii) and so forth, as well as to enable every one to be his own detective by referring to Farley's Rogues' Gallery,
but of course Detective Farley was writing an entertainment as well, nor
would the steel-engraving "portraits" with descriptions appended really
have enabled anyone to be his own detective. The full-page engravings
were only not quite cartoons. The descriptions consisted of height
(tending to be a standard 5′6″ to 5′8″ for men, 5′3″ for women), weight

(tending to 160 pounds for men), and often "nationality" (German, English, etc., but mostly "American"), as:

### JOHN MALONEY

Is a confidence man. He is 40 years of age, 5 feet 8 inches high, of stout build, with sandy complexion, blue eyes and brown hair.

### "SCOTCH MAG"

Is 28 years of age, 5 feet 3 inches high, slightly pock-marked, and a pickpocket.

### "JOE" MURRAY

Is a burglar and a desperate man.

### SOPHIA LEVY

Is 30 years of age, 5 feet 3 inches high, has black hair, black eyes, is a Jewess and a pickpocket.

### LIZZY SMITH

Is English and a pickpocket. She is 35 years of age, stout built [sic], has dark hair, a round face and good teeth.

(But in the accompanying portrait Lizzy has her mouth closed.)

Moreover, the enunciated intentions aside, the continuous effort of Detective Farley's book, insinuatively but certainly, was toward humanizing these embezzlers and forgers and pickpockets, whom Detective Farley seemed to know well. He would occasionally go off to a saloon with one or another of them, so he said. Thus he detected, but thus also he was a companion. And Farley himself was one of the more corrupt members of the New York Detective Bureau, according to the historian Larry K. Hartsfield, allegedly having profited very well from two of the major crimes of the nineteenth century: the robbery of the Ocean Bank of New York in 1868, and the forgeries committed by an American ring on the Bank of England in 1873.[2] To err was human. To commit theft not only was human, but was to obey natural law, as in effect Detective Farley said in the wonderfully appropriate epigraph to his *Criminals of America*, from Shakespeare's *Timon*:

> The sun's a thief, and with his great attraction
> Robs the vast sea; the moon's an arrant thief
> And her pale fire she snatches from the sun

—and so on forward to the lesson, "each thing's a thief . . . All that you meet are thieves," after which, what might there be which was not exculpable, what not actually to enjoy, along with the announced endeavor to prevent crime.

And there was former New York City detective George W. Walling, who testified (if perhaps redundantly nonetheless with his own very considerable authority) to what he offered as the general and ordinary practice of collusion between thieves and politicians. Walling had served for almost forty years, rising in the ranks to the position of head of detectives and ultimately to that of "superintendent" of police, before, apparently, being forced to resign, in 1885. He had served conspicuously. It was he who had arrested Ned Buntline on the occasion of the Astor Place riot long ago, in 1849. On loan, he had been largely responsible for securing the safety of Abraham Lincoln when Lincoln traveled from Philadelphia through Baltimore on the way to the inauguration in Washington. Walling had sent detectives to infiltrate the ranks of southern sympathizers, for there had been threats. (Allan Pinkerton would claim that it was he who had discovered and thwarted the plots against Lincoln in Baltimore, and perhaps they both did.) During the Draft Riots of 1863, as a captain of police, Walling had saved some two hundred of the inmates of the Colored Orphan Asylum. He had also once, in 1857, been sent to arrest the mayor of New York, Fernando Wood, when the state had taken over police functions from the city, but on that occasion he had failed.

When in 1887 he published his memoirs, *Recollections of a New York Chief of Police*, Walling evidently was a bitter man, and in any event was not unwilling to confess that sometimes he had been rude in his ways. Distrusting courts and magistrates, he had routinely arrested and held persons in jail without trial. In interrogations he had been particularly direct. Once, as he recalled, he had forced an emetic down the throat of a swindler who had swallowed a counterfeit bill. Thus there was an irony in his concluding recommendations for an ideal police department, to be defined particularly by improved deportment. "I have sometimes fancied," he said,

> that it might not be wholly impossible to attempt to endow policemen with those elegancies and courtesies of life which make refined social intercourse so pleasant and improving. Let us imagine an institution in which the guardian of the peace can learn to make a pleasant bow, to walk with grace, to shake hands with dignity, to lift his hat in a courtly way, or to extend his protecting arm to a lady with Chesterfieldian decorum. Such arts are teachable. (593)

And he looked forward to the time when some great reformer might inaugurate the "Era of National Politeness."

His underlying bitterness and his history of immoderation aside, Walling might have been honest enough, and in any event undoubtedly he did have exceptional evidence of prevailing political corruption. ("Full well do I know the power of that mighty combination—Politics and Police," he said in his Introduction to his *Recollections*. "I attempted to make a stand against it, but the result was most disastrous to myself.") He had held high position during the whole of the time when the Tweed Ring controlled and swindled New York City—and when the police were in charge of counting the votes. Walling had fought with Tweed's man A. Oakey Hall, first District Attorney and then mayor of New York. But whatever else he may have been, Walling was not partisan in his opposition to Tweed's Democrats, for he knew better. "As every one knows," he said, "there are two political factions, so called, in New York—Republican and Democratic—but politics implies principles, and I do not believe that one man in five hundred can explain understandingly the foundation principles of either of the parties mentioned. To call them 'political' parties is clearly a misnomer, for the very simple reason that the only basis underlying their existence, here in New York, at least, is power and plunder"—although apparently the thieves of his acquaintance did make distinctions. "All the sneaks, hypocrites and higher grade of criminals when questioned upon the subject," he said "almost invariably lay claim to be adherents of the Republican party; while, on the other hand, criminals of the lower order—those who rob by violence and brute force—lay claim in no uncertain tones to being practical and energetic exponents of true Democratic principles" (597).

> The city of New York [he said] is actually ruled by some twenty thousand office-holders, most of whom are taken from and controlled by the very worst elements in the community.
>
> Observe the countenances of some of our "City Fathers," court *attachés* and city employés. You will find the square jaw and large back head of the man who rules by brute force rather than by intellect.
>
> Our judiciary and prosecuting officers are elected and controlled in a great measure by the very elements they are called upon to punish and keep in check.
>
> It has been shown most conclusively that there is no small amount of corruption in the office of the Commissioner of Jurors.
>
> I believe that universal suffrage, when applied to the municipal government of large cities, is a failure. (596ff.)

Accordingly it might have followed, as no doubt was intended, that Walling's own confessed ways with the law were justified, as to say that when the law was corrupt then true justice required certain efficiencies, but in fact the basic tendency of Walling's *Recollections*, too, like those of the others, actually went the other way, toward humanizing crime and the criminals. He might be rough with an uncooperative swindler here and there, or issue blanket orders to incarcerate all known pickpockets on the occasion, perhaps, of a parade, but those criminals first of all for forty years had constituted his milieu, and, second, were virtually normative for government itself except that they might be more straightforward in their thievery.

Third, moreover, frequently these criminals were admirable for their professionalism, and it followed that despite occasional sonority and despite some sneering, Walling, too, really was engaged in presenting the pervading, continuously ironic social truth, that crime was the law and that theft was the social integument, from which it followed additionally that "professionalism" within crime was status, properly regarded. As the detective was particularly privileged to know.

So, implicitly, said all of these. For McWatters there had been, for instance, Colonel Novena, "The Prince of Confidence Men," as he called him. "He was a man of brilliant talents," said McWatters, "indeed, great native ability," who might have adorned any profession. He had been an excellent storyteller, presumably a matter of special virtue for "the Literary Policeman". He had known the art of dressing well. He had been a social genius who, in addition, had aided a great many poor people, particularly children, while practicing numbers of swindles and particularly preying upon the affections of women of the upper classes. His widow, a wealthy brothel-keeper who summered in New Jersey, would beg McWatters to consider that "may be, no better man had lived, as surely no more remarkably gifted, elegant, and strange one, than 'Colonel Novena,' had I ever met" (599ff.) For Detective Phil Farley, at his lower station in life, there had been, for other instance, Mabel Wray, "Queen of the Pawn-Ticket Players"—an expert in securing loans from married men whose wives were away, offering worthless pawn tickets as security; and, again, with evident perverse delight, there had been Spence Pettis (shoplifter, pickpocket, embezzler, forger, and pimp) who, while not actually a very good thief, nevertheless stood out in society by having no goodness within him at all, which totality of absence evidently in Farley's view constituted its own distinction (37ff., 245ff.). For Walling, with his better credentials, there had been George MacDonnell, for instance, of the Bank of England forgeries, "the most expert and persistent forger and confidence man that ever exercised his cunning on unsuspecting humanity in this country and in Europe" (172), and Mother Mandelbaum, "Queen of Fences," of whom he said that she was "a wonderful person; she changed character like a chameleon, and was as adept in her business as the best stockbroker in Wall Street in his." Particularly, Mother Mandelbaum had fine knowledge both of criminals and venal policemen, and her "honesty in criminal matters was absolute." She was known not only throughout the United States, but in Canada, Mexico, and Europe. She paid a retainer of five thousand dollars a year to the celebrated criminal lawyers Messrs. Howe and Hummel, and when finally caught (by Pinkerton agents) escaped to Canada where she still resided, quietly, "cheered by frequent visits from emissaries of her council, and saddened by the intelligence of the death of her younger daughter," but the elder daughter meanwhile had married a private detective. Said Walling respectfully,

> Mrs. Mandelbaum depleted her income in good living. She had a cellar of choice wines and liquors and was a liberal patron of the local synagogue, of which she was considered a consistent member. In the winter she frequently gave entertainments to thieves of both sexes and outside friends, and the receptions were conducted with as much attention to the proprieties of society as though Mrs. Mandelbaum's establishment was in Fifth Avenue instead of in a suspicious corner of the East Side. (279ff.)

And as for the general case, said Walling, having been chief of police of one of the greatest cities of the world, he had had personal contact with the most consummate criminals, and knew that a successful criminal had to be an individual of rare cunning and great determination. "Criminals who live by their wits, generally termed swindlers," he said, "are almost without exception persons of winning address and fascinating manners" (321)—this from the exponent of the "Era of National Politeness."

Walling's successor was Thomas Byrnes, first as chief of detectives of New York City (and "inspector of police" at the same time) and later as superintendent of police. Byrnes, too, eventually would be forced to resign. That would be in 1894, in a time of a freshet of reform, when he would be replaced by Captain of Police Max Schmittberger, who had unseated him as a result of his testimony before an investigating committee and who had much to testify to because he himself had been principal collector of bribes in the Tenderloin District. But prior to his disgrace, if such it was, Thomas Byrnes was a famous man, celebrated in fiction and in life.

Tribute was accorded by "Old Cap. Collier," of the dime-novel series of the same name, who recalled that the swindling attorney Flash Jack had been kept out of New York during Inspector Byrnes's regime and

Thomas Byrnes. From Thomas Byrnes, *Professional Criminals of America* (New York: Cassell & Co., 1886), frontispiece.

had returned only "when the great chief of detectives resigned." So said Old Cap. Collier in *The Thugs of the Tenderloin; or, Old Cap. Collier Tracking a Daring Band of Thieves.*

Julian Hawthorne, Nathaniel's son, wrote a series of five popular novels based on Byrnes's cases, prior to his own incarceration in the Atlanta Penitentiary for stock fraud. He composed a Byrnes who was alternately solid and reposeful in manner but nonetheless quick in movement when movement was indicated, who was wonderfully keen in observation, even eerily omniscient, gentle, tough, generous, and a man of rather courtly rectitude, and who as well "evidently enjoys capital health and a sound digestion," as says the author in the novel *The Great Bank Robbery* (45). "He's what I call a man!" says Percy Nolen in the novel *Another's Crime*, and Percy's sister Pauline agrees. "God bless him!" she whispers (241). "He would be a rash man who should venture to assert that there is any thing in New York that the inspector does not know," says the author, again in *The Great Bank Robbery* (44). The financier Mr. Golding, who has been threatened with assassination and blackmail, thanks the inspector for his help and offers to reimburse him for expenses, at the end of *Section 558 or, The Fatal Letter,* but the inspector demurs. "The expenses," says Byrnes, "amount to nothing," and Mr. Golding is surprised:

> "Nothing? No, no," returned Golding. "That's no way to do business, and you'll never be a rich man if you adopt it."
> Inspector Byrnes smiled, and shook his head. "I am just as much obliged to you," he said. "I have simply done my duty as an officer, and the success of my stratagems is my reward."
> "Well, there seems to be a difference between Mulberry Street and Wall Street," remarked the other, with a short laugh. (245)

But Golding surely was mistaken, regarding the supposed difference between Wall Street and Police Headquarters. Julian Hawthorne certainly knew better, which would have been reason for him to write the passage, and in any event the facts were well known. "Crime was a business," said the journalist and reformer Lincoln Steffens in his *Autobiography*, reflecting back on his years as a police reporter in New York in the early nineties, and so equally was detecting (221ff.) Byrnes, with his "saloon nerves" connected with "the big-business brains," in Steffens's characterization, regularly took tribute from prostitutes, saloon-keepers, beggars, homosexuals, and thieves, and had a large and rewarding reputation as well among the elevated classes. He had sent word to thieves to stay within their own territories, north of Fulton Street and the financial district, and was appreciated therefore. He was as well the man to take care of blackmailers, just as Mr. Golding had come to appreciate, as so said Steffens: "Wall Street and 'Society' had suffered from the possession by unscrupulous scoundrels of personal and more or less scandalous facts against its leaders; true stories. Byrnes could deal with them. You told him 'all about it'; perhaps you made one more payment, and—that ended it" (222). Steffens remembered that "they all knew him in Wall Street; big men down there envied me the privilege of knowing personally 'the inspector,' as they still called him." "You see him?" they would say. "Every day? And he talked to you, man to man, like that?" (221). But some of the Wall Streeters seemingly did know Byrnes, for he was said to have accumulated some $350,000 from stock market tips given to him by Jay Gould and others.

Byrnes was a legend in his time not without his own creative effort. He would tell detective stories in which he was the major player, so Steffens also recalled, which stories he had plagiarized; Steffens had discovered Byrnes's cache of detective storybooks. Byrnes would also appropriate the work of other detectives, again taking a hero's part for himself and elaborating plots and clues, seemingly with effect on enunciation. He would speak an English as English as he could make it, so Steffens remembered, using the broad "a," although when moved by temper and not in the storytelling vein, he would fall back into his native Irish. "Did youse did it?" he would ask.

But Byrnes's great imaginative work was his *Professional Criminals of America*, published in 1886.

According to a "Frederick Smyth, Recorder" and former judge, who wrote a prefatory note, the book had been submitted to the public specifically not as a work of fiction but as a true history of the criminal classes. On the other hand and obviously nonetheless, it had been informed by a sensibility and a vision, and surely it was that by which it beckoned a public. In greater part it was a Rogues' Gallery, like the book of Detective Phil Farley, but it was far superior both technically and imaginatively. It was a gorgeous book. It had 204 photographs (not cheap engravings) along with accompanying narratives. Pains had been taken, said Byrnes, "to secure, regardless of expense, excellent reproductions of their photographs, so that the law-breakers can be recognized at a glance," and there for pondering, were: "James Lee, Bogus Custom-House Collector"; "Frederick Bennett, Alias Dutch Fred, Burglar"; "Michael Kurtz, Alias Sheeny Mike, Burglar"; "Margaret Brown, Alias Old Mother Hubbard, Pickpocket and Satchel Worker"; "Louisa Jourdan, Alias Little Louise, Pickpocket and Shop Lifter"; "Rudolph Lewis, Alias Young Rudolph, Shop Lifter"; "Julius Klein, Alias Young Julius, Sneak and Shop Lifter"; "William Peck, Alias Peck's Bad Boy, Pickpocket"; "Albert Wilson, Forger"; "Charles J. Everhardt, Alias Marsh Market Jake, Sneak and Forger"; "Robert Bowman, Alias Hogan, Forger"; among the many others.

Here, clearly, was another kind of expressiveness. Here was an album of reminiscences, a family album offering double implication. As in the usual case with family albums, it spoke first of all to a sense of privileged intimacy, and then second, by way of balance, and also as usual, it suggested something more generous: an offer to share, incorporating in turn the idea that all happy families are alike. It was in fact the manifest truth evident in the photographs, that these rogues had for the most part been very angry when they had faced the camera. Some had smiled and some others obviously were insane, but that was a detail which was erased by the fact of the book itself, as the book imposed its luxurious formality.

Byrnes did say that some of these faces seemed to be contorted, but that was only because the subjects had been trying to cheat the camera—and had failed, the essential man being nevertheless there to be seen. And that allowed Byrnes to say additionally, in response to a supposed inquiry

> Here is where the public err. Their idea of burglars and all that have been gathered from books . . . and they look for Bill Sykeses and Flash Toby Crackitts, whereas the most modest and most gentlemanly people they meet may be the representatives of their very characters. Remember that nearly all the great criminals of the country are men who lead double lives. Strange as it may appear, it is the fact that some of the most unscrupulous rascals who ever cracked a safe or turned out a counterfeit were at home model husbands and fathers. (54)

And so, said Byrnes, there was George Engles, the forger, for instance. "His family lived quietly and respectably, mingled with the best of people and were liked by all they met." And there was George Leonidas Leslie, alias Howard, "who was found dead near Yonkers, probably made away with by his pals, [who] was a fine-looking man, with cultured tastes and refined manners" (54). And so forth through the two hundred and four cases.

This was not quite to say that respectability was a consequence of rascality, but it was emphatically to suggest not only that these rogues might look just like your neighbor, or you, but, more than that, they might well look just like what you aspired to be, and had the secret of success.

So, no doubt reflecting Byrnes's own views, shortly after the publication of *Professional Criminals of America*, Julian Hawthorne would have a character in *The Great Bank Robbery* consider the inspector's actual Rogues' Gallery, in Mulberry Street, and deny what Byrnes's book in fact showed. Looking at those portraits, Hawthorne's character says to an acquaintance, "You will think that you have seldom seen an equal number of intelligent, respectable, self-satisfied persons. Nothing diabolic, nothing brutal, no signs of corroding anxiety or secret agony.

No, Sir! You will find unwrinkled brows, unfurrowed cheeks, untroubled eyes, complacent mouths. Here are people who enjoy their eight or nine hours good sleep." And this is the case, the character goes on to say, beyond apparent irony, because the professional criminal does not wear the burden of usual duties and routine. "My dear fellow," he exclaims, "just fancy for one moment the state of a man who feels that he owes nothing to society! No fear of social opinion—no obligation—no slavery to it! Why, it must be to the mind what annulling the attraction of gravitation would be to the body!" (9–10).

Perhaps inevitably, the one conspicuous stylistic fault in Byrnes's book was its tendency to tribute. Repeatedly the inspector's criminals are persons "well worth knowing." Thus of Julius Klein: "He is a sneak thief well worth knowing." Of Joe Gorman: "He is one of the smartest pickpockets in America, and a man well worth knowing." Of Annie Reilly, Dishonest Servant, " 'Little Annie Reilly' is considered the cleverest woman in her line in America. . . . This woman is well worth knowing. She has stolen more property the last fifteen years than any other four women in America." Of Albert Cropsey: "Cropsey is a very clever hotel and boarding-house thief, and is a man well worth knowing." Or they are the smartest or the most adroit, or one of the most celebrated: "Joe Parish is a Western pickpocket and general thief, and is one of the most celebrated criminals in America"; John Irving, or Old Jack, Burglar, "is one of the most celebrated criminals in America"; Peter Lake, or Grand Central Pete, "is one of the most celebrated and persistent banco steerers there is in America, 'Hungry' Joe possibly excepted." (Hungry Joe Lewis had swindled Oscar Wilde during the latter's lecture tour in America in 1882, but then it was Byrnes's opinion that Oscar Wilde himself, "when he reaped a harvest of American dollars with his curls, sun-flowers and knee-breeches," was no less the swindler only not quite so sharp [42].)[3] Or they make a fine appearance, and when they did not, Byrnes allowed himself a note of regret, as in the instance of Emanuel Marks, alias Minnie Marks, alias The Red-Headed Jew, Bank Sneak, Confidence Man, and Skin Gambler, of whom Byrnes was compelled to say, "Used to dress well, but getting careless of late." Or they were good talkers, as in the instance of Franklin J. Moses, a graduate of Columbia College and also formerly the governor of South Carolina, who had swindled Col. T. W. Higginson out of thirty-four dollars, not that that was his only swindle.

But above all, these persons, at least as a class, were good at what they did. "The professional forger," said Byrnes, "is a man of great ability," while "the class of thieves devoting themselves to robbing rooms in hotels and in fashionable boarding-houses operate according to circumstances and always have their wits about them for any unexpected emergency; the successful ones are men of respectable appearance, good address, and cool and daring fellows." Or, "the leading confidence and banco operators are an industrious set; they are also men of education, possessed of plenty assurance, gifted with a good knowledge of human nature and a fair amount of ingenuity," while "it requires rare qualities in a criminal to become an expert bank-safe robber." "Thieves of this high grade," said Byrnes, "stand unrivaled among their kind. The professional bank burglar must have patience, intelligence, mechanical knowledge, industry, determination, fertility of resources, and courage—all in high degree,"—like Charley Adams, alias Langdon W. Moore, and William Robinson, alias Gopher Bill, and Mark Shinburn, he of the Ocean Bank robbery years ago, who "always stops at first-class hotels" (19, 40, 2).

In a word, and with all of their implication in ordinary ways of success, and as in fact promised by the title of his book, Byrnes considered that these persons were "professionals". "Robbery is now classed as a profession," so he said directly to the point, "and in the place of the awkward and hang-dog looking thief we have to-day the intelligent and thoughtful rogue" (53).

Obviously in this way of thinking, it took a professional not even necessarily to catch a professional, for that appeared really to be a matter of secondary relevance, but to recognize a professional, meaning not merely someone who was good at the job. "Professional" conveyed its own social and moral status, not entirely a matter of greater privilege but meaning more genuine, closer to the inner secrets of things. To be a professional criminal was, in refreshing paradox, to be one of those who actually did the business of society beyond both naiveté and hypocrisy, and thus to be a professional detective was to be the same. The world of both cops and robbers was of course a different world, in which however was to be discovered suggestion that after all it was the real one. It was different and it was the same. It had essentiality. It might have seemed to have its own ethical system, but really did not. The difference was that it had achieved candor.

Thus as had said the wise George S. McWatters, certainly there was "honor among thieves, as among other business men." There must be a certain degree of it, he had said, "else business itself would die out or go into anarchy," and it followed that the detective could not afford to have less. Thus the detective, so he observed, "is a sort of prince, in the thieves' opinion. He is the only man for whom they have any real respect," (661) not because he was good at catching them but because he was one of them.

Six male thieves. From Thomas Byrnes, *Professional Criminals of America* (New York: Cassell & Co., 1886), following page 164.

| 127 | 128 | 129 |

ANNIE REILLY,
ALIAS LITTLE ANNIE.
DISHONEST SERVANT.

SOPHIE LYONS,
ALIAS LEVY,
PICKPOCKET AND BLACKMAILER.

KATE RYAN,
PICKPOCKET.

| 130 | 131 | 132 |

ANNIE MACK,
ALIAS BOND.
SNEAK AND SHOP LIFTER.

LOUISA JOURDAN,
ALIAS LITTLE LOUISE.
PICKPOCKET AND SHOP LIFTER.

CATHARINE ARMSTRONG,
ALIAS MARY ANN DOWD, ALIAS DILLON.
PICKPOCKET.

Six female thieves. From Thomas Byrnes, *Professional Criminals of America* (New York: Cassell & Co., 1886), following page 203.

It had been professionalism that had distinguished Allan Pinkerton, too, even in his earliest ambitions. It had been that rather than ideas of justice or of vengeance, or sympathy for victims of crime, not that such sentiments were absent in the man. The Pinkerton National Detective Agency ("We Never Sleep") saw everything and did not shed a tear. The Agency was more knowing than the Business which, as a business, it served, and strove to be different if at all only by being more businesslike. Thus in a time when to say Business was to say Railroads, the chief source of income for the Pinkerton Agency was railroads and express companies. Thus it was that Pinkertons pursued the Reno Gang, and the Jameses and Youngers, and the Wild Bunch, who robbed railroads, thereby to counter the romance of social banditry with the equal persuasiveness of a professionalism which was beyond good and evil.

Allan Pinkerton's first large case, and the subject of his first book, had to do with the 1858 theft of fifty thousand dollars from the Adams Express Company by its agent in Montgomery, Alabama, one Nathan Maroney, and it was revealing that Pinkerton's attitude in this instance tended toward fretfulness if not indeed jealousy of a sort. Maroney had proved to be elusive. It had taken two years for Pinkerton's agents to trap him, but then beyond what might have been conveyed by that frustration, it is the evidence of the book that Pinkerton conceived virtually a competition with the man, for, particularly, a kind of respectability. Taking up the case, Pinkerton wrote in *The Expressman and the Detective*, "from the meagre reports I had received I found I had to cope with no ordinary man, but one who was very popular, while I was a poor nameless individual, with a profession which most people were inclined to look down upon with contempt" (24–25), and when at the end Maroney had been trapped into a confession (by a cellmate who was a Pinkerton agent), Pinkerton's own confessed satisfaction specifically was in the fact that he had salvaged his own professionalism. He said, "There are quacks in other professions as well as in mine, and people should lay the blame were it belongs, upon the quacks, and not upon the profession" (261), while as for himself he had rewarded his employer's confidence.

Nor did Pinkerton moralize in any conventional way, neither here nor elsewhere, except indeed in his antislavery statements, but that was morality of a different order.[4] If he might say as occasionally he did, that crime was an alien thing, "an element as foreign to the human mind as a poisonous substance is to the body" (in *Bucholz and the Detective*, a tale of the robbery of a rich man by his valet, who will be trapped by a cellmate who is actually a Pinkerton agent), that observation was much more a shrewdness than a judgment, for it would follow that "the criminal, yielding to a natural impulse of human nature, must seek for sympathy," and there would be the Pinkerton agent ready to hear a confession (xii–xiii). Certainly there was little indication that, to extend the trope, diseased though the criminal might be, he was morally revolting. The peculiar Maroney case perhaps excepted, there was little animus in Pinkerton's telling of his tales, at least so far as individuals were concerned.

The Pinkerton Agency soon would be notorious for its union-busting, following especially upon its providing guards and scabs for the bloody Homestead Strike of 1892, although and as was likely given its Business bias, it had supplied infiltrators in the earlier days as well. But even here, in the matter of labor conflict, for Pinkerton, individuals largely were to be exempted from blame even if they were also not quite so well respected as were, say, bank robbers. So in his account of the railroad strikes of 1877 (*Strikers, Communists, Tramps and Detectives*), in which Pinkerton agents had played a minor part, there were culprits, like P. M. Arthur, grand chief engineer of the Brotherhood of Locomotive Engineers, and Robert Ammon, of the Trainmen's Union, but the personal guilt, if such it was, largely was absorbed into a kind of fortuitousness. The source of the great troubles was, variously, the Paris Commune of 1871, refugees from which had been discovered among the strikers, or the "International Society," in Pinkerton's phrase, founded in 1863 in London by "one George Odger, a defeated aspirant for parliamentary honors," with the assistance of Dr. Karl Marx, who read a manifesto to the convention, or the source was the European institution of the "strike." The peril in any event had been "everywhere; it was nowhere." "A condition of sedition which can be located, fixed, or given boundaries," said Pinkerton, "may, by any ordinary community or government, be subdued," but this was different.

> This uprising, in its far-reaching extent, was so alarmingly sudden that it seemed like the hideous growth of a night. It was as if the surrounding seas had swept in upon the land from every quarter, or some sudden central volcano had upraised its hideous head and belched forth burning rivers that coursed out upon the country in every direction. No general action for safety could be taken. Look where we might, some fresh danger was presented. No one had prophesied it; no one could prevent it; no one was found brave enough or wise enough to stop its pestilential spread. Its birth was spontaneous; its progress like a hurricane; its demise a complete farce. (Strikers 13–14)

But this prose, with its unaccustomed excitement, was to convey intrusion, fluke, as against a customary assured and knowing competence.

And as with Pinkerton himself, so with the Agency. It was a business, emphatically and deliberately, characterized by its curtailment of personality. "The business of investigating crime and evil-doing generally, is by no means always active," said Pinkerton, by way of introduction to a collection of random pieces, *Bank-Robbers and Detectives.* "Just as merchants at times find themselves pressed with orders beyond their means of supply, and at others are fated to days and weeks of idleness, so with my business" (11). While, moreover, the books had such titles as, *The Gypsies and the Detectives, The Spiritualists and the Detectives, The Mollie Maguires and the Detectives*, and so on, within the organization the Pinkerton agents were called "Operatives," meaning a worker or, in the factory sense, one of the machine hands, as the Pinkerton historian Frank Morn has pointed out, with any potential of glamour deliberately having been subtracted in advance. The rules of the Agency, moreover, were very strict, at least in design. Operatives in the field were never to accept gratuities. All travel and other expenses were to be agreed upon in advance, in consultation with the client. Operatives in the field, far from being on their own, were required to submit a daily report, from which (according to Morris Friedman, the ex-stenographer in the Denver office) the Operative's superintendent would know "when the operative rose in the morning, whether he worked at the client's plant during the day, what time he quit work, when he had his supper, whether he spent the evening trying to obtain information, what time he retired, how much money he spent, and what for" (16), and then the Agency in its various divisions and sections would make its corporate decisions.

Labor spying was the main source of revenue for the Agency, as said Friedman in his 1907 book *The Pinkerton Labor Spy*, but the so-called "Secret Operatives," who were the labor spies and who were themselves not very well paid, were for the most part recruited from the ranks of salesmen, as would have been a likelihood. And even the few seemingly independent adventurers who worked for the Agency tended to regard themselves according to the Agency's basic terms. There had been Tom Horn, a western gunman, former Indian fighter, and primarily, notoriously, a killer. "Killing is my specialty," he said, adding, "I look at it as a business proposition, and I think I have a corner on the market."

Tom Horn eventually would be hanged. Colorful characters were not likely to last, in one way or another of an ending to their careers or their tales or their lives. He had quit the Pinkertons, commenting, "My work for them was not the kind that exactly suited my disposition; too tame for me. There were a good many instructions and a good deal of talk given the operative regarding the things to do" (Horn

222). But then it would seem to have been a not very different kind of ambition, only more entrepreneurial, that had done him in. He had been working for the Wyoming Cattleman's Association, at the rate of six hundred dollars a killing. He was hanged for the murder of a fourteen-year-old boy whom he had mistaken for a sheepherder. And there had been Charles A. Siringo, author in 1915 of: *Two Evil Isms: Pinkertonism and Anarchism, By a Cowboy Detective Who Knows, as He Spent Twenty-Two Years in the Inner Circle of Pinkerton's National Detective Agency.* Siringo too, finally, was not quite the renegade his title promised him to be. Certainly he did not share the principled spite of Morris Friedman of a few years before, who had been writing at the time of the Steunenberg trial with the intention chiefly of exposing the role of the Pinkerton Agency and of James McParlan in particular. For Siringo there were confusions. He had been in Haymarket Square in Chicago in 1886 at the time of the riot, as a Pinkerton Operative, and subsequently, so he said, had been disgusted by the false stories which were written about the Anarchists. On the other hand, by "Anarchism" Siringo seems to have meant lawlessness in general. In a general way he accused the Pinkerton Agency of bribing juries, fixing elections, corrupting police officers and other officials, kidnapping witnesses, railroading men to prison or the gallows, and so forth, and accused the Agency thus of "anarchism" in his meaning of the word. As for specifics, however, most of his indictment consisted of allegations of company-approved inflation of expense accounts, perhaps indicating that he was a company man after all, zealous mostly for internal reform.

Charlie Siringo would seem to have drunk truly from the source, despite his opting out and despite the gesture of exposé. The Agency had shaped his character. As he presented himself in his defiance, pitched against both of his evil "isms," he was a certain kind of a hero, not bold nor courageous nor a good citizen. Rather, he was a knowing, efficient, cunning, cynical, and in that way a modest man. In so fundamental a way he was all business, the business being society itself, and he had learned so well that he had advice for negotiating the business of society. By way of valediction he said,

> As it does not fall to the lot of every mortal to spend nearly a quarter of a century as a sleuth, in all the walks of life, from the lowest to the highest, I will here record my advice for the upbuilding of society, and the protection of unfortunate souls who are ignorant of the snares set to catch "suckers."
>
> Never bet at another man's game. If he couldn't beat you, he wouldn't be in the business. (103)

# 10   Hammett

DASHIELL Hammett had his special authority for writing about Private Eyes. He had himself been in the business, as a Pinkerton Operative. He knew the truth of the ways and the lives of detectives.

It had been only for a few years, and then off and on, when he was in his twenties, but he had been there. In 1915 in Baltimore, at the age of twenty and out of work, he had answered an ad at the Pinkerton Agency, having dropped out of school at the age of fourteen and having had a number of other knockabout jobs. At first he had been a clerk, then an Operative, and had remained with the Agency until 1921, based initially in Baltimore, then Spokane, then San Francisco. Discounting some time out spent in the Army, after which there was a hospital confinement for tuberculosis, for he was a "lunger," he had been an Operative for a total of only about four and a half years, some of that time part-time—not nearly so long that being an Operative might have figured as a career for him, but on the other hand he had stayed with that job of work longer than he would with any other. Except indeed for his writing, but the Private-Eye writing in obvious ways would be a reflection upon and an extension of the same job. As a writer, according to his own explicit testimonies, he did draw on his detective experiences for characters and plot movements and the authentic details of detecting—hence, so it was said, one of the reasons for his superiority to the others in the trade. He really knew. As a reviewer of detective novels (for two years, from 1927 to 1929, for *Saturday Review of Literature*), he regularly took the measure of those others who, for instance, didn't know anything about the impact of a .45.

Evidently, moreover, the detective experience had presented him with deep satisfactions quite beyond both the data and the matter of the edge he had on the competition. Says the Continental Op in one of the early stories, "The Gutting of Couffignal": "Now I'm a detective because I happen to like the work. . . . That's the fix I am in. I don't know anything else, don't enjoy anything else, don't want to know or enjoy anything else"—not that the Op necessarily always spoke for Hammett, but undoubtedly they understood each other. And as a Private Eye Hammett had indeed had more than a job and more than sport. There was plausible fulfillment there.

Detectives knew things, as everybody knew that they knew, that second instance of awareness being much to the point. As Hammett would have known along with everybody else, detectives were peculiarly privileged persons: they had the integrity of their disenchantment. They knew how society really worked particularly in America and particularly now, and they lived life accordingly. They knew the urban and industrial geographies, and the nature of business and politics in America, not even to speak of human nature. And this was a matter of heritage, which would be to say that the basics of the wisdom of the Continental Op and of the few others of Hammett's detectives already were in place. Just behind the Pinkerton Operative Dashiell Hammett, within the few years constituting modern times (and whether or not as a matter of his specific knowledge although in fact Hammett was proud of the esoteric reaches of his knowledge), there had been the accumulating lore and response of character—including the adventures of the great James McParlan with his supple and affectless adaptability, and "the Literary Policeman" George S. McWatters together with Detective Phil Farley and Chief of Police George Walling and Inspector Thomas Byrnes and the others with their genuine profundities of cynicism, not to speak of Allan Pinkerton himself with his perfectly ironic business morality. All of this and these added up to a wisdom already become public but which nonetheless, as everyone would acknowledge, was possessed especially by those who had charge of crime in America. Detectives knew better than anyone else and knew for certain that "crime" was an ethical quibble.

It was Hammett's genius, then, to take what was already a common wisdom and to make of it an elegant, stylized joke—if literature, then something along the lines of Restoration Comedy, granted the American accents. What Congreve did for adultery, Hammett did for murder. Crime was an amusement subject to witty elaborations and twists and sardonic exaggerations, set forth in a remarkably sharpened prose. Hammett would sometimes have inclinations toward profundity, but typically and at his defining best he resisted original thinking. He did not reflect nor did he probe, but was wry, cynical, and parodic—with the result no doubt that the horror was doubled, because moralizing disappeared into the wit.

There had been as well the so-called "Black Mask School," a remarkably self-conscious literary enterprise of the 1920s, of which Hammett was a member and which contributed some other implications to what he was doing.

The pulp magazine *Black Mask*, originally the creation of H. L. Mencken and George Jean Nathan (who in the same motion and for the same reason had founded the magazines *Parisienne* and *Saucy Stories*), had been taken over by a succession of other owners and editors, a couple of whom had ambitions for the detective story. Mencken and Nathan had founded and sold the magazine in 1920. Hammett, using a pseudonym, had begun writing for it in 1922. Erle Stanley Gardner said it was Phil Cody, editor of *Black Mask* from 1924 to 1926, who, having a keen appreciation of literature, was the first to appreciate the genius of Dashiell Hammett. Cody's successor was Captain Joseph Thompson Shaw, late of the United States Army, who was a dull novelist, a champion fencer, and, as the event would prove, a great promoter. It is Shaw who is usually credited with the making of the "Black Mask School" as such. Taking Hammett's early stories for an initial and approximate model, according to Philip Durham in his authoritative account of this matter, Shaw set forth the rules for what he said was a new kind of detective story, different from the tale of ratiocination which Poe had invented. In the new tale simplicity would be basic principle, "simplicity," in his words, "for the sake of clarity, plausibility, and belief." There would be no fat in the language. There would be no incredibility of action. Characters would be realistic. And Shaw assembled a group of writers including Raymond Chandler (with Philip Marlowe), Lester Dent (creator of Doc Savage), Horace McCoy (begetter of "Captain Jerry Frost" of the Texas Rangers), Frederick Nebel (creator of "Donny Donahue"), and some others, all of whom, in Shaw's words, shared "the *Black Mask* spirit and the *Black Mask* idea of what a short story should be." Hammett by Shaw's nomination was the primary exemplar of the new tale, but Hammett by the same stroke was thus part of a group effort, of which Shaw was the leader, and to some extent Hammett must have agreed, as did the others. The first of Hammett's five novels, *Red Harvest*, would be dedicated to Shaw. In 1944 Chandler would dedicate a collection of stories to: "Joseph Thompson Shaw with affection and respect, and in memory of the time when we were trying to get murder away from the upper classes, the week-end house party and the vicar's rose-garden, and back to the people who are really good at it."

*Black Mask*, said Lester Dent years afterward, "was akin to a writer's shrine," and most of all apparently it was the language, in its details and as a matter of rhythms and syntax and the little words, that was the important thing (although that would have had everything to do with social class), and within the words it was something basic beyond occasional instances of thieves' cant—it was the language that mattered most and not, as the event proved, merely the toughness of the tough guys. The acknowledged first inventor of the hard-boiled private eye was Carroll John Daly, creator of "Terry Mack" and "Race Williams"—the latter "a swaggering illiterate with the emotional instability of a gun-crazed vigilante," in the appreciative words of the historian of these matters William F. Nolan. Race was a dead shot, a rat with women, was powerful and was brutal, but was stilted and uncertain in his language, as, apparently, so was his author, and that made for the crucial difference. Terry Mack when he speaks says: "I'm looking for a gink what drove a car last night," "So I play a high-class joint for a feed," and, reaching for a conceit but embarrassed when he finds it, "When I look out that window, that street is as deserted as a poetry graveyard" (in "Three Gun Terry," reprinted by William Nolan). Hammett wrote core, minimalist precisions, which by the stroke of the reduction itself would activate the ironies:

> "Exit Arlie," he said.
> "R.I.P.?"
> "Yep."
> "How?"
> "Lead."
> "Our lad's?"
> "Yep."
> "Keep till morning?"
> " Yep."
> "See you at the office," and I went back to sleep. ("$106,000 Blood Money")

> She was probably twenty. Her eyes were blue, her mouth red, her teeth white, the hair-ends showing under her black-green-and-silver turban were brown, and she had a nose. Without getting steamed up over the details, she was nice. I said so. ("The Big Knockover")

And it was Hammett (who was an attentive reader of Henry James and who would say later that it was to James that he owed his conception of literary style) who came to define both *Black Mask* and a genre. It

was to the Icelandic sagas, Hammett would say, that he owed his idea
of tone.

Hammett was the group's "ace performer," said Chandler, but
then Chandler went on to say, as would others, that there was nothing in Hammett's work that was not implicit in the early novels of
Hemingway—but in this Chandler was mistaken. Nick Adams and Jake
Barnes by their deliberate simplicities of speech clearly implied sto-
icism. They have reduced utterance following upon disappointment,
probably spiritual, while Hammett's Private Eyes in fact hold back very
little but have very little to say because they are beyond opinions and
reflections. Their inspiration is not loss as of a lost generation, but
rather acceptance of terminations, moral and civic. (And insofar as
Chandler had meant to imply that Hammett derived from Hemingway,
the dates should have been troublesome. Hammett had been publishing
his stories regularly for a couple of years prior to the 1924 appearance of
Hemingway's *In Our Time*.) But then just as certainly Chandler was right
in saying that Hammett was part of "a rather revolutionary debunking of
both the language and the material of fiction" which had been going
on for some time, writing as he did in the new common language,
namely American. Perhaps it took a transplanted Englishman to notice.
And by that much once again Hammett, in the particulars of his craft,
echoed large realizations. ("The *Black Mask* revolution was a real one,"
Ross MacDonald would say later on in agreement. "From it emerged
a new kind of detective hero, the classless, restless man of American
democracy, who spoke the language of the street" [299].)

In fact much of that manifold self-conscious American avant-garde
activity of the 1910s and 1920s which would be said to constitute "renaissance" involved deliberate recognition of American things, particularly
as opposed to English things. The detective story was one of those
English things, with, in Chandler's words, its "heavy crust of English
gentility." English detective stories had neither tang nor substance,
nor did they bear very much reality. (Said Robert Graves and Alan
Hodge in their history of Great Britain between the Wars, English
detective novels "were no more intended to be judged by realistic stan-
dards than one would judge Watteau's shepherds and shepherdesses
in terms of contemporary sheep-farming" (290), wherefore, they said,
Hammett was not much read in Great Britain.) In greater particular,
American speech was more than a medium; it was a banner and a
cause, promising fresh knowledge. The first edition of H. L. Mencken's
*The American Language* had appeared in 1919, setting forth scholarly
authority for separation of the two English tongues. (And Mencken
had been Hammett's first editor.) And there had been William Carlos

Williams's tireless insistence upon the integrity of a native poetical speech, and also the practices of such less rationalizing poets as Edgar Lee Masters and Vachel Lindsay and Carl Sandburg. The vulgate, again, including although not restricted to language, was manifesto for the self-proclaiming "Young America" group, including such figures as Van Wyck Brooks, Paul Rosenfeld, Alfred Stieglitz, Randolph Bourne, Waldo Frank, and Lewis Mumford, as it was also for the writers of the socialist left who were associated with the journal confidently called *Masses*. And there had been Sherwood Anderson at one level of assertion, and Gertrude Stein at another—visiting Los Angeles in 1935, it was Hammett whom Stein particularly wanted to meet, so she said in her *Autobiography*, presumably on the basis of fellow feeling.

In none of these instances was naive patriotism the issue, nor, of course, nativism. (Challenged to name the source of that American language which he was defending, Williams said that it came "from the mouths of Polish mothers.") American language was a signal. To have it as literary medium was to deny smoothness, in metaphysics as well as in literature, which denial arguably was the major tendency in all of the avant-gardes of the moment of so-called "renaissance." Chandler was right still once again when he said of Hammett that "he had style" even though his audience may not have recognized it, and that "he wrote scenes that seemed never to have been written before," but that on the other hand the style did not belong to Hammett nor to any individual writer, but was broadly "the American language (and not even exclusively that any more)." There was a general aim here, toward the low and the undeniable—the real versus the ideal, the hard versus the soft, which in the case of the special amusement of detective stories would implicate the city versus the country house, the Private Eye versus Dupin and Holmes and the other dandies of their stripe.

By so much *Black Mask*, too, had a kind of certification of boldness. It marched in the ranks and took part in something more than itself, and then ironically enough, of all of the schools and the hot little movements, from "Imagism" to "Vorticism" to "Objectivism," and of all of the groups that gathered in all of the brave little magazines from *Seven Arts* to *Others* to *Little Review* to *The Dial* to *Contact* to *Broom*, it was only the Black Mask School that persisted through the years and into the other literary media, crossing into movies and television, becoming a datum central to culture. Contemporary poets there are who trace descent from Objectivism, but Black Mask is there every evening.

Behind Hammett there was the trope of detective knowledge of modern society, and as complement to such knowledge there was the prevailing tone of an avant garde, which then Hammett refined and reduced to almost continuous, almost perfect irony—doubling irony, indeed, because the constant message was that things are never better nor even more interesting than ever they seem to be.

The irony, for one thing, was in the advertised attitude toward his own authority. Hammett was a Private-Eye writer who really had been a Private Eye, as was made known, and as a writer of fiction he did draw on cases and characters he had known, as was also made known, but as a usual thing, and as he would testify, the original of a given character was always lesser, in the measure of reality, or was perhaps oddly, whimsically corrupt and therefore lesser still. "I followed Gutman's original in Washington," he would write in a Modern Library introduction to *The Maltese Falcon*, "and I never remember shadowing a man who bored me so much," although and for whatever little interest the fact might have had, the man "was suspected of being a German spy." (But probably was not a German spy, that was to say.) To the same effect, Sam Spade's secretary, the "good girl" Effie Perine, was taken from a woman who "once asked me to go into the narcotic smuggling business with her in San Diego." Gabrielle Leggett, the Continental Op's client in *The Dain Curse*, who is a morphine addict, who tries to commit suicide, who is molested and accused and betrayed on every side, and who may have committed murder, was the switchboard operator at Albert Samuel's jewelry store in San Francisco, where Hammett wrote advertising. A little more intricately, early on he had adopted a pen name, "Peter Collinson." "Peter Collins," as Hammett himself later pointed out, was criminal slang for "a nobody," and therefore "Peter Collinson" was the son of a nobody.

All of this was a kind of pleasure of inside joking which now was made public not at all in order to spoil the story but in its way to confirm it. In this play there was an invitation to that common sense which knows that reality mostly is banal although sometimes it is sordid, and that the rest is fiction, and that was what the fictions said as well.

Hammett was droll, again, regarding devices and skills for thief-catching, and the thrills of the pursuit, which would be to say as regards the authenticating details of his supposed expertise. In 1923 in an essay of a sort in Mencken's *Smart Set*, a magazine for sophisticates, he would present twenty-nine brief observations on detective life as he had known it, enumerated and unrelated except by mordancy of tone. "I know an operative," said he in observation Number 4, "who while looking for pickpockets at Havre de Grace race track had his wallet stolen. He later became an official in an Eastern detective agency." And in Number 13: "I know a detective who once attempted to disguise himself thoroughly. The first policeman he met took him into custody." "Pocket-picking," he said in Number 18, "is the easiest to master of all the

criminal trades. Anyone who is not crippled can become adept in a day."
And Number 19: "In 1917, in Washington, D.C., I met a young lady who
did not remark that my work must be very interesting." And famously,
in Number 28: "I know a man who once stole a Ferris-wheel." Such was
Hammett's genuine authority, so it was to be inferred, confirmed even
by the shape of the essay, which was sequence without development.

André Gide was one of Hammett's admirers. He especially liked *Red
Harvest*, for its "implacable cynicism" as he said in one of his journal
entries in the early 1940s, and then again, as he said in one of his
"Imaginary Interviews" of the same time, he liked the novel for its
being "the last word in atrocity, cynicism, and horror." He thought that
"the amazing *Red Harvest*" was far superior to *The Maltese Falcon* and
*The Thin Man*, although he realized at the same time that subtleties
of dialogue might have escaped him—and the kind of the judgment
would indicate that indeed something subtle but crucial had got away
from him. (In that same "Interview" Gide had noted his appreciation
of the "instinctive optimism" of Herman Melville, who never had an
optimistic day in his life.)

And Hammett himself was not immune to occasional ambitions
for wisdom, notably by way of parables meant to incorporate morals for
his tales.

In *The Thin Man* there would be the story of Alfred G. Packer, the
1870s prospector who had turned to cannibalism. Lost in the mountains
in Colorado, Packer had killed his companions and eaten five of them.
In the version of the tale that Nick Charles offers to young Gilbert,
taken, as said, from Maurice Duke's *Celebrated Criminal Cases of America*,
Packer had confessed not only to the cannibalism but to appetite as
well; "I had grown fond of human flesh," he had said, "especially that
portion around the breast."

In *The Glass Key* Janet Henry will have a dream, also happening to
involve food. She dreams that Ned Beaumont and she, like a Hansel
and a Gretel, wander in the woods and come upon a house filled
with delicious foods, as can be seen through the window, but when
they open the door they see hundreds of snakes. In her second and
presumably truthful version of the dream, Janet Henry adds that when
in the dream she and Ned tried to relock the door in order to keep
the snakes inside, the key had shattered because it was made of glass
and all of the snakes had come out and slithered over them, and she
had awakened screaming.

In *The Maltese Falcon* Sam Spade tells Brigid O'Shaughnessy the
story of the man named Flitcraft, who one afternoon in Tacoma had almost been hit by a beam falling from an office building under construction. Thereupon he had left his wife, children, house in the suburbs,

real-estate business, golf game, and new Packard car, eventually to settle down in Spokane, where he had married a woman much like the first Mrs. Flitcraft, had secured a new business, this time selling automobiles rather than real estate, had become father to a child again, played golf, presumably had another new car, and had a house in the suburbs. "I don't think he even knew he had settled back naturally into the same groove he had jumped out of in Tacoma," says Spade. "But that's the part of it I always liked. He adjusted himself to beams falling, and then no more of them fell, and he adjusted himself to them not falling."

None of this was beyond decoding. Albert Packer had *liked* the taste of human flesh. It was more a matter of his eating his companions or starving, says Gilbert, who is young and eager and fundamentally innocent despite a taste of his own for gore, but Nick Charles stops him short. Not unless you want to believe Packer, he says, as Nick himself clearly will not, for he has long ago learned the paradox of the likelihood of human perversity in its extremes. Ned Beaumont for his part knows that once you let the snakes out, there is no stopping them. (There is surely sexual content here, as critics, including Sinda Gregory, have pointed out, but that comes to the same thing.) Flitcraft for his part is there to confirm Sam Spade's ancient knowledge that the universe is perfectly random, with particular implications for the plotting of the novel that, first, appearances are deceiving, and that, second, sentiment (romantic love, the more particularly) falsifies.

None of this was beyond decoding although in fact in each instance the primary auditors are made not to understand, presumably in order to signify meaning beyond the common reach and of the order of profundity. Young Gilbert is said to be disappointed with the Packer story. (But so was Hammett's companion Lillian Hellman, according to Richard Layman.) It is just a thing in a book, says Gilbert, and turns his attention elsewhere. Janet Henry had been impressed by her dream, by Hammett's arrangement. She had awakened screaming. But when Ned Beaumont tells her to forget it, she does so immediately, and interpretation does not follow. Brigid O'Shaughnessy's response to the Flitcraft story is three words, "How perfectly fascinating," after which she turns her attention to the matter at hand, namely the further seduction of Sam Spade, while a reader, however, is invited to ponder.

But it might well be said that young Gilbert has the right of it after all, along with the others who are set forth to not understand. Beyond or besides being, in André Gide's words, "the last word in atrocity, cynicism, and horror," as might have been implied by those parables, finally the novels mocked even such pretension as that. The horror has its special quality. What is asserted even by way of atrocity is also dismissed, although it might be seen that just for that reason atrocity becomes atrocious.

For one thing, atrocity becomes fiction in these tales, and does so, for one thing, by excess. "Bodies Piled Up" is the title of one of the early Op stories, no doubt at once defining Hammett's appreciation of what in the instance he had wrought and setting forth a rule for the art. Halfway through the action of *Red Harvest*, in the town called Personville, the Op pauses to reflect. "This damned burg's getting me," he says. "There's been what? A dozen and a half murders since I've been here," but when he counts them up ("Donald Willsson; Ike Bush; the four wops and the dick at Cedar Hill," etc.), in fact there are only sixteen, and it is the gesture of the approximation—of numbers of corpses, after all—that tells the tale, that says more than would an accuracy. It's a joke. One body would have been enough, had the purpose been to establish evil, or tragedy, or anything of that nature, but that is not the purpose. This moment has other special importance, it happens, because the Op is led here to reflect on his own possible involvement in the human condition, but then the tone of his reflection is not even so much as solemn. The Op is fretful, rather. "I've arranged a killing or two in my time, when they were necessary," he says. "But this is the first time I've ever got the fever. It's this damned burg," named Personville. And he says, "Play with murder enough and it gets you one of two ways. It makes you sick, or you get to like it," directly after which notion occurs to him, and only not quite dismissively, he goes back to business such as it is.

In the story "The Scorched Face" it is said: "At the base of a tree, on her side, her knees drawn up close to her body, a girl was dead. She wasn't nice to see. Birds had been at her." It is said in "$106,000 Blood Money": "At ten o'clock that morning, into busy Market Street staggered a man who was naked from the top of his battered head to the soles of his blood-stained feet. From his bare chest and sides and back, little ribbons of flesh hung down, dripping blood. His left arm was broken in two places. The left side of his bald head was smashed in. An hour later he died." And, "Her body was drawn up in a little heap, from which her head hung crookedly, dangling from a neck that had been cut clean through to the bone," it is said in "The Golden Horseshoe."

And the same then with *The Dain Curse*, although with slightly another kind of fancy. The novel is an anthology of gothic clichés, frankly derivative, heightened, and thereby undermined. There is the curse itself. There is suspicion of matricide, long ago and in Paris. The murdered man had escaped from Devil's Island, on a flimsy raft.

The second of the novel's three parts takes place in "The Temple of the Holy Grail," a place where ancient Gaelic mysteries are unfolded, where poor Gabrielle Leggett is imprisoned, where the Op is drugged and where he sees a ghost—"The thing was a thing like a man who floated above the floor, with a horrible grimacing greenish face and pale flesh that was not flesh, that was visible in the dark, and that was as fluid and as unresisting and as transparent as tidal water," which really is a stage trick, the creation of one Tom Fink. The cream of this jesting is in the fact that the primary murderer will turn out to be a novelist friend of the Op's, Owen Fitzstephen, who is to be presumed to have virtuoso knowledge of just such conventions and conceits as constitute this novel, and who furthermore, as Hammett's biographer Diane Johnson has pointed out, bears resemblance to Hammett himself. (Owen Fitzstephen was "a long, lean sorrel-haired man of thirty-two," it is said, "who pretended to be lazier than he was, would rather talk than do anything else, and had a lot of what seemed to be accurate information and original ideas on any subject that happened to come up, as long as it was a little out of the ordinary.") In any event, the Op with his street imagination is there at every turn to call attention to the fictiveness of the tale in which he is engaged, thus to undermine what does not topple of its own weight. "How's the literary grift go?" he asks Fitzstephen.

When at the end of *The Thin Man*, again, the remains of the murdered man are uncovered, they are not a pretty sight—"He'd been sawed up in pieces and buried in lime or something so there wasn't much flesh left on him"—and that too is a joke. Lacking flesh, he is the thin man. "What was that joke about a guy being so thin he had to stand in the same place twice to throw a shadow?" asks the attending cop, and by way of answer Hammett offers the comic literalness. And then the same with the fat man who with comic redundancy is named Gutman, in *The Maltese Falcon*. As the thin man is thin to the last extreme, the fat man is fat:

> The fat man was flabbily fat with bulbous pink cheeks and lips and chins and neck, with a great soft egg of a belly that was all his torso, and pendant cones for arms and legs. As he advanced to meet Spade all his bulbs rose and shook and fell separately with each step, in the manner of clustered soap-bubbles not yet released from the pipe through which they had been blown. His eyes, made small by fat puffs around them, were dark and sleek. Dark ringlets thinly covered his broad scalp.

Meanwhile the several Private Eyes run counter to type, further multiplying the comic ironies. The Continental Op is forty years old, is five-foot-six, and weighs an unmuscular either 180 or 190 pounds, depending on the text, and is therefore neither a hero of romance nor a tough guy. Sometimes he is called "Fat Shorty." Sam Spade is an evil-looking fellow, "his chin a jutting v under the more flexible v of his mouth. His nostrils curved back to make another, smaller, v. His yellow-grey eyes were horizontal. The v *motif* was picked up again by thickish brows rising outward from twin creases above a hooked nose, and his pale brown hair grew down—from high flat temples—in a point on his forehead." He has the look of the blade of a spade, that would be to say, although he is several times referred to as a "blond satan," but in either event this first paragraph of description is to have the effect of playing against expectations: that first of all, rather than the establishing of a new type for myth. Nick Charles in *The Thin Man*, meanwhile, is a forty-one-year-old premature retiree who is living on his wife's money, who wants a drink, paragraph by paragraph, and who inhabits a usual state between being "tight" and being hung over. Still at the end, the case solved, time to leave New York and go back to San Francisco, and where the moral of the tale might be and perhaps is, he says to Nora, "Let's stick around awhile. This excitement has put us behind in our drinking." In what was once the notorious line of dialogue in the novel, Nora says to Nick, "Tell me something, Nick. Tell me the truth: when you were wrestling with Mimi, didn't you have an erection?" and he answers, "Oh, a little," but the irresistible implication of everything that has gone before is that Nick's response is itself a pretension, for he resists excitements of whatever sort. With some seeming daring, in 1934, the novel implied that Nick and Nora had the kind of marriage in which there was an understanding, but then in fact the novel went further than that by neutralizing sex itself. Comparison here with Jake Barnes might be apt, but where Jake is rueful and stoical having been damaged by modern history, Nick is charming. Disengagement has become a matter of taste. Impotence is his style.

And if Nick in his usual state wants a drink, the Continental Op who precedes him craves sleep. "I decided I needed sleep," says the Op in the middle of an action in *Red Harvest*, and then reminds himself of the same repeatedly. "I looked at the vacant white bed," he says. And, "Another tub of cold water did me so little good that I almost fell asleep in it." And again, "I went over to my hotel, thinking about that neat white bed." And so on until the climax of his adventures consisting of "twelve solid end-to-end hours of sleep." Indeed it is a fairly consistent irony that the detectives are weary men, wearied not only with a general world-weariness, which they also have, but also locally and particularly with respect to the actions in which they are engaged and of which they are the protagonists, the weariness being a device of the wit. They put forth minimum effort. They will plead that what they do is merely a job. "What's the use of getting poetic about it?" says the Op, in *Red Harvest.* "If you've got a fairly honest piece of work to be done in my line, and you want to pay a decent price, maybe I'll take it on. But a lot of foolishness about smoking rats and pig-pens doesn't mean anything to me."

The assertion is taken sometimes to indicate honor, but that is an inversion, as to say that these are modest heroes who honorably do the jobs for which they have been subscribed. But to the contrary, in fact, these private eyes are professionals only. They are expert, knowing well that all the world's a thief, or is so in any event where they live, and it is by the rules of their expertise that they deny value beyond the job. Invested with professional knowledge of corruption, they know the folly of looking further, beyond the little action which is the tale. If any of these various protagonists might be said to be socially engaged, it would seem to be Ned Beaumont, in *The Glass Key*, in his function as strategist for the political boss Madvig, but then he, too, is an outsider. In the plotting of the tale he is an outsider in fact (he has come to San Francisco from New York, and at the end will return to New York), and he is an outsider on principle. He has been a gambler and therefore has had his privileged knowledge of the human community both in its greed and its triviality (which will account for his fine political instincts), and therefore like the Op, and like the others, he too begins at a level of social cynicism, which incidentally will allow no possibility either of surprise or development. To consider the two of the seemingly more explicitly socially concerned novels, *Red Harvest* and *The Glass Key*, at the end of the one, the corrupt town is put under martial law, with the distinct promise that when the militia leaves, the corruptors will return, and at the end of the other, the city is returned to the machine political boss with his patronage and his protection racket, with the distinct lesson that what looks like civic reform is the more dishonest.

The vision is conservative, no matter Hammett's own subsequent involvement with left-wing politics. It is conservative in the classical and absolute sense of acceptance of depravity, while the style of the envisioning is weary, cool, knowing, and aloof. The protagonists are essentially and fundamentally apart, and so is the author, who in his aplomb can both assert and dally with the cultural realities. These are the mean streets and not the rue Morgue, "mean" in the sense not only nor finally of a viciousness, which might demand response, but of the low, real, sordid, and dismissable commonplace.

There can be no question that at the time of the writing at least of the novels, in the late 1920s and early 1930s, Hammett's own citizenly convictions were liberal at the least, and tending further to the left. He was a Marxist. By 1930 he had established his relationship with Lillian Hellman, who was committed to the hard left. Eventually, in 1951, he would be jailed for his supposed association with Communist Party activities. But that did not mean that there was no amusement in contemplation of the likelihoods of civil affairs.

He was evidently amused by the nationalities, for instance.

The political boss in *The Glass Key* is named Paul Madvig and his primary rival is named Shad O'Rory, in both instances as is likely because politics in the city is ethnic and is attached to names such as these. In *The Glass Key* that social fact is thus established and is if anything approved. It is "Judge Henry," an "aristocrat" and a real American, who lives in the suburbs, who is the villain of the novel. On the other hand, there is no ethnic privileging here. There is comedy, rather, of a certain sort. In the same way there is the instance of "Miss Wonderly" in *The Maltese Falcon*, who really, merely, vulgarly is Brigid O'Shaughnessy. (To the punk Wilmer Cook, come from Irish-Catholic New York to San Francisco, Sam Spade says, "you're not in Romeville now. You're in my burg.") The little homosexual Joel Cairo, again, is Levantine, with implication that it is appropriate that he be such. Casper Gutman besides being a fat man is probably a Jew.[1] Nick Charles is really, originally, Charalambides, a Greek. To Nora he will say in passing, "Everybody trusts Greeks"— and Nora pays no attention presumably because this is a private sarcasm to which she does not have the key. In one of the items of his *Smart Set* essay in 1923 Hammett had laid it down as a matter of his detective experience that "Of all the nationalities hauled into the criminal courts, the Greek is the most difficult to convict. He simply denies everything, no matter how conclusive the proof may be." In the paired stories "The Big Knockover" and "$106,000 Blood Money," the brains behind the gang of thieves is one, Papadopoulis, who betrays everyone including the members of his own gang.

The prose was flat, wry, and dismissive, but it also chuckled. For all of the seeming straightforward efficiency of the prose, Hammett practiced what clearly he considered to be artifice. In his late unfinished autobiographical novel *Tulip* he would recall having "written a story on a Möbius band, designed to be read from any point in it on around to that point again"—whether truly or not, but in any event some years before the novelist John Barth tried the same. An early article on the art of advertising, retrieved by Richard Layman, was entitled "Have You Tried Meiosis?" And in the tales and the novels he caressed funny names and planted puns. There are: "Romaine Frankl," a pretty Moravian girl in the story "This King Business," "Bruno Gungen" and "Coughing Ben" in "The Main Death," "Levi Oscant" (for Oscar Levant) in *The Thin Man*. It is a punster who, in the first paragraphs of *Red Harvest*, contemplates the Montana mining town called Personville and sees a pair of buttocks with a fetid notch in between:

> The city wasn't pretty. Most of its builders had gone in for gaudiness. Maybe they had been successful at first. Since then the smelters whose brick stacks stuck up tall against a gloomy mountain to the south had yellow-smoked everything into uniform dinginess. The result was an ugly city of forty thousand people, set in an ugly notch between two ugly mountains that had been all dirtied up by mining. Spread over this was a grimy sky that looked as if it had come out of the smelters' stacks.

("Personville" was based on Anaconda, where Hammett had done some sleuthing in his Pinkerton days. It was also the residence of his wife's parents.) He read the masters, widely and appreciatively, for the purposes of the art of the fiction. Particularly, according to Diane Johnson, he surprised people with his minute acquaintance with the works of Henry James. He had startled James Thurber, particularly, one evening in a New York speakeasy, telling him that most of all he had been influenced by James and that in particular in writing *The Maltese Falcon* he had been influenced by *The Wings of the Dove*—perhaps his heart had stirred for a bird.

And it was a pleasantry of the same order of doubling amusement that in *The Maltese Falcon*, Gutman's genealogy of the bird is historically accurate, almost. It is the case that in the year 1530 there was an agreement between the Order of the Hospital of St. John of Jerusalem, later called the Knights of Rhodes and other things, just as Gutman says, whereby the island of Malta was given over to the Order in consideration of the nominal and peculiar annual payment of one Maltese falcon. Hammett would say that he had read about this odd agreement somewhere, as no doubt he had, but he also had to have had books and notes in front of him as he composed Gutman's tale. Gutman names strange and esoteric texts in several languages, which were real enough although not necessarily containing the information which Gutman says that they contain.[2] There was in any event agreeable byplay here; it is a pleasant and complicated joke that the antique learning is not quite fraudulent but at the same time (in the book of Sam Spade) is pretentious.

Altogether, Hammett wrote tales which are ironically aware of themselves at every turn, likely to undermine themselves at every turn:

in their cool and arbitrary way of piling on, by function of the dismissive prose, in their anti-heroic insistences, in their punning and in the several other ways of their self-consciousness, all within a genre which catered supposedly to straightforward lust for violence, or perhaps lust for lust.

In fact it was recognized almost from the beginning that Hammett was something more than a writer for the pulps. He had begun his publishing in H. L. Mencken's *Smart Set*. The novels were accepted for publication by the distinguished firm of Alfred A. Knopf through the particular intervention of Blanche Knopf, who had a celebrated eye for merit. Persons of certified literary distinction approved Hammett early on, including Gide, who himself was led to Hammett by André Malraux, and including Gertrude Stein. And there can be no doubt that Hammett took himself seriously, as a writer. The autobiographical *Tulip* amply so testifies, but perhaps the most pointed proof resides in the fact that no sooner had he achieved some fame as a writer of detective fictions than he abandoned detective fictions. He had published the first of his *Black Mask* stories in 1923. Four of the five novels were published in the two years 1929 to 1931, followed by *The Thin Man* in 1934—and although he would continue to write for the next twenty-six years of his life, *The Thin Man* marked the end of this main part of his career.

And that in turn was to prove that like other great American writers, from Horatio Alger, Jr., to Owen Wister, he had written much better than even he knew, despite the amount of his self-awareness. As had been the case with those others, he had made fictions which transcended their texts, and protagonists the same.

His inventions would persist, that of no other writer more imperatively. In fictions, and in radio in the early days, and in movies and television and comic strips, the Continental Op would be insistent, along with Nick Charles, and with Sam Spade perhaps most insistent of all. The later Private Eyes would be derivations of course, but remarkably and as a usual thing not indeed very far from type, and equipped with the distinct style of knowledge of contemporary life of the originals: mordant, witty, wry, aslant, more tired than cynical, curtailed and disengaged (episodic, in fact), or engaged, rather, in creating amusements from the materials of modern crime and punishment.

Were there no profundity in that, then the fictions would not have endured. That the type is not only originally but fundamentally American, no one will dispute, while the perseverance of the type testifies to continued activity of understanding. The Continental Op and the others are in fact loaded with an American history in which the question of what constitutes crime, which is to say the question of ethics itself, becomes perfectly paradoxical. It was Hammett's genius, whether he knew it or not, to take an appalling knowledge and to retrieve the same as an American humor. He retrieved civic despair as style.

# Notes
# Bibliography
# Index

# Notes

### Part I: Introduction

1. See "Horatio Alger," *Getting Creamed on Wall Street*, 1985, and *Coming Back on Wall Street*, 1986 (both Burlington, Vt.: Fraser Pub. Co.).

### Chapter 1. Alger

1. Gary Scharnhorst and Jack Bales, *Horatio Alger, Jr.: An Annotated Bibliography of Comment and Criticism* (Metuchen, N.J.: Scarecrow Press, 1981), p. 76; Edwin P. Hoyt, *Horatio's Boys: The Life and Works of Horatio Alger, Jr.* (Radnor, Penn.: Chilton Book Co., 1974), p. 251.

### Chapter 2. Adrift in New York

1. Alger's letter to Adams is quoted in Ralph D. Gardner, *Horatio Alger, or The American Hero Era* (Mendota, Ill.: Wayside Press, 1964), pp. 188–89.

2. In Gary Scharnhorst and Jack Bales, *The Lost Life of Horatio Alger, Jr.* (Bloomington: Indiana University Press, 1985), p. 77.

3. This trend was to continue into the twentieth century. See Ira Rosenwaike, *Population History of New York City* (Syracuse: Syracuse University Press, 1972), pp. 55–63.

4. Ibid., pp. 67, 71.

5. See Thomas Adams et al., *Population, Land Values and Government: Studies of the Growth and Distribution of Population and Land Values: and of Problems of Government* (New York: Regional Plan of New York and Its Environs, 1929), vol. 2, p. 56.

6. In Herbert Asbury, *The Gangs of New York: An Informal History of the Underworld* (New York: Alfred A. Knopf, 1928), p. 174.

### Chapter 4. Royalty

1. In Don Russell, *The Lives and Legends of Buffalo Bill* (Norman: University of Oklahoma Press, 1960), pp. 324ff.

197

## Chapter 5. Roosevelt

1. Quoted in G. Edward White, *The Eastern Establishment and the Western Experience: The West of Frederic Remington, Theodore Roosevelt, and Owen Wister* (New Haven: Yale University Press, 1968), pp. 126–127.
2. See ibid., pp. 154–55.
3. Theodore Roosevelt, *Cowboys and Kings: Three Great Letters by Theodore Roosevelt.* Ed. Elting E. Morison (Cambridge: Harvard University Press, 1954), p. 12.

## Chapter 6. The Lessons of Deadwood Dick

1. See Albert Johannsen, *The House of Beadle and Adams and Its Dime and Nickel Novels: The Story of a Vanished Literature* (Norman: University of Oklahoma Press, 1950–1962), vol. 2, p. 171.
2. Johannsen, above, is the indispensable reference for these biographical materials.
3. See John Cawelti, *Adventure, Mystery, and Romance: Formula Stories as Art and Popular Culture* (Chicago: University of Chicago Press, 1976), pp. 210–11.
4. See the anonymous introduction to Calamity Jane, *Life and Adventures of Calamity Jane, by Herself* (1896: Fairfield, Wa.: Ye Galleon Press, 1969.)

## Chapter 7. Wister

1. Fanny Kemble Wister, Introduction, Owen Wister, *Owen Wister Out West: His Journals and Letters* (Chicago: University of Chicago Press, 1958), pp. x–xii.
2. Wister, *Owen Wister Out West*, p. 246.
3. Roosevelt would say that Wister's article on the Pennsylvania National Guard had influenced his own essay "True American Ideals." See Forrest G. Robinson, "The Roosevelt-Wister Connection: Some Notes on the West and the Uses of History," *Western American Literature* (Summer 1979): 109, 110.
4. Wister, *Owen Wister Out West*, pp. 32–35.
5. Ben Merchant Vorpahl, *Frederic Remington and the West: With the Eye of the Mind* (Austin: University of Texas Press, 1978), p. xiii. Remington's letter is in Peggy and Harold Samuels, *Frederic Remington: A Biography* (New York: Doubleday & Co., 1982), p. 177.
6. Frederic Remington, "Cracker Cowboys of Florida" and "Artist Wanderings Among the Cheyennes," *Frederic Remington Selected Writings.* Ed. Peggy and Harold Samuels, and Frank Oppel (Secaucus, N.J.: Castle, 1981), pp. 82, 108. See also Samuels, *Frederic Remington*, p. 148.
7. Wister, *Owen Wister Out West*, p. 209.
8. Owen Wister, "The Evolution of the Cow-Puncher," in Ben Merchant Vorpahl, *My Dear Wister: The Frederic Remington–Owen Wister Letters* (Palo Alto: American West Publishing Co., 1972), p. 80.
9. Henry James, "To Owen Wister," 7 August 1902, *Henry James Letters.* Ed. Leon Edel (Cambridge: Harvard University Press, 1984), vol. 4, pp. 232–34.

## Chapter 8. McParlan

1.  Howard Haycraft, *Murder for Pleasure: The Life and Times of the Detective Story* (New York: D. Appleton-Century, 1941), p. 316.

2.  This is to repeat the sane cautions of J. Walter Coleman, writing in the 1930s. See Coleman, *The Molly Maguire Riots: Industrial Conflict in the Pennsylvania Coal Region* (Richmond: Garrett & Massie, 1936).

3.  Some sources put the figure as high as four thousand, but a membership of five or six hundred would, first, seem to be more reasonable given the necessity for secrecy, and, second, comes from a credible source, namely Franklin B. Gowen, arguing for the prosecution at the several trials of the Mollies. If Gowen were biased in this matter, it would have been in the direction of exaggeration. Had not the Mollies been exposed, he said, "This organization now numbering in this country five or six hundred," would have swelled its numbers. *Report of the Case of the Commonwealth vs. John Kehoe et al.*, rep. R.A. West (Pottsville: Miners; Journal Book and Job Rooms, 1876), p. 177.

4.  For the history of the Mollie Maguires in Ireland, including discussion of the fretted question of the origin of the name, see Wayne G. Broehl, Jr., *The Molly Maguires* (Cambridge: Harvard University Press, 1964), pt. I. Broehl's is also the clearest and most comprehensive of modern accounts of the Mollies.

5.  See ibid., p. 361.

6.  See for instance Pinkerton's preface to his account of his agency's involvement in the railroad strikes of 1877:

> In reciting these facts and considering their lesson, I believe that I of all others have earned the right to say plain things to the countless toilers who were engaged in these strikes. I say I have *earned* this right. I have been all my lifetime a working man. I know what it is to strive and grope along, with paltry remuneration and no encouragement save that of the hope and ambition implanted in every human heart. I have been a poor lad in Scotland, buffeted and badgered by boorish masters. I have worked weary years through the "prentice" period, until, by the hardest application, I conquered a trade. . . . I know what it is, from personal experience, to be the tramp journeyman; to carry the stick and bundle; to seek work, and not get it; and to get it, and receive but a pittance for it, or suddenly lose it altogether and be compelled to resume the weary search. (x–xi)

Pinkerton employed ghostwriters and there is no knowing to what extent the words are his, but presumably he agreed with the sentiments. Allan Pinkerton, *Strikers, Communists, Tramps and Detectives* (1878; New York: Arno Press and New York Times, 1969), pp. x–xi.

7.  See the personal recollection recorded by Arthur H. Lewis, *Lament for the Molly Maguires* (New York: Harcourt, Brace & World, 1964), p. 34.

8.  See Broehl, *Molly* 277–78. Broehl's source is a letter from the superintendent of Pinkerton's Philadelphia office, addressed to the district attorney of Schuylkill County.

## Chapter 9. Detectives

1. The "Metropolitan Police" was created by the New York state legislature in 1857, in order to wrest control of the police from the mayor, Fernando Wood. The city briefly in 1857 had two police forces, which fought each other, climaxing in a police riot in June of that year. The Municipals won the battle, but the courts ruled in favor of the Metropolitans. In 1869, when the Tweed machine came to control both city and state, police authority reverted to the city. See George W. Walling, *Recollections of a New York Chief of Police.* With an introduction by James F. Richardson. (1887; Montclair, N.J.: Patterson Smith, 1972), pp. ixff., 54ff.

2. See Larry K. Hartsfield, *The American Response to Professional Crime, 1870–1970* (Westport, Conn.: Greenwood Press, 1985), pp. 48–49.

3. See Richard Ellmann, *Oscar Wilde* (New York: Alfred A. Knopf, 1988), p. 200. Ellmann says that the swindler's name was "Hungry Joe" Sellick, but Ellmann was mistaken.

4. In the early years, in Dundee, Illinois, Pinkerton had been active in underground railroad activities. For a year plus a few months during the Civil War, he was head of the Federal Secret Service, a position which he secured through the agency of his friend General George McClellan. Pinkerton had known McClellan when the latter had been the president of one of the railroads which had employed Pinkerton. When McClellan was relieved of command, so was Pinkerton.

## Chapter 10. Hammett

1. An early draft for a novel, to be called "The Secret Emperor," contains the notation:

> [The villain is] Seth Gutman, 50, black-haired, ivory skin, no lines in his suavely strong face, hawk nose, smooth-shaven, broad sloping forehead, hair thick and curly, oval face with something suggesting an Egyptian drawing in it, fairly plump but in perfect shape, except perhaps a bit soft. Dark, large and intelligent eyes. Low musical voice, charming personality. Since, being a Jew, he may not be president, he decides to be secret emperor of the U.S.

And he has a ravishing wife whose name is Tamar. In Diane Johnson, *Dashiell Hammett: A Life* (New York: Fawcett Columbine, 1985), pp. 56–57.

2. J. Delaville Le Roulx's *Les Archives, La Bibliothèque et le Trésor de l'Lordre de Saint Jean de Jérusalem a Malte* contains an account of the library at Malta but no mention of the falcon; Lady Francis Verney's *Memoirs of the Verney Family during the Seventeenth Century* (not the actual title) also contains no mention of the bird, but, then, Gutman says that it does not.

Hammett perhaps struck upon this trail in his reading of Arthur Symons's *The Symbolist Movement in Literature,* published in 1919, a book which anyone in the 1920s who was serious about contemporary writing was likely to have read. In it Hammett would have found an account of the nineteenth-century poet Villiers de l'Isle d'Adam, who was a lineal descendent of the Villiers de l'Isle d'Adam who as Grand Master of the Order of Saint John of Jerusalem had obtained the concession of Malta from Charles V. Said Symons about the poet Villiers: "For Villiers, to whom time, after all, was but a metaphysical abstraction, the age of the Crusaders had not passed." Which would seem to be Gutman's sense of things as well.

# Bibliography

## Part I. Rags To Riches

Adams, Thomas, et al. *Population, Land Values and Government: Studies of the Growth and Distribution of Population and Land Values; and of Problems of Government.* 4 vols. New York: Regional Plan of New York and Its Environs, 1929. Vol. 2.

Aiken, George L. *Fergus Fearnaught, the New York Boy; A Story of the Byways and Thoroughfares by Daylight and Gaslight.* New York: Beadle's Half Dime Library, Vol. 11, no. 261. 1882.

Aldrich, Thomas Bailey. *The Story of a Bad Boy.* 1870. New York: Garland Publishing, 1976.

"Alger, Horatio." *Coming Back on Wall Street.* Burlington, Vt.: Fraser Pub. Co., 1986.

"Alger, Horatio." *Getting Creamed on Wall Street.* Burlington, Vt.: Fraser Pub. Co., 1985.

*Alger Street: The Poetry of Horatio Alger, Jr.* Ed. Gilbert K. Westgard II. Boston: J. S. Canner, 1964.

Asbury, Herbert. *The Gangs of New York: An Informal History of the Underworld.* New York: Alfred A. Knopf, 1928.

Brace, Charles Loring. *The Dangerous Classes of New York, and Twenty Years' Work Among Them.* 3d ed. New York: Wynkoop and Hallenbeck, 1880.

Brace, Charles Loring. *The Life of Charles Loring Brace: Chiefly Told in His Own Letters.* Ed. His Daughter. New York: Charles Scribners, 1894.

Bremner, Robert H. *From the Depths: The Discovery of Poverty in the United States.* New York: New York University Press, 1956.

Browne, Junius Henri. *The Great Metropolis: A Mirror of New York.* 1869; New York: Arno Press, 1975.

Buel, J. W. *Mysteries and Miseries of America's Great Cities, Embracing New York, Washington City, San Francisco, Salt Lake City, and New Orleans.* San Francisco: A. L. Bancroft, 1883.

Campbell, Mrs. Helen, Col. Thomas W. Knox, and Inspector Thomas Byrnes. *Darkness and Daylight: or Lights and Shadows of New York Life.* Hartford: A. D. Worthington, 1891.

Cawelti, John G. *Apostles of the Self-Made Man: Changing-Concepts of Success in America.* Chicago: University of Chicago Press, 1965.

Cowdrick, J. C. *Broadway Billy, the Bootblack Bravo; or, Brought to Bay by a Bold Boy.* New York: Beadle's Half Dime Library, 1886. Vol. 19, no. 490.

Cowley, Malcolm. "The Alger Story." *The New Republic* (10 Sept. 1945): 319–20.

Gardner, Ralph D. *Horatio Alger, or The American Hero Era.* Mendota, Ill.: Wayside Press, 1964.

Gruber, Frank. *Horatio Alger, Jr.: A Biography and Bibliography.* West Los Angeles: Grover Jones Press, 1961.

Holbrook, Stewart H. "Horatio Alger Was No Hero." *The American Mercury* 51 (Oct. 1940): 203–9.

Holland, Norman N. "Hobbling with Horatio, or the Uses of Literature." *Hudson Review* 19 (Winter 1959): 549-57.

Howe, William F., and Abraham H. Hummel. *In Danger; or, Life in New York. A True History of a Great City's Wiles and Temptations. True Facts and Disclosures by Howe and Hummel, the Celebrated Criminal Lawyers.* New York: J. S. Ogilvie, 1888.

Hoyt, Edwin P. *Horatio's Boys: The Life and Works of Horatio Alger, Jr.* Radnor, Penn.: Chilton Book Co., 1974.

Huber, Richard M. *The American Idea of Success.* New York: McGraw Hill, 1971.

Mayes, Herbert R. *Alger: A Biography Without a Hero.* New York: Macy-Masius, 1928.

Needham, George C. *Street Arabs and Gutter Snipes: The Pathetic and Humorous Side of Young Vagabond Life in the Great Cities, with Records of Work for Their Reclamation.* Boston: D. L. Guernsey, 1887.

"One Who Knows." *The Spider and the Fly; or, Tricks, Traps, and Pitfalls of City Life.* New York: C. Miller & Co., 1873.

Peck, George W. *Mirth for the Million: Peck's Compendium of Fun, Comprising the Immortal Deeds of Peck's Bad Boy and His Pa, and All the Choice Gems of Wit, Humor, Sarcasm and Pathos, from the Prolific Pen of George W. Peck.* Chicago: Belford, Clarke & Co., 1883.

Peck, George W. *Peck's Bad Boy and His Pa.* 2 vols. Chicago: Belford, Clarke & Co., 1883.

Pierce, Jo. *Bob o' the Bowery; or, The Prince of Mulberry Street.* New York: Beadle's Half Dime Library, 1885. Vol. 16, no. 397.

Poole, Ernest. *Child Labor—The Street.* New York: Child Labor Committee, 1903.

Riis, Jacob. *How the Other Half Lives: Studies Among the Tenements of New York.* 1890. Rpt. *Jacob Riis Revisited: Poverty and the Slum in Another Era.* Clifton: Augustus M. Kelley, 1973.

Riis, Jacob. *Nibsy's Christmas.* New York: Charles Scribners, 1893.

Roosevelt, Theodore. *An Autobiography.* New York: Macmillan, 1916.

Rosenwaike, Ira. *Population History of New York City.* Syracuse: Syracuse University Press, 1972.

Rovere, Richard H. *Howe & Hummel: Their True and Scandalous History.* New York: Farrar, Straus, 1947.

Scharnhorst, Gary. *Horatio Alger, Jr.* Boston: Twayne Publishers, 1980.

Scharnhorst, Gary, and Jack Bales. *Horatio Alger, Jr.: An Annotated Bibliography of Comment and Criticism.* Metuchen, N.J.: Scarecrow Press, 1981.

Scharnhorst, Gary, and Jack Bales. *The Lost Life of Horatio Alger Jr.* Bloomington: Indiana University Press, 1985.

Seelye, John. "Horatio Alger Out West: A Marriage of Myths." Introduction. *The Young Miner; or, Tom Nelson in California.* By Horatio Alger, Jr. 1879. San Francisco: The Book Club of California, 1965. v–xix.

Seelye, John. "Who Was Horatio? The Alger Myth and American Scholarship." *American Quarterly* 17 (1965): 749–56.

Slotkin, Richard. *The Fatal Environment: The Myth of the Frontier in The Age of Industrialization, 1800–1890.* New York: Atheneum, 1985.

Smith, Mrs. Elizabeth Oakes (Prince). *The Newsboy.* New York: J. C. Derby, 1854.

*Snares of New York; or, Tricks and Traps of the Great Metropolis, Being a Complete, Vivid and Truthful Exposure of the Swindles, Humbugs and Pitfalls of the Great City.* New York: Jesse Haney & Co., 1879.

Spargo, John. *The Bitter Cry of the Children.* 1906. New York: Johnson Reprint Corp., 1969.

Tebbel, John William. *From Rags to Riches: Horatio Alger, Jr., and the American Dream.* New York: Macmillan, 1963.

Weiss, Richard. *The American Myth of Success: From Horatio Alger to Norman Vincent Peale.* New York: Basic Books, 1969.

Wheeler, Edward L. *Fritz, the Bound-Boy Detective; or, Dot Leetle Game mit Rebecca.* New York: Beadle's Half Dime Library, 1881. Vol. 9, no. 209.

Wohl, R. Richard. "The 'Country Boy' Myth and Its Place in American Urban Culture: The Nineteenth-Century Contribution." *Perspectives in American History.* New York: Cambridge University Press, 1969. Vol. 3, pp. 75–156.

Wyllie, Irvin G. *The Self-Made Man in America: The Myth of Rags to Riches.* New Brunswick, N.J.: Rutgers University Press, 1954.

Zuckerman, Michael. "The Nursery Tales of Horatio Alger." *American Quarterly* 24 (1972): 191–209.

## Part II.  Westerns

Aiken, Albert W. *Dick Talbot the Ranch King, or, The Double Foe.* New York: Beadle's Dime Library, Nov. 9, 1892. Vol. 57, no. 133.

Armstrong, Margaret. *Fanny Kemble: A Passionate Victorian.* New York: MacMillan Co., 1938.

Blackstone, Sarah J. *Buckskins, Bullets, and Business: A History of Buffalo Bill's Wild West.* New York: Greenwood Press, 1986.

Bold, Christine. *Selling the Wild West: Popular Western Fiction, 1860 to 1960.* Bloomington: Indiana University Press, 1987.

Bowen, Cromwell. *The Elegant Oakey.* New York: Oxford University Press, 1956.

*Buffalo Bill and the Wild West.* The Brooklyn Museum [and] Museum of Art, Carnegie Institute, [and] Buffalo Bill Historical Center. Pittsburgh: University of Pittsburgh Press, 1981.

Buntline, Ned. *Buffalo Bill and His Adventures in the Wild West.* New York: J. S. Ogilvie Publishing Co., 1886. Rpt. of *Buffalo Bill: The King of the Border Men,* 1881.

Buscombe, Edward. "Painting the Legend: Frederic Remington and the Western." *Cinema Journal* 23 (Summer 1984): 12–27.

Cawelti, John. *Adventure, Mystery, and Romance: Formula Stories as Art and Culture.* Chicago: University of Chicago Press, 1976.

Cody, William F. *The Life of Hon. Wm. F. Cody, Known as Buffalo Bill.* 1879; New York: Indian Head Books, 1991.

Drinnon, Richard. *Facing West: The Metaphysics of Indian-Hating and Empire-Building.* Minneapolis: University of Minnesota Press, 1980.

Dyer, Thomas G. *Theodore Roosevelt and the Idea of Race.* Baton Rouge: Louisiana State University Press, 1980.

Ellis, Edward S. *Seth Jones.* 1860. In *Dime Novels.* Ed. Philip Durham. Indianapolis: Odyssey Press, 1966.

Estleman, Loren D. *The Wister Trace: Classic Novels of the American Frontier.* Ottawa, Ill.: Jameson Books, 1987.

Etulain, Richard W. *Owen Wister.* Boise: Boise State College, 1973.

Horn, Tom. *Life of Tom Horn, Government Scout and Interpreter: Written by Himself.* 1904; University of Oklahoma Press, 1964.

Ingraham, Col. Prentiss. *Buck Taylor, or, The Raiders and the Rangers: A Story of the Wild and Thrilling Life of William L. Taylor.* New York: Beadle's Half Dime Library, Feb. 1, 1887. No. 497.

Ingraham, Col. Prentiss. *Captain Ku Klux, The Marauder of the Rio, or The Buckskin Pards' Strange Quest.* New York: Beadle's Half Dime Library, Nov. 28, 1887. No. 540.

James, Henry. *The American Scene.* 1907; New York: Horizon Press, 1967.

James, Henry. "To Owen Wister." 7 August 1902. *Henry James Letters.* Vol. 4. Ed. Leon Edel. Cambridge: Harvard University Press, 1984.

Jane, Calamity. *Life and Adventures of Calamity Jane, by Herself.* 1896; Fairfield, Wa.: Ye Galleon Press, 1969. Afterword anon.

Johannsen, Albert. *The House of Beadle and Adams and Its Dime and Nickel Novels: The Story of a Vanished Literature.* 3 vols. Norman: University of Oklahoma Press, 1950–62.

Jones, Daryl. *The Dime Novel Western.* Bowling Green: Popular Press, 1978.

Lindsay, Vachel. "Roosevelt." 1924. *The Poetry of Vachel Lindsay.* Ed. Dennis Camp. 3 vols. Peoria: Spoon River Poetry Press, 1984–86.

"Men in Evidence." Editorial. *Harper's Weekly* 21 July 1894: 678–79.

Monaghan, Jay. *The Great Rascal: The Life and Adventures of Ned Buntline.* Boston: Little, Brown, 1952.

Payne, Darwin. *Owen Wister: Chronicler of the West, Gentleman of the East.* Dallas: Southern Methodist University Press, 1985.

Pearson, Edmund. *Dime Novels; or, Following an Old Trail in Popular Literature.* Boston: Little, Brown, 1929.

Remington, Frederic. "Chicago Under the Mob." *Harper's Weekly* 21 July 1894: 680–81.

Remington, Frederic. *Crooked Trails.* 1898; Freeport, N.Y.: Books for Libraries, 1969.

Remington, Frederic. *John Ermine of the Yellowstone.* 1902; Ridgewood, N.J.: The Gregg Press, 1968.

Remington, Frederic. *Selected Writings.* Ed. Peggy and Harold Samuels, and Frank Oppel. Secaucus, N.J.: Castle, 1981.

Robinson, Forrest G. "The Roosevelt-Wister Connection: Some Notes on the West and the Uses of History." *Western American Literature (Summer 1979): 95–114.*

Roosevelt, Theodore. *An Autobiography.* New York: Macmillan Company, 1916.

Roosevelt, Theodore. *Cowboys and Kings: Three Great Letters by Theodore Roosevelt.* Ed. Elting E. Morison. Cambridge: Harvard University Press, 1954.

Roosevelt, Theodore. *Hunting Trips of a Ranchman: Sketches of Sport on the Northern Cattle Plains.* New York: G. P. Putnam's Sons, 1885.

Roosevelt, Theodore. *Ranch Life and the Hunting Trail.* 1888. Ann Arbor: University Microfilms, 1966.

Roosevelt, Theodore. *The Strenuous Life: Essays and Addresses.* New York: The Century Co., 1901.

Roosevelt, Theodore. *The Winning of the West.* 4 vols. 1889–1896; New York: G. P. Putnam's Sons, 1900.

Russell, Don. *The Lives and Legends of Buffalo Bill.* Norman: University of Oklahoma Press, 1960.

Samuels, Peggy and Harold. *Frederic Remington: A Biography.* New York: Doubleday & Co., 1982.

Slotkin, Richard. *The Fatal Environment: The Myth of the Frontier in the Age of Industrialization, 1800–1890.* New York: Atheneum, 1985.

Slotkin, Richard. *Gunfighter Nation: The Myth of the Frontier in Twentieth-Century America.* New York: Atheneum, 1992.

Smith, Henry Nash. *Virgin Land: The American West as Symbol and Myth.* 1950; New York: Vintage Books, n.d.

Tompkins, Jane. *West of Everything: The Inner Life of Westerns.* New York: Oxford University Press, 1992.

Vorpahl, Ben Merchant. *Frederic Remington and the West: With the Eye of the Mind.* Austin: University of Texas Press, 1978.

Vorpahl, Ben Merchant. "Henry James and Owen Wister." *The Pennsylvania Magazine of History and Biography* (July 1971): 291–338.

Vorpahl, Ben Merchant. *My Dear Wister: The Frederic Remington–Owen Wister Letters.* Palo Alto: American West Publishing Co., 1972.

Wheeler, Edward L. *Deadwood Dick in Boston or, The Cool Case.* New York: Beadle's Half Dime Library, April 24, 1888. No. 561.

Wheeler, Edward L. *Deadwood Dick Jr. in Chicago or, The Anarchist's Daughter.* New York: Beadle's Half Dime Library, July 10, 1888. No. 572.

Wheeler, Edward L. *Deadwood Dick Jr. in Coney Island, or, The "Piping" of Polly Pilgrim.* Beadle's Half Dime Library, Jan. 22, 1889. No. 600.

Wheeler, Edward L. *Deadwood Dick on Deck.* 1878. *Dime Novels.* Ed. Philip Durham. Indianapolis: Odyssey Press, 1966.

Wheeler, Edward L. *Deadwood Dick Jr. in Denver or, Cool Kate, the Queen of the Crooks.* New York: Beadle's Half Dime Library, Oct. 2, 1888. No. 584.

Wheeler, Edward L. *Deadwood Dick Jr. in Gotham or, Unraveling a Twisted Skein.* New York: Beadle's Half Dime Library, Mar. 6, 1888. No. 554.

Wheeler, Edward L. *Deadwood Dick in New York, or "A Cute Case," A Romance of To-Day: To Which the Attention of Metropolitan Police, and All Detectives Is Respectfully Called.* New York: Beadle's Half Dime Library, Aug. 18, 1885. No. 421.

Wheeler, Edward L. *Deadwood Dick Jr. in Philadelphia or, The Wild West Detective Among the Crooks.* New York: Beadle's Half Dime Library, June 5, 1888. No. 567.

Wheeler, Edward L. *Deadwood Dick, The Prince of the Road; or, The Black Rider of the Black Hills.* New York: Beadle's Half Dime Library, Oct. 15, 1877. Vol. 1, no. 1.

Wheeler, Ed [sic] L. *Deadwood Dick, Jr., or The Sign of the Crimson Crescent.* New York: Ivers & Co., 1886.

Wheeler, Edward L. *Wild Ivan, the Boy Claude Duval; or, The Brotherhood of Death.* New York: Beadle's Half Dime Library, 1878. Vol. 2, no. 35.

White, G. Edward. *The Eastern Establishment and the Western Experience: The West of Frederic Remington, Theodore Roosevelt, and Owen Wister.* New Haven: Yale University Press, 1968.

Wister, Owen. *The Jimmyjohn Boss and Other Stories.* 1900; New York: Garrett Press, 1969.

Wister, Owen. *Lady Baltimore.* New York: Macmillan Co., 1906.

Wister, Owen. *Lin McLean.* 1897; New York: A. L. Burt Company, 1907.

Wister, Owen. *Members of the Family.* New York: Macmillan Co., 1911.

Wister, Owen. "The National Guard of Pennsylvania." *Harper's Weekly* (1 Sept. 1894): 824–26.

Wister, Owen. *Owen Wister Out West: His Journals and Letters.* Ed. Fanny Kemble Wister. Chicago: University of Chicago Press, 1958.

Wister, Owen. *Philosophy 4: A Story of Harvard University.* 1903; New York: Macmillan Co., 1924.

Wister, Owen. *Red Men and White.* 1896; New York: Garrett Press, 1968.

Wister, Owen. *Roosevelt: The Story of a Friendship: 1880–1919.* New York: Macmillan Co., 1930.

Wister, Owen. *The Virginian: A Horseman of the Plains.* 1902; New York: New American Library, 1979.

Wister, Owen. *Watch Your Thirst: A Dry Opera in Three Acts.* New York: Macmillan Co., 1923.

Wister, Owen. *When West Was West.* New York: Macmillan Co., 1928.

## Part III. Private Eyes

Adamic, Louis. *Dynamite: The Story of Class Violence in America.* 1931; rev. ed. 1934; Gloucester: Peter Smith, 1963.

Bailey, W. H., Sr., LL.D. *The Detective Faculty, as Illustrated from Judicial Records and the Actualities of Experience.* Cincinnati: The Robert Clark Co., 1896.

Barzun, Jacques. "Detection and the Literary Art." *The Mystery Writer's Art.* Ed. Francis M. Nevins, Jr. Bowling Green: Bowling Green University Press, 1970. Pp. 248–62.

Bassan, Maurice. *Hawthorne's Son: The Life and Literary Career of Julian Hawthorne.* Columbus: Ohio State University Press, 1970.

Bimba, Anthony. *The Molly Maguires.* 1932; New York: International Publishers, 1950.

Boyer, Richard O., and Herbert M. Morais. *Labor's Untold Story.* 1955; New York: United Electrical, Radio & Machine Workers of America, 1984.

Bradford, Ernle. *The Shield and the Sword: The Knights of St. John.* London: Hodder and Stoughton, 1972.

Broehl, Wayne G., Jr. *The Molly Maguires.* Cambridge: Harvard University Press, 1964.

Bruce, Robert V. *1877: Year of Violence.* 1959; Chicago: Ivan R. Dee, 1989.

Byrnes, Thomas. Inspector of Police and Chief of Detectives, New York City. *Professional Criminals of America.* New York: Cassell & Co., 1886.

Cawelti, John G. *Adventure, Mystery, and Romance: Formula Stories as Art and Popular Culture.* Chicago: University of Chicago Press, 1976.

Chandler, Raymond. "The Simple Art of Murder." *The Simple Art of Murder.* New York: Vintage Books, 1988. Pp. 1–18.

Christopher, J. R. "Poe and the Tradition of the Detective Story." *The Mystery Writer's Art.* Ed. Francis M. Nevins, Jr. Bowling Green: Bowling Green University Press, 1970. Pp. 19–35.

Coleman, J. Walter. *The Molly Maguire Riots: Industrial Conflict in the Pennsylvania Coal Region.* Richmond: Garrett and Massie, 1936.

Crapsey, Edward. *The Nether Side of New York; or, The Vice, Crime and Poverty of the Great Metropolis.* New York: Sheldon & Co., 1872.

Dewees, F. P. *The Molly Maguires: The Origin, Growth, and Character of the Organization.* 1887; New York: Burt Franklin, 1969.

Durham, Philip. "The *Black Mask* School." *Tough Guy Writers of the Thirties.* Ed. David Madden. Carbondale: Southern Illinois University Press, 1968. Pp. 51–79.

Farley, Detective Phil. *Criminals of America; or, Tales of the Lives of Thieves. Enabling Every One To Be His Own Detective. With Portraits, Making a Complete Rogues' Gallery.* New York: Author's Edition, 1876.

Friedman, Morris. *The Pinkerton Labor Spy.* New York: Wilshire Book Co., 1907.

Gide, André. *Imaginary Interviews.* Trans. Malcolm Cowley. New York: Alfred A. Knopf, 1944.

Gide, André. *The Journals of André Gide.* Vol. 4: 1939–1949. Trans. Justin O'Brien. New York: Alfred A. Knopf, 1951.

Gilbert, Elliot L. "The Detective as Metaphor in the Nineteenth Century." *The Mystery Writer's Art.* Ed. Francis M. Nevins, Jr. Bowling Green: Bowling Green University Press, 1970. Pp. 285–94.

Graves, Robert, and Alan Hodge. *The Long Week End: A Social History of Great Britain 1918–1939.* New York: Macmillan, 1941.

Grebstein, Sheldon Norman. "The Tough Hemingway and His Hard-Boiled Children." *Tough Guy Writers of the Thirties.* Ed. David Madden. Carbondale: Southern Illinois University Press, 1968. Pp. 18–41.

Gregory, Sinda. *Private Investigations: The Novels of Dashiell Hammett.* Carbondale: Southern Illinois University Press, 1985.

Guillot, Ellen Elizabeth. *Social Factors in Crime: As Explained by American Writers of the Civil War and Post Civil War Period.* Ph.D. dissertation, University of Pennsylvania, 1943.

Hartsfield, Larry K. *The American Response to Professional Crime, 1870–1917.* Westport, Conn.: Greenwood Press, 1985.

Hawthorne, Julian. *An American Penman. From the Diary of Inspector Byrnes.* New York: Cassell & Co., 1887.

Hawthorne, Julian. *Another's Crime. From the Diary of Inspector Byrnes.* New York: Cassell & Co., 1888.

Hawthorne, Julian. *The Great Bank Robbery. From the Diary of Inspector Byrnes.* New York: Cassell & Co., 1887.

Hawthorne, Julian. *Section 558, or The Fatal Letter. From the Diary of Inspector Byrnes.* New York: Cassell & Co., 1888.

Hawthorne, Julian. *A Tragic Mystery. From the Diary of Inspector Byrnes.* New York: Cassell & Co., 1887

Haycraft, Howard. *Murder for Pleasure: The Life and Times of the Detective Story.* New York: D. Appleton-Century, 1941.

Haywood, William D. *Bill Haywood's Book.* New York: International Publishers, 1929.

Heilbrun, Carolyn. "Keynote Address: Gender and Detective Fiction." *The Sleuth and the Scholar: Origins, Evolution, and Current Trends in Detective Fiction.* Ed. Barbara A. Rader and Howard G. Zettler. New York: Greenwood Press, 1988. Pp. 1–8.

Hellman, Lillian. Introduction. *The Big Knockover.* By Dashiell Hammett. New York: Random House, 1966. Pp. vii–xxi.

Horan, James D. *Desperate Men: Revelations from the Sealed Pinkerton Files.* New York: G. P. Putnam's Sons, 1949.

Horan, James D. *The Pinkertons: The Detective Dynasty that Made History.* New York: Bonanza Books, 1967.

Horn, Tom. *Life of Tom Horn, Government Scout and Interpreter: Written by Himself.* 1904; Norman: University of Oklahoma Press, 1964.

Johnson, Diane. *Dashiell Hammett: A Life.* New York: Fawcett Columbine, 1985.

Kaplan, Justin. *Lincoln Steffens: A Biography.* New York, Simon & Schuster, 1974.

Layman, Richard. *Shadow Man: The Life of Dashiell Hammett.* New York: Harcourt Brace Jovanovich, 1981.

Lc Roulx, J. Delaville. *Les Archives, La Bibliothèque et le Trésor de l'Ordre de Saint-Jean de Jérusalem a Malte.* Paris, 1883.

Lewis, Arthur H. *Lament for the Molly Maguires.* New York: Harcourt, Brace & World, 1964.

McDonald, Ross (Kenneth Millar). "The Writer as Detective Hero." *The Mystery Writer's Art.* Ed. Francis M. Nevins, Jr. Bowling Green: Bowling Green University Press, 1970. Pp. 295–305.

McWatters, George S. *Knots Untied: Ways and By-Ways in the Hidden Life of American Detectives: A Narrative of Marvelous Experiences Among All Classes of Society,— Criminals in High Life, Swindlers, Bank Robbers, Thieves, Lottery Agents, Gamblers, Necromancers, Counterfeiters, Burglars, Etc., Etc., Etc.* Hartford: J. B. Burr and Hyde, 1871.

Madden, David. "Introduction." *Tough Guy Writers of the Thirties.* Ed. David Madden. Carbondale: Southern Illinois University Press, 1968. Pp. xv–xxxix.

Marcus, Steven. Introduction. *The Continental Op.* By Dashiell Hammett. New York: Random House, 1974. Pp. ix–xxix.

Morn, Frank. *The Eye That Never Sleeps: A History of the Pinkerton National Detective Agency.* Bloomington: Indiana University Press, 1982.

Nolan, William F. *The Black Mask Boys: Masters in the Hard-Boiled School of Detective Fiction.* New York: William Morrow, 1985.

Nolan, William F. *Dashiell Hammett: A Casebook.* Santa Barbara: McNally & Loftin, 1969.

Pinkerton, Allan. *Bank-Robbers and Detectives.* 1882; New York: G. W. Carleton & Co., 1883.

Pinkerton, Allan. *Bucholz and the Detectives.* New York: G. W. Carleton & Co., 1880.

Pinkerton, Allan. *The Expressman and the Detectives.* 1875; New York: Arno Press, 1976.

Pinkerton, Allan. *The Molly Maguires and the Detectives.* New York: G. W. Carleton & Co., 1877.

Pinkerton, Allan. *Strikers, Communists, Tramps and Detectives.* 1878; New York: Arno Press and New York Times, 1969.

Rahn, B. J. "Seeley Regester: America's First Detective Novelist." *The Sleuth and the Scholar: Origins, Evolution, and Current Trends in Detective Fiction.* Ed. Barbara A. Rader and Howard G. Zettler. New York: Greenwood Press, 1988. Pp. 47–61.

*Report of the Case of the Commonwealth vs. John Kehoe et al.,* stenographically reported by R. A. West. Pottsville: Miners' Journal Book and Job Rooms, 1876.

Rovere, Richard H. *Howe and Hummel: Their True and Scandalous History.* New York: Farrar, Straus, 1947.

Rowan, Richard Wilmer. *The Pinkertons: A Detective Dynasty.* Boston: Little, Brown, 1931.

Schermerhorn, E. W. *Malta of the Knights.* New York: Houghton Mifflin, 1929.

Siringo, Charles A. *A Cowboy Detective: A True Story of Twenty-Two Years With a World-Famous Detective Agency.* 1912. Introduction, Frank Morn. Lincoln: University of Nebraska Press, 1988.

Siringo, Charles A. *Two Evil Isms: Pinkertonism and Anarchism, By a Cowboy Detective Who Knows, as He Spent Twenty-Two Years in the Inner Circle of Pinkerton's National Detective Agency.* 1915. Introduction, Charles D. Peavy. Austin: Steck-Vaugn Co., 1967.

Steffens, Lincoln. *The Autobiography of Lincoln Steffens.* New York: Harcourt, Brace & Co., 1931.

Stein, Gertrude. *Everybody's Autobiography.* 1937; New York: Vintage Books, 1973.

Stowe, William W. "Hard-Boiled Virgil: Early Nineteenth-Century Beginnings of a Popular Literary Formula." *The Sleuth and the Scholar: Origins, Evolution, and Current Trends in Detective Fiction.* Ed. Barbara A. Rader and Howard G. Zettler. New York: Greenwood Press, 1988. Pp. 79–90.

Symons, Julian. *Dashiell Hammett.* New York: Harcourt Brace Jovanovich, 1985.

*The Thugs of the Tenderloin; or, Old Cap. Collier Tracking a Daring Band of Thieves,* n.p., *Old Cap Collier Library,* 1897. *The Dime Novel Detective.* Ed. Gary Hoppenstand. Bowling Green: Bowling Green University Popular Press, 1982. Pp. 71–98.

Thurber, James. "A Guide to the Literary Pilgrimage." *Vintage Thurber.* Vol. 1. London: Hamish Hamilton, 1963. Pp. 430–34.

Thurber, James. "The Wings of Henry James." *Vintage Thurber.* Vol. 1. London: Hamish Hamilton, 1963. Pp. 593–603.

Verney Family. *Letters and Papers of The Verney Family.* Ed. John Bruce, Esq. London, 1853.

Walling, George W. *Recollections of a New York Chief of Police.* 1887; Montclair, N.J.: Patterson Smith, 1972. Introduction by James F. Richardson.

Widmer, Kingsley. "The Way Out: Some Life-Style Sources of the Literary Tough Guy and the Proletarian Hero." *Tough Guy Writers of the Thirties.* Ed. David Madden. Carbondale: Southern Illinois University Press, 1968. Pp. 3–12.

Winks, Robin W. Foreword. *The Sleuth and the Scholar: Origins, Evolution, and Current Trends in Detective Fiction.* Ed. Barbara A. Rader and Howard G. Zettler. New York: Greenwood Press, 1988. Pp. ix–xiii.

Winks, Robin W. *Modus Operandi: An Excursion into Detective Fiction.* Boston: David R. Godine, 1982.

# Index